CAMBRIDGE AIR SURVEYS
Series editor David R. Wilson

THE GEOGRAPHY OF BRITAIN FROM THE AIR
General editors David R. Wilson *and* Robin Glasscock

Natural Landscapes of Britain from the Air
Nicholas Stephens (*ed.*)

Britain's Changing Environment from the Air
Tim Bayliss-Smith *and* Susan Owens (*eds.*)

Historic Landscapes of Britain from the Air
Robin Glasscock (*ed.*)

HISTORIC
LANDSCAPES OF
BRITAIN
FROM THE AIR

EDITED BY ROBIN GLASSCOCK

Historic
Landscapes of
Britain
from the air

CAMBRIDGE
UNIVERSITY PRESS

Published by the Press Syndicate of the University of Cambridge
The Pitt Building, Trumpington Street, Cambridge CB2 1RP
40 West 20th Street, New York, NY 10011–4211, USA
10 Stamford Road, Oakleigh, Victoria 3166, Australia

First published 1992

Printed in Great Britain by BAS Printers Limited, Over Wallop, Hampshire

A catalogue record for this book is available from the British Library

Library of Congress cataloguing in publication data
Historic landscapes of Britain from the air
  edited by Robin Glasscock
          p.   cm. – (Cambridge air surveys)
Includes bibliographical references and index.
ISBN 0 521 32533 1 (hardback)
1. Great Britain – Historical geography – Pictorial works.
2. Historic sites – Great Britain – Pictorial works.
3. Landscape – Great Britain – Pictorial works.
4. Great Britain – Aerial photographs.
I. Glasscock, Robin E. (Robin Edgar)
II. Series. DA600.H53   1992.
914.1′0022′2 – dc20   92-4892   CIP

ISBN 0 521 32533 1 hardback

Frontispiece:
Features of the rural landscape of the English Midlands dating
from different periods are to be seen in this photograph of a
Roman road, the Foss Way, heading north-eastwards across the
cultivated farmland of south Warwickshire. Regular fields and
straight hedgerows dating from Parliamentary Enclosure overlie
ploughed-out furlongs and ridges of the medieval open fields.
Remnants of old woodland exist alongside parkland, new
plantations and hedgerow trees. The parishes in the foreground,
divided by the Foss Way are Wellesbourne (to the left) and
Combrook (to the right). Beyond Combrook is the wooded
Compton Verney estate, site of a deserted medieval village and
even now in the process of change as plans are formulated to
build a new opera house in the landscape park designed for the
Verneys by Capability Brown   BSY 15   June 1975

Contents

Preface

This volume in the Cambridge Air Surveys concludes a three-part sub-series on the geography of Britain from the air which began with physical geography – *Natural Landscapes of Britain from the Air* (ed. Nicholas Stephens, 1990) – and continued with the contemporary environment – *Britain's Changing Environment from the Air* (ed. Tim Bayliss-Smith and Susan Owens, 1990). These three books have their origins in Cambridge where both the General Editors are based: Robin Glasscock as a University Lecturer in Geography and David Wilson as Curator in Aerial Photography. Cambridge, uniquely among British universities, is fortunate in having its own Aerial Photography Unit. The photographic library it has built up over the last 45 years is now of first importance as a record of the changing geography of post-war Britain. From this archive has been selected the majority of photographs used to illustrate the various themes explored in these books.

The General Editors wish to place on record their thanks to all their contributors, to the individual volume editors, to Julia Darrell and Ruth Nossek at the Cambridge University Collection of Air Photographs, and to Peter Richards and Christine Matthews of the Cambridge University Press. Acknowledgements to other individuals and institutions who have helped in the supply of information and photographs will be found within each volume.

Introduction

With the help of aerial photographs this book is a contribution towards recording, explaining and understanding the past. Aerial photographs, although now familiar through their increasing use in the press, are a comparatively new source of information; not only do they bring new perspectives (seldom available to most people) but they record and illustrate more comprehensively than maps the legacy of past activity in the present landscape. Not infrequently, they add information to what is already known from archaeology and written records.

We cannot claim, however, except in a very limited sense, that the 'past' survives in the present. Many man-made features have disappeared without trace, ploughed away or buried beneath built-up areas. They cannot be revealed by aerial photography any more than can the people and their beliefs and decisions which produced the remains that are still visible. Indeed, it has been observed that aerial photographs tend to dehumanise the landscape; big buildings rather than small people show up from a great height. Thus, an aerial photograph of the ruins of an abbey (photo 44) may be of considerable interest for what it shows of the ground plan, surviving buildings and earthworks but it tells us very little about Christianity, the monastic life, or the date of the foundation. For such information we depend upon other sources, mainly written. Similarly, a photograph of part of a city (photo 96) shows the extremely high density of Victorian housing without revealing the inhabitants, their way of life and their poverty. When looking at aerial photographs it is therefore important to bear in mind that they are apt to give a false impression of the past and sometimes to romanticise it. This does not, of course, negate their value *per se*; rather, it means that they must be used with the same care and caution that is brought to any other form of historical evidence.

For these reasons this book does not consist simply of a series of photographs with explanatory captions. Instead, the photographs are integrated chapter by chapter into interpretations of the changes which have happened over time; they are used to illustrate aspects of the past which may still be seen today and to comment on the societies and their motivations which may have produced them. These concerns are fundamental to historical geography which aims both to reconstruct and to interpret geographies of the past.

Of the many thousands of aerial photographs which have been taken in Britain only a small number have revealed features which were previously unknown. Such photographs have, however, an importance out of all proportion to their number for they have added immensely to knowledge, particularly of the prehistoric, Romano-British, Anglo-Saxon and medieval periods.

Most new discoveries have been made through the photography of cropmarks. In dry summers, and given certain soil conditions, some crops, cereals especially, will grow more vigorously over sub-surface features such as former ditches and pits which, although filled in and covered over, still retain available moisture and nutrients. Conversely crops grow less well and grass dries out when deprived of moisture because of the nearness of bed-rock or of man-made foundations of stone, brick or gravel not far below the surface. Parchmarks are then revealed; usually they are more easily seen on the ground than are cropmarks but both are clearer from the air and are best recorded by aerial photography.[1]

New discoveries in the early days of aerial photography in the 1920s alerted scholars to the importance of this new source of evidence for the past. The field archaeologist O. G. S. Crawford, working in Wessex, made a major contribution to the interpretation of the prehistory of Wiltshire through his recognition of the value of cropmarks in revealing sub-surface features. For example, on photographs taken in 1921 by members of the RAF, he recognised marks which he felt to be those of the missing eastern part of the Stonehenge avenue. Testing by excavation he subsequently found the ditches of the avenue exactly where they had been indicated on the photographs.[2] Nothing had been visible on the ground. Similarly, it was cropmarks which led to the discovery in 1925–6 of 'Woodhenge', so-called because of the similarity of its plan to that of Stonehenge despite the fact that its only surface expression was in ripening cereals.

New discoveries continue to be made through the photography of cropmarks. In the summer of 1979, D. N. Riley discovered a huge circle of interrupted ditch around the great neolithic mound at Duggleby Howe in east Yorkshire and recognised possible traces of a neolithic causewayed enclosure on the site of a large henge (itself an aerial discovery) at Newton Kyme, near Tadcaster.[3] Similarly, in 1989 D. R. Wilson recorded extra-mural streets and a triple ditch-system on the east side of the Roman city of *Venta Icenorum* at Caistor St Edmunds in Norfolk (photo A). This echoed similar discoveries made in 1960 by J. K. S. St Joseph on the south side of the city; it is evident that in the second century AD the built-up area was more extensive than that contained by the surviving third-century walls and that it had its own defensive circuit comprising an earthen bank and multiple ditches.

In this century conflicts the world over have led to increasing surveillance from the air and thereby to a greater use of aerial photography and, more recently, of satellite imagery. In Britain, RAF vertical coverage, particularly of the national survey of 1946–7, is especially valuable despite being taken from high level and sometimes obscured by cloud cover. Recognition of the value of aerial photography for teaching and research in many disciplines led the University of Cambridge in 1949 to set up a committee to promote the development of the subject.

Dr J. K. S. St Joseph was appointed the first Curator in Aerial Photography; he was succeeded by D. R. Wilson, General Editor of this series, in 1980. It was St Joseph who first saw and photographed complex and intriguing cropmarks at Yeavering in Northumberland in the very dry summer of 1949.[4] At that time the recognition and identification of the signs of Anglo-Saxon timber buildings from the air had hardly begun. The potential importance of the site was appreciated not only by St Joseph but also by B. Hope-Taylor who, in subsequent excavations over many seasons, revealed both the prehistoric origins of the site and its importance as a centre of kingship in the middle Anglo-Saxon period.[5]

Yeavering, discovered by aerial photography, was soon to become a major land-mark again not only for what it revealed of Anglo-Saxon society in that particular place but through its contribution to the increasing importance of archaeological aerial photography in post-war Britain and in particular to Anglo-Saxon studies. For example, distinctive types of royal hall excavated at Yeavering could be recognised from the air as cropmarks at places as far away as Malmesbury in Wiltshire[6] and Atcham in Shropshire.[7]

Many sub-surface remains of the Romano-British period have also been detected through cropmarks and parchmarks; plans and internal details are sometimes revealed with remarkable clarity by photographs taken at exactly the right time and under ideal light conditions. Two examples are the villas at Lidgate, Suffolk and Chignall, Essex[8] (photo B) both first discovered by observant agricultural workers and only later photographed from the air. A photograph of a Roman fort in Dyfed and its associated road system, revealed under similar conditions, is included later in this volume (photo 13).

Cropmarks appear infrequently, sometimes maybe for only a few days in each generation; many no doubt disappear again unrecorded. Their discovery depends upon a photographer being 'up' at the right moment. Fields at Glenlochar, near Castle Douglas, photographed in July 1949 by St Joseph revealed with exceptional clarity the plan of a large Roman fort; photographed in the same month four years later there was nothing to be seen and no hint of what lay beneath the surface.[9] The infrequency with which cropmarks appear underlines the need for continuing aerial reconnaissance, especially in dry summers. Discoveries continue to be made in places which have been over-flown many times before. In just two weeks in early July 1989, for example, over 300 previously unknown archaeologial sites were discovered; this in a summer, like those of 1949, 1959, 1975, and 1976, in which unusually dry conditions favoured the occurrence of cropmarks in cereal crops and of parchmarks in pasture.

A This photograph illustrates two phases in the defences of the Roman town of *Venta Icenorum*. The parish church of Caistor St Edmunds (Norfolk) stands just within the over-grown remains of the third-century town wall. In the field to the east (in the centre of the picture) three parallel linear marks indicate the course of a triple ditch belonging to an earlier earthwork defence. Pale marks in the crop reveal the position of Roman streets and buildings. The street system conforms to the earlier de-fences but is overridden and cut off by the town wall, with the exception of the nearest street which passes through the east gate.

B A Roman villa at Chignall St James, Essex, showing up with remarkable clarity in a grow-ing crop in the summer of 1976. The courtyard ground plan is almost entirely visible as are the internal and external walkways and the arrangement of the internal rooms and passages.

Cropmarks may be recorded from the air but in themselves they tell us little of the communities which produced the features they show. It is often not clear even to the most experienced interpreter what they represent and it is impossible to assign them a date of origin with any confidence. In any case, they may be of many periods and the results of long occupation and/or cultivation of the same site. Even now, most recorded cropmarks remain unexcavated although an increasing number are being explored on the ground by field walking in winter and spring in the search for fragments of building materials and pottery turned up by the plough.

For medieval England the main contribution of aerial photography has been somewhat different insofar as photographs have mainly been of buildings and of earthworks which are visible at ground level. While many medieval settlements, like their Anglo-Saxon predecessors, have been ploughed out, the remains of others, particularly in the English midlands, may still be seen as earthworks under pasture. ('Earthworks' is something of a misnomer for these remains often conceal stone foundations.) The remains of many deserted villages have only survived because the irregularities on the surface have been enough to deter farmers from ploughing them. Unfortunately, with the increasing power and size of agricultural machinery this is no longer an obstacle and in some arable areas almost all the earthworks of medieval settlements have been ploughed up in recent years. In Norfolk, for example, only two good sites of deserted medieval villages now remain, at Pudding Norton and Godwick.[10]

Aerial photographs of earthworks frequently clarify and enhance what can be seen at ground level and sometimes reveal slight undulations which may have been missed in ground survey and photography. It is for these reasons that the Cambridge Aerial Photography Unit, among others, has routinely photographed deserted sites which have already been identified from documents, maps and ground visits. Oblique aerial views taken at the correct angle relative to the light often bring out features which are very hard to see on the ground; several photographs of such sites are included in this book (photos 37, 41, 49, 50, 51). However, despite their clarity, even the best photographs may mislead. It is tempting to see a fine set of settlement earthworks as representing the remains of houses and enclosures which were abandoned at the same time. Experience has shown, however, that this is rarely the case; excavations of deserted villages have invariably shown the visible earthworks to be a palimpsest and representative of different stages in the life of a settlement. Some features may even be of prehistoric origin while others are Saxon or medieval in date. Excavation has demonstrated the complexity of such sites and shown that all is not as it may appear on the surface, as for example at Wharram Percy, Yorkshire.[11] Aerial photographs may also mislead in another way. At first glance the splendid photograph of Gainsthorpe (photo 51) may give the impression that the whole of the abandoned settlement has been preserved in earthworks. A closer look shows, however, that features continue into the surrounding ploughed fields and it is known from written sources that the settlement was once more extensive. Much of the site has already been ploughed away and what we see today is only part of the village. The same has been shown to be true of a 1980 photograph of the village earthworks at Kingerby in the same county where the remains are less extensive than they were in a ground survey carried out only a year before.[12] These examples serve as reminders that aerial photographs must be interpreted with the help of other sources of information.

Nevertheless, aerial photography is valuable in showing man-made ground disturbance be it from settlements, cultivation or non-agricultural activities such as stone-quarrying and mining. While the photographs themselves tell us little of how communities lived and worked they are sometimes the key to unlocking such information; in conjunction with ground survey they may be used to determine archaeological priorities and excavation strategies. Aerial photographs have also been used to good effect in the study of monastic houses and castles, both of which have been the subject of earlier volumes of Cambridge Air Surveys.[13] Not only do the photographs convey the fascination of the 'bird's eye view' — and with it a new appreciation of ground plans and the relationship of main buildings to outworks — but occasionally they reveal traces of buildings, walls, fishponds and watercourses which have not previously been recognised. They have been of particular value for those monastic sites almost completely destroyed after the Dissolution.

It could be argued that for the medieval and early modern periods aerial photography has been of most value in recording abandoned sites where only earthworks are left on the surface. An interesting and perhaps less familiar example is provided by abandoned gardens such as those at Harrington, Northamptonshire (photo C). Photographs such as this have been of great assistance in the emergence of 'garden archaeology' and the study of garden history.

Aerial photographs take on a different significance when used to illustrate the increasingly urbanised and industrialised societies of Victorian and modern Britain. Photographs, especially those taken before World War II, have now

C An oblique air photograph of earthworks in a pasture field at Harrington, Northamptonshire shows with remarkable clarity the surviving terraces of a Baroque garden, probably of the late seventeenth century. The house stood below the terraces; its foundations with a sunken garden beyond may be seen to the right of centre. The terraces above were different in detail; a lower one receded in a curve while the two above had a trapezoidal pond and smaller ponds or, perhaps, fountains. Two paths which cut diagonally across the top terraces presumably led to some kind of 'eye catcher'. To the right are other earthworks (?medieval fishponds) which look to be earlier in date and, in the foreground, ridge-and-furrow remains of medieval ploughing.

D The Potteries at Longton, Staffordshire, photographed in June 1960 when coal-fired bottle kilns were still a distinctive feature of the landscape. Even by then the number of bottle kilns in the Potteries had halved from the thousand or so in 1939. As they disappeared in the post-war period, replaced by electric and gas-fired kilns, so also did the pall of smoke which formerly hung over the area during firing. In 1960 many of the small potteries, seen here with bottle kilns in their enclosed yards, still survived; most have now gone, as have the Victorian terrace houses recorded here at a time of very active urban renewal and modernisation.

become an invaluable record of urban and industrial landscapes which have changed over the last thirty years; they are now historical artefacts in their own right. For example, hardly a bottle kiln now remains in the Potteries in contrast to the situation in 1960 (photo D) when the area is seen in the process of industrial change and urban renewal. The same is true of the photographs of the dramatic changes in the City of London (photos 119 to 121), its Docklands (photo 94) and in inner cities (photos 96, 97). These more recent changes are explored in the last two chapters of this book and in a companion volume in this series.[14]

As the Cambridge Aerial Photography Unit did not start up until after World War II and because the emphasis of its work has been on rural rather than urban landscapes, some photographs from other collections have been used in this volume and are gratefully acknowledged.

1   The prehistoric and Roman periods

The British Isles exhibit a rich and diverse mosaic of landscapes reflecting a long and complex sequence of development. Despite the quickening pace of change within both rural and urban areas, the imprint of the past can still be identified embedded within or submerged beneath the modern landscape. The remnants of the past within the landscape constitute a finite and diminishing resource, yet their significance is constantly being reassessed as a result of changing research methodologies and the emergence of new conceptual frameworks. Interpretations of the prehistoric and Roman periods[1] have been substantially revised in recent years in response to a rapidly expanding data base, the development of inter-disciplinary research programmes which have demonstrated the intricate ecological relationships of prehistoric communities, and through the attempted explanation of the social dimensions of the archaeological record.

THE SPATIAL FRAMEWORK: PROCESSES OF DESTRUCTION AND DISCOVERY

In recent years a quantitative and qualitative explosion of information has transformed our understanding of the spatial distribution, density and character of prehistoric and Roman activity and has also promoted a more critical awareness of the processes of destruction and the subsequent recovery of archaeological sites and landscapes. The survival of archaeological features in the present landscape is far removed from the original pattern. Indeed, the operation of a wide range of destructive processes, both natural and anthropogenic, has generated a relict and fragmentary pattern which presents many problems of interpretation.

Each successive phase in the development of the human landscape, whilst contributing new elements, also destroyed many earlier components. Thus, areas which have been continuously and intensively exploited over long periods, often exhibit little surface evidence of their earliest phases of activity. Land use change in particular can have important repercussions in terms of the survival or destruction of archaeological features. The retreat of cultivation from many upland areas and their relative isolation in recent years, has frequently led to the preservation of landscape information, whilst intensive arable activity in lowland zones has erased such detail from the ground surface. Prehistoric landscapes may also be hidden beneath later deposits. Thus, colluviation and alluviation, often initiated or accentuated by forest clearance and cultivation, can lead to the removal of archaeological evidence in the topsoil in upland areas and on hill slopes, whilst sediments deposited in valley floors may obscure early occupation levels. Similarly, peat growth or the deposition of marine sediments can mask yet also preserve intact the archaeological surfaces beneath them. An awareness of the

15

1 Plowden, the Long Mynd, Shropshire. Earthwork features of many periods can be identified on the southern fringes of the Long Mynd plateau. A field system of uncertain date, characterised by broadly rectangular fields 60 to 90 m across and defined by lynchet banks, extends across the undulating pasture land (between 250 and 325 m in altitude). Two trackways form an integral part of the field system; one emerges from a steep-sided valley (left foreground), the other (on the right of the photograph) joins the Portway, an important prehistoric routeway which climbs northwards along the crest of the Long Mynd. A circular enclosure, 70 m in diameter overlies part of the field system but also remains undated. At least three later phases of activity can be identified. The enclosed field with parallel ridges overlooking the steep western scarp slope, suggests arable activity, perhaps reflecting pressure on land during the Napoleonic Wars. However, a rabbit warren and sheep grazing appear to have been the most important later land uses. The small rounded embankment (18 m long) in front of the circular enclosure is a pillow mound constructed for the trapping of rabbits probably between the fifteenth and eighteenth centuries AD. A warren is identified here in 1808. The rectangular structure incorporating the stone foundations of a small building (centre left) may also be associated with the warren or may indicate the site of a shepherds' hut. A changing reappraisal of resources, from an agricultural to a recreational context, can be seen in the four small areas of levelled ground which represent the remnants of a former private golf course developed by the land owner; a forerunner of the increasing recreational use of the Long Mynd in recent years.

differential impact of such destructive forces is of great importance in evaluating the significance of landscape survivals.

The great potential of the uplands as zones of survival is currently being clarified through the integration of field survey and aerial reconnaissance, the latter being particularly important in inaccessible and difficult terrain. Large tracts of prehistoric landscapes including settlements, field systems and land boundaries have been identified fossilised within moorland environments for example on Dartmoor and Bodmin Moor and in the Cheviots and Pennines. These landscapes of early abandonment, although sometimes recolonised during the medieval period, can often provide valuable insights into the layout and organisation of settlements and field systems, not only in the uplands, but also in lowland zones where the earliest phases of activity have been extensively modified or destroyed. Paradoxically the recognition of the significance of these upland reservoirs of archaeological data comes at a time when they are increasingly at risk, especially through the improvement of agricultural land, a dilemma which can be seen at Plowden in Shropshire. First recognised from the air in 1938, the oblique angle and good winter lighting conditions of the aerial view highlights a series of small earthwork features including trackways, field boundaries and enclosures (photo 1).

The landscape at Plowden demonstrates the potential of aerial photography in the recovery of complex landscapes, yet also illustrates a range of interpretative problems and contemporary pressures which are frequently encountered within upland environments. Firstly, despite the range of features revealed, their chronological and functional significance remain tantalisingly obscure. Although it has been suggested that the field system may have been in use in the late prehistoric or Romano-British period, without excavation this hypothesis remains unproven.[2] The relationships between the field system and the other landscape components is also uncertain. Secondly, recent developments at Plowden illustrate the destructive pressures affecting both the ecological and archaeological heritage of many upland areas. Plowden is incorporated within An Area of Outstanding Natural Beauty in recognition of its landscape and amenity value, and was also included in the Long Mynd Site of Special Scientific Interest (SSSI), designated in 1953 to safeguard the area's distinctive geology, botany and wildlife. It is particularly unfortunate, therefore, that since 1965 Plowden has been subject to considerable modification through agricultural improvement. The formerly open landscape (as seen in photo 1) has now been fenced, the pasture ploughed and reseeded, new access roads have been constructed and the earthworks considerably reduced. When the Long Mynd SSSI was redesignated in 1990, the boundaries were redrawn, excluding the improved land at Plowden. The ecological impact of upland improvement in Shropshire has recently been documented and the net loss in the area and diversity of semi-natural habitats has been highlighted.[3] The archaeological features at Plowden were not scheduled and thus lacked any degree of protection. The growing pressures on fragile upland landscapes such as these and the conflicting demands on land use has promoted a growing awareness of the common interests shared by archaeologists, nature conservationists and other groups concerned with the interpretation and protection of the British landscape.[4]

In areas which have been subject to intensive agricultural development over long periods, aerial reconnaissance coupled with ground inspection provides the

most powerful tool for the discovery of features which have been erased from the contemporary land surface, but which are revealed in certain circumstances as soil marks and patterns of differential crop growth which can only be fully appreciated from the air.[5] The expansion of aerial survey following the pioneer work of O. G. S. Crawford and Major G. W. G. Allen[6] in the 1920s and 1930s, and of Professor J. K. S. St Joseph from 1945 has clearly demonstrated the great value of aerial photography in archaeological contexts. 'Upstanding' field monuments have been shown to represent a mere fragment of what was originally a much more complex and extensive pattern of early settlement and land use (photo 2). The recovery of soil and crop mark information has led to a massive

2 Berghill, Whittington, Shropshire. At Berghill on the North Shropshire Plain, at least two major phases of land organisation can be identified. Between 1847 and 1873 the field boundaries were extensively remodelled, an earlier pattern of small fields being replaced by the larger more regular layout evident in the photograph. Lying beneath the modern landscape, however, an earlier phase can be identified. The well drained sandy and loamy soils formed above an island of glacio-fluvial drifts, combined with a cereal crop, provided excellent conditions in July 1979 for the development of extensive crop marks which create a 'window' on an earlier agrarian pattern. Positive crop marks, caused by more luxuriant crop growth, appear darker on the photograph and reflect the position of buried ditches delineating a variety of features. The light coloured fields reveal two clearly defined rectilinear enclosures, the largest of which exhibits an annexe and is bounded on its eastern side by a trackway which broadens to form a triangular green; in the background a darker crop reveals a circular enclosure and a number of linear features. To the east the crop-mark sequence is truncated by an unresponsive crop. The aerial photograph poses considerable problems of interpretation. What type of upstanding structures are implied by these patterns of differential crop growth? What were the functional relationships between the various enclosures? To what extent can chronological depth be identified through the presence of overlapping detail? With four hillforts within a 12 km radius and the Roman city of Wroxeter (*Viroconium Cornoviorum*) 19 km to the south-east, an Iron Age or Romano-British date for these crop marks can be hypothesised. Conclusive evidence could only be provided by an intensive programme of field analysis and excavation.

increase in the numbers of known archaeological sites, particularly in the sands and gravels of many river valleys, in chalk and limestone landscapes, and in areas characterised by glacial outwash deposits.[7] These discoveries have led to a fundamental reappraisal of the number, density and distributional patterns of prehistoric and Roman settlement. The traditional concept of the archaeological 'site' has also been found wanting in many lowland areas where extensive landscapes comparable to those discovered in upland environments have been identified, often exhibiting multi-period phases of development.

Whilst the great value of aerial reconnaissance in augmenting the archaeological data base has been recognised, there has been a growing awareness in recent years of the often serious problems inherent within the aerial photographic record. From the spatial viewpoint it has become clear that the distributional anomalies of landscape evidence caused by differential destructive processes are equally apparent in aerially derived data due to the differential patterns of recovery. Thus, the spatial pattern of soil and crop mark features reflects many variables including soil type, weather conditions, land use and the intensity of aerial reconnaissance. It is important, therefore, to recognise that apparent negative areas caused by heavy soils, unresponsive land uses, or air traffic restrictions

3 Fengate, Peterborough, Cambridgeshire. Within the expanding industrial fringe of Peterborough, excavation of crop marks discovered through aerial reconnaissance has revealed a complex sequence of prehistoric occupation located where the gravel terraces of the River Nene meet the western margins of the peat Fens. The expansion of Peterborough New Town provided the stimulus for large-scale excavation in the 1970s. The buried ditches which lay beneath the crop marks have been exposed within the two excavated areas in the upper portion of the photograph; they form part of a planned rectilinear system of ditched enclosures and track-ways established on the gravel terraces at right angles to the fen edge in the early second millennium *bc*. The excavation of these two areas confirmed the general pattern of the crop mark features but generated a dramatic reappraisal of their function and dating. It has been suggested that a trans-humance cycle was in opera-tion, exploiting contrasting yet complementary ecological zones. During the wet winter months the enclosures on the flood-free river terraces would have functioned as cattle pad-docks while in summer the rich grasslands along the margins and islands of the Fenland pro-vided grazing. The complex tangle of features in the third area (lower centre of photo-graph) was largely invisible to the aerial camera due to al-luvial deposition in the third century AD. Only the most re-cent Romano-British phase ap-peared as a crop mark, the circular houses of the earlier Iron Age settlement being revealed only through bore-hole surveys and excavation.

are not necessarily blank areas in the archaeological record.[8] Drought conditions, land use change, longer term aerial surveillance and detailed field work con-sistently reveal the distributional limitations of aerially derived data. The analysis of soil and crop mark distributions needs therefore to be presented in a spatial context which illustrates both the opportunities and constraints for aerial survey and also relationships with other sources of archaeological information.

The interpretative problems, particularly of soil and crop marks, remain severe. Each individual aerial photograph provides a transient indication of a range of buried features, the pattern of which varies according to season, weather and land use. Even when a cumulative picture can be achieved based on a sequence of photography, invariably the aerial view will reveal only a fraction of the buried landscape, nor can it provide any firm evidence concerning function and dating. Excavation can clarify many of these problems and also provides a cautionary insight into the limitations of the aerial view. Thus, at Fengate, the excavation of a dense pattern of crop marks revealed a landscape exhibiting much greater chronological depth and complexity than was initially thought, including areas of occupation which did not appear on the aerial photograph because of the masking effect of alluviation (photo 3).[9]

4 The Polden Hills, Somerset. From the narrow limestone ridge of the Polden Hills, the landscape of the Somerset Levels provides little evidence of the prehistoric past. However, encapsulated and preserved within the waterlogged peat deposits of the Brue valley, numerous wooden trackways have been identified which bear witness to the activity patterns of prehistoric groups from the fourth millenium *bc*. The trackways linked permanently settled dry points, including the Polden Hills and adjacent 'islands' of rock and sand, and provided safe passage through an evolving sequence of reed swamp, fen woodland and the blanket bog in the intervening lowlands. The trackways permitted the exploitation of these contrasting ecological zones, linking the natural and coppiced woodlands, grazing and arable land of the uplands, the rich seasonally flooded meadows or 'hangings' at the interface of hill slope and marsh, and the fish and game supplies of the wetter areas.

Whilst the important role of excavation can be seen at Fengate, the vast quantity of aerially derived information and the increasing pressure on archaeological resources make it unlikely that many sites will ever be excavated on such a scale as this. There is, therefore, an urgent need to develop additional methodologies which will enable the potential of aerial photography to be fully exploited. The most promising way forward appears to be in the integration of aerial photography with other non-excavational methods, for example field walking and the examination of surface debris, sedimentological analysis of the plough soil, and geophysical survey to clarify the nature of subsurface structures. These approaches require the specialist skills of both archaeologists and environmental scientists, and can provide a complementary approach to the traditional, destructive, and expensive technique of excavation.

ENVIRONMENT AND LANDSCAPE

The changing appreciation of the density and pattern of prehistoric activity has been paralleled by a fuller recognition of the abilities of prehistoric groups to use, modify and manage environmental resources. Through the application of a wide spectrum of palaeoecological perspectives, environmental patterns and processes can be monitored and the difficult task of isolating the role of human agency as an instigator and catalyst of ecological change can be attempted.

A prime example of the successful integration of palaeoecological and archaeological research can be seen in the Somerset Levels Project. The peat deposits of the Levels provide excellent conditions for the preservation of organic materials, including a series of prehistoric wooden trackways and a wide range of palaeobotanical data. The excavation of the trackways, initially revealed through commercial peat extraction, has been complemented by specialist environmental studies of peat types, fossil pollen, plant and insect assemblages, dendrochronology and radio-carbon dating.[10] As a result, the changing ecological pattern and the nature of human response and adaptation have been identified. (photo 4).

The wooden trackways are of significance, not only as artefacts, but also as important sources of environmental evidence in their own right. The types of wood used evoke the character of the prehistoric woodlands, and provide tangible evidence for the woodland clearance revealed in local pollen diagrams, particularly those from the hill slopes of the Poldens and the light sandy soils of the Burtle 'island'. The trackways also exhibit considerable wood-working skills, and above all reveal the active management of woodland resources particularly through the coppicing of hazel, oak and ash from *c.*3200 *bc* onwards. The building and maintenance of the trackways also implies the existence of permanently settled and well-organised communities, probably located on the Polden Hills and adjacent 'island' sites. A sustained prehistoric presence has thus been demonstrated within an area which on the ground and from the air appeared to possess little archaeological significance.[11]

The abilities of prehistoric groups to control and manage environmental resources can also be seen in the impressive degree of planning and organisation within many prehistoric landscapes, particularly in the physical layout of field

5 Yar Tor Down and Holne Moor, near Dartmeet, Dartmoor, Devon. The field boundaries extending from Yar Tor Down (368 m) and beyond the River Dart gorge to the Holne Moor plateau (*c*.330 m), form part of the Dartmeet parallel reave system, one of the finest prehistoric field systems in Britain. The coaxial reave boundaries extend across a varied tract of countryside (*c*.3200 ha) with a common north-east to south-west orientation, regardless of topography. The reave system forms part of a wider territorial unit incorporating the sheltered Upper Dart basin to the west and with access also to the higher moorland to the north and south. The field system, with its planned and organised layout, was abandoned during the first millennium *bc*. Land hunger in the medieval period promoted a partial recolonisation; the curved pattern of medieval lynchets, resulting from cultivation of the sheltered hill slopes of Holne Moor (bottom right), contrasts with the prehistoric field layout.

systems and land boundaries.[12] Although prehistoric field patterns are very varied,[13] the existence of regular and planned layouts, often described as coaxial or cohesive systems, has been recognised in a growing range of geographical and temporal contexts.[14] Many examples have been discovered, preserved and fossilised, within moorland and pastoral environments. Thus, on Dartmoor, which has been described as 'one of Britain's last great reservoirs of ancient landscapes',[15] a highly organised system of land division has been identified. The long, low, stony boundaries, known as reaves, were recognised in the nineteenth century, but their extent, pattern and chronological context have only recently been established (photo 5).[16] The Dartmoor reaves appear to have been established over a short time span *c*.1300 *bc*, as part of an extensive, planned system of land division within an area which had previously functioned as a casually used common. However, although the pattern is now recognised, an understanding of its purpose and the manner in which it was delineated prove more problematical. It has been suggested that increasing pressure on grazing land and the need to control and manage resources more effectively, provided the stimulus for the reave systems, thus reducing conflict between competing groups.[17]

The location of the Dartmeet system on the central Dartmoor massif has ensured its survival. At lower levels the reaves have been engulfed within the modern landscape. However, elements of linearity and the common orientation of field boundaries often provide glimpses of the earlier, underlying pattern. Indeed, the survival of coaxial prehistoric field systems preserved within modern landscapes should not be underestimated even within more intensively exploited lowland zones. Thus, the topographical analysis of field patterns in areas of 'ancient countryside',[18] characterised by long continuity in landscape development, has revealed extensive, coaxial field systems, probably of late prehistoric or Roman date, still providing the framework of the modern landscape in parts of East Anglia and Essex.[19]

In many arable areas, however, aerial reconnaissance has recovered coaxial field systems erased and submerged beneath modern field layouts and exhibiting considerable geographical and chronological diversity. Reference has already been made to the planned rectilinear field system at Fengate which dates from *c*.2000 *bc* and was apparently designed to maximise the capacity of valuable winter grazing land along the Fen edge (photo 3). However, some of the most impressive examples are located on the chalk downlands of southern Britain, where large coaxial systems extend over several kilometres irrespective of topography.[20] A unitary, deliberately planned pattern of land allotment is suggested which may have its origins in the second millennium *bc*. A final example of the aerial discovery and particularly the mapping of an extensive coaxial field system can be seen in south Yorkshire and north Nottinghamshire, where the light soils of the Bunter sandstones provide excellent conditions for soil and crop mark formation.[21] Although restricted excavation has demonstrated a Roman use for part of this system, a prehistoric origin may well be a possibility in some areas.

Organisation and management of land and resources is also suggested by the existence of linear land boundaries. Whether surviving in the landscape or occurring largely as soil and crop marks, the individual boundaries usually form part of a wider system. Interpretations of their function vary. In some areas these boundaries appear to be associated with a change from an arable to a more pastoral economy, perhaps defining areas of controlled grazing. Elsewhere they appear to delineate distinctive territorial units. An impressive sequence of linear land boundaries can be seen on the North York Moors (photo 6).

A hypothetical model of territorial organisation in the north-west of the North York Moors has been proposed following a detailed survey of archaeological features and their position within the landscape.[22] It is suggested that declining fertility in the uplands, combined with population pressure, may have generated the emergence of a territorial system between 1700 *bc* and 1300 *bc*. Natural boundaries, particularly watersheds, appear to be augmented by symbolic boundaries defined by burial sites in the form of round barrows. Each territory integrated the permanent settlements in valley locations with seasonal occupance of the uplands. During the first millennium *bc*, linear earthwork systems emerged in some areas, most notably on the Tabular Hills.[23] Here the dyke systems delineate land divisions with a varied resource potential, incorporating moorland access, arable land on the south facing slopes, and rich pastures and water meadows at the junction of hill and vale.

6 The Scamridge Dykes, Yorkshire. Prehistoric boundaries cross the fertile farmland of the Tabular Hills, terminating in an escarpment overlooking Troutsdale and the heather moorland and afforested areas of the North York Moors. The contrasting modern landscapes reflect the divergent potential of the two areas in prehistoric times. In the northern uplands, woodland clearance, combined with climatic deterioration, led to decreasing soil fertility, the gradual replacement of woodland by heather moorland and a decline in the intensity of prehistoric activity c.1000 bc. The productive limestone soils of the Tabular Hills, however, continued to provide a focus for settlement throughout the prehistoric period, culminating in the construction of substantial linear earthworks in the first millennium bc. Running southwards from the scarp slope, the dykes then extend along the sides of valleys opening to the Vale of Pickering.

The evaluation of the palaeoecological record and the physical evidence of the landscape itself enables the profound and cumulative impact of prehistoric communities to be monitored. Through the clearance and management of woodlands, the development of arable and pastoral economies, and the establishment of field systems and land boundaries, the transition from a natural landscape to one increasingly modified by human activity was achieved. A mosaic of prehistoric environments was created exhibiting great diversity over time and space. In some regions a continuous process of landscape evolution can be identified, while in other areas colonisation and settlement were followed by decline and abandonment. The contraction of prehistoric activity in northern and western Britain is well documented in the first millennium *bc*, the derelict field systems of Dartmoor and the declining exploitation of the North York Moors being just two examples of a more widespread pattern. Although climatic deterioration between 1400 and 600 *bc* would have been felt most keenly within the Highland zone, the vulnerability of many upland ecosystems had already been accentuated by clearance and agricultural activities. The removal of the protective woodland cover was often followed by declining soil fertility, soil erosion and the spread of heathland and bog. Indeed, many of the open landscapes of northern and western Britain, which are now highly valued for the recreational and amenity potential of what are often considered 'natural' landscapes, developed through the complex interplay of climatic and anthropogenic factors in the prehistoric period.

In lowland Britain the impact of climatic deterioration was less significant, and many areas exhibit a more sustained process of landscape development. Woodland clearance and environmental modification were equally profound, but greater fertility and more resilient soils frequently resulted in the creation of relatively stable and intensively used agrarian landscapes. A good example is provided by the Wessex chalklands where the wealth of archaeological field evidence is complemented by a growing range of palaeoecological research illustrating the long term, often irreversible, changes wrought by prehistoric communities.[24] The analysis of pollen and mollusc assemblages, often derived from old land surfaces sealed beneath Neolithic and Bronze Age structures, has demonstrated that the initial clearance of the natural mixed oak forests often resulted in the emergence of the permanently open landscapes so characteristic of the chalk downlands throughout their subsequent history. Although the pattern of clearance was varied, many areas were largely deforested by the middle of the second millennium *bc*. The physical evidence of open conditions can also be seen in the emergence of formalised field sytems during this period. Lynchets, formed by the downslope accumulation of soil hastened by ploughing within these arable plots, were formerly widespread on the downlands. Although subsequent cultivation has been highly destructive, extensive areas of prehistoric fields can be recovered through aerial reconnaissance (photo 7).

Both the longevity of agrarian activity on the chalklands and some of the associated environmental problems have been demonstrated through the analysis of colluvial deposits in valley locations.[25] Colluviation, resulting from the downslope movement of soil accentuated by cultivation, was initiated in some areas during the second millennium *bc* and increased in the later first millennium *bc*

7a, b Beacon Hill and Ladle Hill, Hampshire. At the northern margins of the Hampshire chalk plateau, an impressive array of prehistoric field monuments survive within pockets of downland protected as Sites of Special Scientific Interest. Aerial photography demonstrates that these features are remnants of an extensive prehistoric landscape largely destroyed through the cultivation of the former downland. The earliest visible features are burial sites in the form of round barrows, probably constructed within an already open landscape in the second millennium *bc*. Prehistoric fields, defined by well preserved lynchets, survive on the steep eastern slopes of Beacon Hill, while those on the gentler western slopes are being destroyed through cultivation. Ploughed out lynchets indicate the original scale of the field system. Although traditionally described as 'Celtic' fields, these small, rectangular plots exhibit a broad chronological span extending from the second millennium *bc* through to the Romano-British period. A linear ditch or land boundary, probably dating from the early first millennium *bc*, traverses the escarpment rim from Great Litchfield Down northwards to Ladle Hill, where it was subsequently incorporated within the unfinished hillfort. The whole landscape is dominated by the hillfort on Beacon Hill which must have functioned as an important territorial focus within the densely occupied countryside of the later prehistoric period.

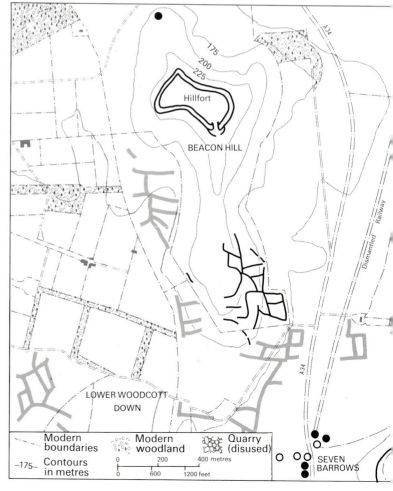

26

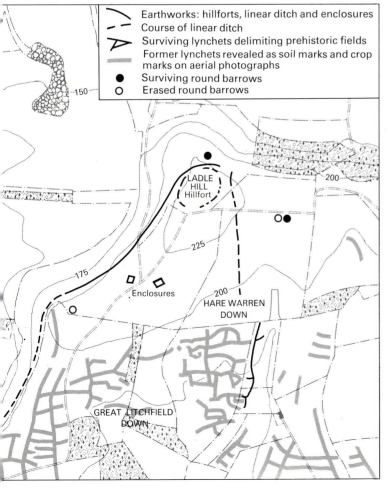

Earthworks: hillforts, linear ditch and enclosures
Course of linear ditch
Surviving lynchets delimiting prehistoric fields
Former lynchets revealed as soil marks and crop marks on aerial photographs
● Surviving round barrows
○ Erased round barrows

—150

—200

LADLE HILL Hillfort

○●

—225

—175

□ □
Enclosures

—200
HARE WARREN DOWN

○

GREAT LITCHFIELD DOWN

An aerial photographic interpretation of the prehistoric landscape of Beacon Hill and Ladle Hill, Hampshire.

8 The Butser Ancient Farm Project, Bascomb Copse, Chalton, Hampshire. The farm, established in 1972 at Butser Hill and transferred in 1990 to nearby Bascomb Copse, functions as 'an open air laboratory' within which the farming practices of an Iron Age Chalkland community can be simulated and scientifically evaluated. The most ambitious of the three Iron Age houses rebuilt within the octagonal enclosure can be seen under construction in the form of concentric rings of wooden posts, recreating a substantial roundhouse excavated at Longbridge Deverill Cowdown in Wiltshire. A large rectangular area edged by wattle fences provides arable plots in which prehistoric cereal types and legumes are grown. A variety of livestock, including sheep, goats and cattle represent the important pastoral dimension of Iron Age farming. As the project evolves, the buildings and enclosures will provide a three-dimensional model of the late prehistoric countryside, usually glimpsed only through earthwork, soil mark and crop mark evidence.

as a result of agrarian intensification. However, while sediment deposition increased valley productivity, the erosion of soil on hill tops and slopes lessened their fertility, leading in some areas to the conversion of former arable land to pasture and the incorporation of new arable areas on heavier soils. Colluvial deposits can be identified within the chalk landscape of Beacon Hill and Ladle Hill (photo 7), most noticeably on Hare Warren Down, through the broad, dark soil marks which delineate the greater soil depth accumulated within the curving, coalescing pattern of dry valleys.

The mapping of the field evidence, soil and crop marks provides a partial and discontinuous representation of a multiperiod prehistoric landscape. Blank areas on the map may merely reflect unfavourable soil and crop conditions and the destructive impact of intensive and long established cultivation at lower levels; they may, however, indicate significant contrasts in prehistoric land use, for example grazing or woodland zones leaving little evidence of their former existence. Although the precise chronological relationships of the individual components are difficult to define, the overall impression is of a closely delineated and intensively exploited farmscape.[26] The character of the agricultural systems practised within the prehistoric landscape can often be clarified through excavation which may reveal agricultural implements, traces of the crops grown and livestock kept, and may even produce the physical evidence of ground preparation and cultivation in the form of grooves carved in the subsoil by prehistoric ploughs. An important complementary perspective is provided by experimental approaches in which the hypotheses suggested by excavation can be tested in a practical manner (photo 8).

Various long-term research programmes are in progress at the Ancient Farm Project including investigations into building construction, cultivation methods, the performance of cereals and livestock of prehistoric type, the operation of underground pits for bulk storage of grain, and problems of weed infestation and soil exhaustion. The experimental work, although restricted to chalkland environments in the Iron Age (when soil and climate were broadly comparable to the present), suggests a successful and stable agricultural economy with considerable potential for surplus production and storage.[27]

MONUMENTS IN THE LANDSCAPE

The fuller delineation of the prehistoric landscape made possible through intensive fieldwork, aerial reconnaissance and more sophisticated excavation methods, has revealed a countryside which was densely occupied, closely demarcated and often highly organised. However, an understanding of the human groups who created and operated within this landscape is more difficult to achieve. The attempted progression from the description of the physical remnants of past communities, towards an appreciation of the functioning of the societies which produced them, is hindered both by the incomplete and constantly changing nature of the evidence available and also by the difficulties of comprehending the motivations and priorities of prehistoric groups. Nevertheless, considerable progress has been made in inferring the social implications of archaeological data.[28] Many hypotheses relating to social organisation and social change have been generated from a consideration of the substantial monuments which form an important component of the archaeological record at certain periods in the past. Many of these structures, whether funerary, ceremonial or more utilitarian in character, are impressive in scale, exhibit considerable organisational and building skills, and must have absorbed large amounts of time and energy. An examination of the character of these monuments and the roles they played may well permit the elucidation of some aspects of the social complexity of the prehistoric period.

The emergence of substantial communal tombs in the third and second millennia *bc* is of particular interest, these structures often constituting the earliest prehistoric feature to survive within any landscape. Frequently incorporating large earthen mounds or stone cairns which would have formed imposing landmarks, the impressiveness of these monuments is often accentuated by their location in prominent geographical positions. It would appear, therefore, that these communal tombs were not only of significance in the burial of the dead, but also functioned as important symbols within the landscape of the living communities which built them. Although it has been suggested that these monuments reflect the culmination of stable and successful farming communities, it has also been argued that they are more likely to be associated with periods characterised by increasing pressure on vital but restricted resources.[29] The tombs in providing a link with past generations would not only have functioned as a territorial focus, but may also have strengthened and legitimised the use and control of land by the local community.

A high density of communal tombs, known as chambered cairns, occurs in the Orkney Islands. The tombs were built within an open landscape broadly comparable to that of the present day, the original vegetation of birch and hazel scrub being replaced from 3000 *bc* by open grassland and heath. Nevertheless, the prehistoric population was able to exploit a diverse habitat including rich pasture lands, light sandy soils suitable for cultivation, and an abundant marine life. Seventy-seven chambered cairns have been located, widely dispersed throughout

the Orkney Islands. Many are prominently sited overlooking extensive areas of land, and may well have functioned as focal points for surrounding communities, perhaps symbolising their ownership over key areas of arable land. The cairn sequence is dominated by Maes Howe, its size, elaboration and geographical setting distinguishing it from the smaller tombs with their probable community function (photo 9).

The scale of concentrated communal effort involved in the building of Maes Howe is immense, an estimated 100,000 construction hours being required for the chamber tomb whilst the henges, known as the Ring of Brodgar and the Stones of Stenness would have absorbed between 50,000 and 80,000 hours each. It has been suggested that the construction of these major monumental features may reflect changes in the social organisation of the Orkney Islands, perhaps mirroring a progression from a society characterised by small, equal status groups towards the development of a more centralised, hierarchical system in the late third millennium *bc*. The location of the most elaborate chamber tomb and two henges in close proximity within an impressive natural landscape would certainly appear to define an important focal point for the Orkney Islands as a whole.[30]

The Orkney henges are notable examples of a new group of communal monuments which develop in the later third millennium *bc*, including henges, stone circles and the linear bank and ditch features known as cursus monuments. While many of these structures survive in the modern landscape, aerial reconnaissance has recovered many additional examples in areas of intensive arable activity (photo 10). Although these monuments vary widely in size and prove difficult to interpret in a functional sense, many reflect an ability to mobilise and channel substantial resources in the building of large and imposing structures. It has been argued that henges, stone circles, cursus monuments and the earlier causewayed enclosures of southern England and the east Midlands may provide a tangible expression of the power and prestige of broader territorial groupings. Functioning as 'monuments for the living', which proclaimed and reinforced the authority and status of the leaders of organised regional communities, these monuments may have fulfilled a variety of interrelated religious, social and political roles.[31]

From the mid second millennium *bc* the resources formerly channelled into the construction of communal monuments appear to be applied to more practical concerns, particularly the intensive development of the agrarian landscape. Formal field systems permitting the fuller and more efficient use of land became more widespread. The organisational and engineering skills once devoted to the building of funerary, ritual and ceremonial structures can now be seen in large coaxial field patterns, such as the Dartmoor Reaves (photo 5), and in the extensive field systems of the chalk downlands of Wessex (photo 7). The degree of control and management thus imprinted on the landscape suggests a concomitant level of social organisation, characterised by groups or individuals able to plan and implement such developments.

The subsequent remergence of large-scale monuments in the landscape again demonstrates more utilitarian interests, energies now being channelled into hilltop enclosures, culminating in the widespread development of hillforts between 800 and 400 BC. Although very varied in character, many hillforts were substantial constructions involving a considerable investment of labour, were densely

9 Maes Howe, Mainland, the Orkney Islands. Maes Howe constitutes the most elaborate stage in the Orcadian tradition of communal tomb building. The structure is characterised by the high quality of stonework within its central chamber and passage-way, and the substantial covering mound (35 m wide and 7 m high) built on a levelled circular platform encircled by a low bank and ditch. Situated amongst some of the richest agricultural land in the Orkney Islands, Maes Howe lies in close proximity to the isthmus between the sheltered inland lochs of Harray and Stenness, an impressive amalgam of land and water and an area with great accessibility to the islands as a whole. Two enclosures or henges, the Ring of Brodgar and the Stones of Stenness, are located at either end of the isthmus.

10 The Milfield Basin, Northumberland. West of the abandoned Milfield airfield, an intricate mixture of archaeological and geomorphological crop marks occur within deep well drained soils overlying glacio-fluvial drift in the valley of the River Till. A sequence of dark bands reflect the complex pattern of drainage and deposits associated with the ice-dammed lake which developed here at the end of the last glaciation. The polygonal crop marks (foreground), superficially similar to an early field pattern, are fossilised ice wedges originating in periglacial conditions. The circular crop mark of the Coupland henge (70 m in diameter), and two broadly parallel linear crop marks delineating an avenue running through the henge, can be seen superimposed on the natural features. The avenue extends approximately 2 km on a constant north to south axis, linking three of the nine hengiform structures discovered. The diagonal light coloured crop mark (bottom left) marks the course of a North Sea gas main.

occupied, and were clearly defensive in function. Excavation suggests that many hillforts possessed a considerable food storage capacity, often in excess of the apparent requirements of the resident community and beyond the productive capacity of the immediate area. The emergence of hillforts may reflect an increasing pressure of population against resources accentuated by declining productivity associated with land exhaustion and climatic deterioration. New patterns emerge within the settlement hierarchy between 400 and 100 BC. While many hillforts go out of regular use, others appear to increase in status and achieve a pre-eminent position.[32] The character of these 'developed' hillforts may be exemplified by the excavations at Danebury where the hillfort was massively refortified around 400 BC. Supporting a large population within a well organised interior, the hillfort exhibited a substantial grain storage capacity and may also have functioned as a centre of manufacturing and exchange.[33] In Wessex, 'developed' hillforts are regularly spaced, each dominating a clearly defined territorial unit within which they may have provided an important focus of economic, social and political organisation.

The hillfort at Beacon Hill (photo 7) is un-excavated and its status is therefore uncertain. Located at the junction of the Hampshire chalk plateau with the valley of the River Kennet to the north, the surrounding area afforded diverse agricultural resources. The open chalk downlands provided grazing for sheep and cattle; many of the small rectangular fields would have been under arable cultivation; woodland may have been managed on the steep escarpment slopes providing fuel, building materials and grazing for cattle and pigs. The better watered lands below the northern fringes of the escarpment may have provided additional cattle grazing and arable areas.[34] A dense pattern of small agricultural settlements can be envisaged within this varied landscape, their presence now recoverable only through field survey and aerial reconnaissance. The nature of the relationships between the hillfort and surrounding settlements remains speculative; however, the sense of physical domination, engendered by the impressive location and defensive capability of the hillfort, may well have been paralleled by other forms of control and influence.

TRADE AND CONQUEST: THE IMPACT OF ROME

In the last century BC, the internal processes of social and economic change within Iron Age Britain were strongly affected by external stimuli, particularly the increasing level of continental trade. Metals, grain, hides, and manpower in the form of slaves were in strong demand from the consumer markets of the Roman world. Old established trade routes were revitalised, with Hengistbury Head functioning as the major port of call.[35] The extension of Roman control to the whole of Gaul in the late first century BC, not only boosted demand but led to a reorientation of trade routes towards south-eastern Britain focusing particularly on the Thames Estuary. New centres of population and wealth, known as *oppida*, emerge in the south and east at this period, while the majority of hillforts in the region appear to be abandoned. Characterised by large nucleated populations, *oppida* are typically situated in lowlying positions commanding routeways, thus contrasting strongly with the typical hillfort location. *Oppida* appear to have functioned as nodal points within an expanding system of long distance trade, through which the flow of British raw materials and reciprocated luxury items may have been controlled by elite groups. Within the more fully developed market economy of the south-east, a number of *oppida* achieved considerable importance, combining not only commercial and industrial functions but serving also as centres of political authority within territorially distinct tribal groupings. These settlements, which include Colchester, Silchester, Chichester, St. Albans and Bagendon, appear functionally to represent an indigenous pattern of urban or proto urban development.

Some *oppida* were surrounded by impressive dyke systems. Although often defensive in character, these systems do not always form a continuous circuit and may have symbolised the status and prestige of the controlling groups and provided a means of regulating trade movements perhaps defining a mercantile zone. At Stanwick in North Yorkshire, an extensive dyke sequence, traditionally interpreted as a centre of anti-Roman resistance, may well be comparable to the *oppida* of south-eastern England (photo 11).[36] The ramparts at Stanwick were constructed over a short time period in the mid first century AD, before the Roman advance into the region. Located at the junction of north-south and trans-Pennine routeways, Stanwick would have been well placed to control the flow of commodities required by the expanding Roman markets to the south. The recovery of a wide array of Roman prestige goods suggests a wealthy population able to exploit

11 Dyke system at Stanwick, North Yorkshire. A complex sequence of dykes, 8 km in length and enclosing 350 ha, surrounds the parish church at Stanwick, forming one of the most impressive earthwork sequences in northern England. The stone faced ramparts are well preserved, reaching 5 m in height, due largely to their position within the former parkland of Stanwick Hall. Although the structural sequence is unclear the dykes appear to delineate four interconnecting enclosures, two of which are included within the photograph. An oval enclosure, known as The Tofts, can be seen to the right of the church, the south-western boundary being well preserved within a tree plantation. A large broadly rectangular enclosure, partially delineated by tree covered ramparts, extends from the base of Henah Hill behind the church into the foreground of the photograph. The parallel strips of medieval rigg and furrow and traces of the deserted medieval village complicate the earthwork sequences.

12 Dere Street, near Ancrum, Borders Region. Dere Street is a prime example of a long-distance Roman routeway providing the major eastern line of military penetration into Scotland. It can be seen here approaching the Eildon Hills, the summit on the right being surmounted by a substantial and intensively occupied hillfort which is thought to have functioned as an Iron Age tribal capital. The Roman fort of Newstead is located in the valley below, commanding the crossing point of the River Tweed.

34

their position on the periphery of the Roman world through the promotion of trading links.

In AD 43, trading contacts were replaced by Roman conquest. While strong elements of continuity with the past can be identified, the impact of Roman imperialism generated not only new patterns of political authority, but also changed social and cultural relationships, and led to the emergence of a new economic order. Military conquest was enforced and maintained through the development of an efficient transport system and the imposition of control points within the landscape. Arterial highways provided support for the lines of military advance, both facilitating the rapid movement of troops and also serving as supply routes to sustain frontier areas (photo 12). Scattered along these networks, military installations were placed both to fulfil broad strategic considerations and also to control and dominate the immediate locality. The number and distribution of Roman military sites has been substantially increased through aerial reconnaissance, particularly in Wales and Scotland, and new insights have been achieved into the progress of the military campaigns (photo 13).[37]

In much of northern and western Britain, the Roman impact was primarily military in character. Authority was exercised, a fluctuating sequence of frontiers was maintained, and raw materials were exploited. However, the rapid conquest of the more centralised political groupings in the south and east was followed by a civilian phase of development. Administrative control was exerted through urban centres which provided a focus for a surrounding hinterland or *civitas*, usually based on pre-Roman tribal areas. The *civitas* capital was often located in close proximity to an indigenous centre of some importance, whilst others developed from civilian settlements which had emerged on the fringes of forts.

13 Roman fort at Llanio, Ceredigion District, Dyfed. Drought conditions in 1975 revealed the plan of a Roman fort constructed on a low gravel terrace overlooking the Afon Teifi, in an area usually unresponsive to aerial survey. Parch marks in cereal crops delineate the street plan and defences. The central rectangle of the headquarters building or *principia* faces southwards towards the river and traces of long narrow rectangular buildings can be seen in the southern section of the fort. Excavations indicate four phases of building between AD 75–160 followed by abandonment. From the west gate an access road links the fort with Sarn Helen, the main north-south Roman routeway which is partially perpetuated by the modern road. An excavated bath house can be seen to the south of the fort.

14 Caerwent (*Venta Silurum*), Gwent. The *civitas* capital of Caerwent, located at the western fringes of the civilian zone, was centred along the major east-west routeway linking the legionary fortresses of Gloucester and Caerleon; this thoroughfare which continues in use today bisected the Roman town, the southern portion only being visible on the photograph. Masonry walls proclaimed the status of the settlement, controlled access through four gateways and provided security. An outer ditch appears as a darker positive crop mark running parallel to the south wall. The town was divided into twenty rectangular blocks or *insulae* by a planned grid of streets, one of which can be seen as a parch mark emerging westwards from beneath the churchyard. Excavation revealed public buildings, commercial premises and substantial town houses, some of which can be seen as parch marks west of the church. Faint indications of house structures are evident in the pasture field, but the adjacent, more responsive cereal crop provides some excellent house plans.

In addition to their administrative and economic functions, the *civitas* capitals performed an important cultural role in the diffusion of Romanisation. Impressive public buildings were set within planned and regular street layouts, and a wide range of amenities including bath houses, piped water supplies, amphitheatres and substantial town houses demonstrated the attractions and benefits to be derived from a Roman life-style (photo 14).[38]

Forts and urban creations were not only important symbols within the cultural landscape, they also stimulated considerable economic change. The army of occupation and the expanding urban areas provided a substantial consumer market for a variety of goods especially foodstuffs, thus encouraging increased agricultural productivity. Incorporation within the Roman imperial system also imposed taxation demands necessitating the generation of an agricultural surplus. The diffusion of agricultural innovation in the form of new implements and farming methods, settled conditions and an efficient road network also provided beneficial conditions for agricultural expansion. The development of a surplus based, profit orientated agricultural system is reflected in the construction of villas.[39] Despite numerous problems of definition, the term 'villa' usually implies an agricultural unit whose native owners had adopted a Romanised life-style and were operating within a commercially orientated rural economy. Profits accumulated through the invigorated agricultural system were channelled into Romanised buildings and luxury items, thus proclaiming the increasing wealth and status of the occupants.

Aerial reconnaissance has led to the discovery of many previously unrecorded villas, often revealing their ground plans with great clarity.[40] Aerial survey can sometimes play an even more important role in placing a villa within the broader context of the Romano-British landscape. Thus the aerial view may reveal an indigenous settlement beneath or in close proximity to a villa, or may enable the partial reconstruction of an associated field system.[41] Although the chronological and functional associations cannot usually be clarified without excavation, these discoveries pose many interesting questions concerning the relationships between indigenous and Romanised settlements, the development of villas over time and the nature of their surrounding landscapes. Thus, at Lockington (photo 15), the closely juxtaposed indigenous settlement may represent the precursor of the villa or may constitute one of a series of contemporaneous settlements forming part of a larger agricultural unit or estate organised around the villa. Intriguing issues of land ownership and tenurial relationships are also raised at sites such as these.[42]

Villas are concentrated within the lowland zone, often exhibiting particular concentrations around urban centres with which they were so closely linked economically. Villas represent only one aspect of the Roman impact on the countryside. Field survey and aerial reconnaissance have demonstrated an intensification of rural settlement in many parts of Britain reflecting the increasing demand for foodstuffs and the advent of more settled conditions. Major land-clearance schemes have also been discovered, for example in south Yorkshire and north Nottinghamshire, and in parts of East Anglia and Essex, where extensive, regular field systems suggest a deliberately organised and planned extension of farming areas in the Roman period. Roman organisational and engineering skills

were also applied to substantial land reclamation projects, most notably within the Fenlands of eastern England where the construction of drainage channels, including the impressive Car Dyke catch water drain, allowed the productive use of large areas of formerly ill-drained land. Aerial survey has permitted the reconstruction of much of the landscape which developed following drainage, a landscape devoted to intensive cattle rearing and salt production.[43] Landscape change was not confined to the rural sector. The increasing exploitation of minerals, the quarrying of stone and the development of manufacturing, particularly of pottery, also led to the creation of distinctive industrial landscapes. Thus the incorporation of much of Britain within the Roman imperial system, whilst building on the already complex indigenous patterns of the Iron Age, also introduced many new stimuli which had a profound impact on social and economic trends and the development of the British landscape.

PROTECTION OF PREHISTORIC AND ROMAN SITES AND LANDSCAPES

The imprint of the prehistoric and Roman period within and beneath the modern landscape is amply demonstrated by aerial reconnaissance. However, the aerial view also reveals the increasing pressures being placed on archaeological sites and landscapes throughout the British Isles. The photographs presented here indicate the wide range of these destructive processes, including plough damage, upland improvement, land drainage, afforestation, urban expansion and redevelopment, gravel extraction and the installation of public utilities.

The archaeological impact of agricultural change is well illustrated within the chalk landscape of Beacon Hill (photo 7). The ancient grasslands of the chalk downs, which had been maintained over generations by sheep grazing and rabbit breeding, incorporated both a rich flora and fauna and a high density of archaeological field monuments. However, changing agricultural practices have led to the large-scale conversion of these grasslands into areas of intensive arable cultivation, profoundly affecting both their ecological and archaeological significance.[44] A simple land use comparison between the first edition Ordnance Survey map of 1877 (1:10560) and the aerial photograph of 1979 in the figure below reveals the dramatic reduction in the extent of the chalk downland. The surviving discontinuous fragments of ancient grassland, largely restricted to the steeper slopes, receive a degree of protection through their designation by the Nature Conservancy Council as Sites of Special Scientific Interest (SSSI). The protected areas are rich botanically including a nationally important stand of juniper on the western fringes of Beacon Hill, and a particularly diverse flora within the varied and protected habitats provided by the earthwork enclosure on Ladle Hill. However, inclusion within an SSSI has not always safeguarded the botanical or the archaeological interest of an area, as can be seen in the encroachment of cultivation on the western slopes of Beacon Hill leading to the destruction of the prehistoric lynchets and the subsequent redrawing of the SSSI boundary.[45] Although the system of SSSI notification and protection has been revised in the 1981 Wildlife and Countryside Act, many practical problems remain in reconciling the often conflicting demands of agriculture and conservation within successful management policies.[46]

15 Iron Age settlement and Roman villa, Lockington, Leicestershire. The aerial view reveals dense crop marks centred on two gravel islands rising above the flood plain of the River Trent. On the left a complex sequence of overlapping enclosures and circular features are aligned along a central droveway. On the right a series of structures grouped around a rectangular building with a projecting northern wing are set within a large trapezoidal enclosure. Although unexcavated, the morphology of the two crop mark complexes suggests an Iron Age settlement comprising hut sites, small closes and field boundaries on the left, contrasting with the more formalised disposition of a Roman villa and its farm buildings on the right. Field walking indicates that the villa was occupied between the mid second and fourth centuries AD.

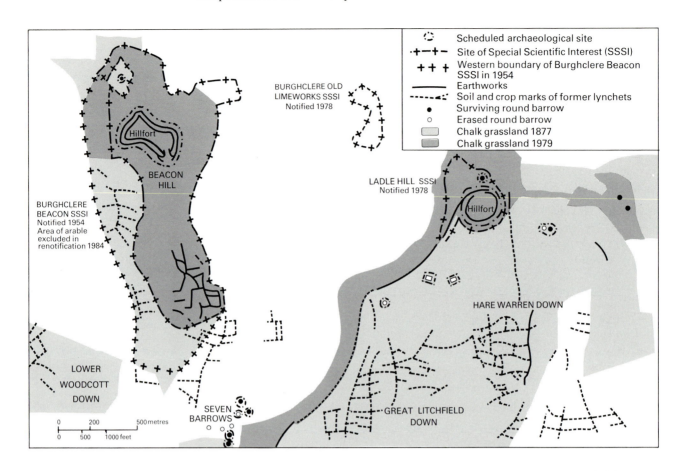

Legend:

- ⌇ Scheduled archaeological site
- ·—+—+— Site of Special Scientific Interest (SSSI)
- + + + Western boundary of Burghclere Beacon SSSI in 1954
- ——— Earthworks
- ------- Soil and crop marks of former lynchets
- • Surviving round barrow
- ○ Erased round barrow
- ▢ Chalk grassland 1877
- ▨ Chalk grassland 1979

BURGHCLERE OLD LIMEWORKS SSSI Notified 1978

BEACON HILL

BURGHCLERE BEACON SSSI Notified 1954 Area of arable excluded in renotification 1984

Hillfort

LADLE HILL SSSI Notified 1978

Hillfort

HARE WARREN DOWN

LOWER WOODCOTT DOWN

SEVEN BARROWS

GREAT LITCHFIELD DOWN

0 200 500 metres
0 500 1000 feet

Land use change, nature conservation and archaeological protection at Beacon Hill and Ladle Hill, Hampshire.

Although the hillfort and well preserved lynchets of a prehistoric field system on Beacon Hill are included within an SSSI, the statutory protection of the archaeological sites is accomplished through scheduling, now enforced through the Ancient Monuments and Archaeological Areas Act of 1979 (amended in England by the National Heritage Act 1983). The scheduled sites are closely delineated, discrete entities contrasting with the broader definition of the SSSIs.[47] Indeed the surviving field monuments are merely the scattered remnants of the once extensive prehistoric landscape originally preserved within the downland pastures and partially mapped in 1931.[48] While the surviving components are still impressive, the totality of the landscape to which they belonged is now visible only in the form of soil and crop marks which reveal the continuous destruction of this fragile 'buried' landscape. The community of interest between archaeology and nature conservation, which can be seen at Beacon Hill, is even more evident within the many threatened upland and wetland environments of Britain.

The survival of field monuments and early landscapes within upland contexts has come under growing pressure as a result of changing agricultural policies, extractive industries, afforestation and sometimes recreational use. Technological developments and the availability of grants and incentives have brought many areas into cultivation which formerly would have been considered marginal. While some of the problems generated by the conversion of moorland into improved grassland have been illustrated at Plowden (photo 1), the process is much more extensive in many areas. Substantial inroads have been made for example into the moorland environments of Exmoor, Bodmin Moor, the Cheviots and the Pennines, with serious repercussions for both their ecological and archaeological heritage. During 1984 and 1985 the Royal Commission on the Historical Monuments of England and the Council for British Archaeology, with the support of the Countryside Commission, undertook a review of the present state of archaeology in the uplands, in which the range of threats was assessed and possible management strategies were evaluated.[49]

Waterlogged environments with their great archaeological potential, as seen in the Somerset Levels Project (photo 4), are also areas at risk. Within the anaerobic conditions of waterlogged deposits a wide range of organic materials are frequently preserved which are rarely found on dryland sites. Detailed palaeoecological studies are thus possible, whilst the survival of wooden artefacts, basketry, textiles and leather for example, permit a much more balanced view of the everyday activities of a prehistoric community. Thus the higher costs incurred in excavating a wetland site are usually rewarded by the quality and quantity of the evidence produced in comparison to the dryland equivalent.[50] Waterlogged environments are however very vulnerable in archaeological terms. Within the Somerset Levels, peat cutting provided the initial stimulus for excavation, but the lowering of the water table through drainage is currently the more serious threat. The resulting dessication of the peat deposits leads to the rapid decay of organic remains and the valuable archaeological and environmental records they contain. Similar problems are encountered within the Fenlands of eastern England where an extensive archaeological programme has revealed numerous important sites, many with well preserved organic remains, most notably at Flag Fen, near Peterborough.[51] Whilst drainage removes the conditions which have ensured organic survival, the resulting shrinkage of the peat deposits can also lead to the re-emergence of once hidden, buried features. Thus at Haddenham extensive barrow-fields, formerly sealed and protected beneath peat and alluvium, are now protruding through the shrinking peat deposits. In 1982 The Fenland Project was established to investigate the archaeological potential of around 400,000 hectares of peats, silts and clays in Lincolnshire, Cambridgeshire, Norfolk and Suffolk, combining field work, environmental studies and excavation with the development of management and scheduling policies.[52]

Destructive processes are equally severe within urban contexts. Urban expansion and the development of New Towns create many problems but can also provide the incentive for archaeological investigation as at Fengate (photo 3). Redevelopment within cities poses particular problems often entailing not only the demolition of the historic urban fabric and topography, but also causing irreparable damage to the underlying archaeological levels. The attempt to facilitate excavation prior to redevelopment through the definition of 'Areas of Archaeological Importance' under Part II of The Ancient Monuments and Archaeological Areas Act of 1979, has been implemented in only five historic centres and has been hampered by lack of funding.

Future progress within urban archaeology is dependent on close cooperation between archaeologists and local planning departments and also on the acceptance by developers that the costs of archaeological investigation should be an integral part of their development proposals.[53]

The quickening pace of land use change generates many conflicts of interest within both rural and urban environments. In many areas the ecological, historical and archaeological resources of the British landscape are seriously threatened. Aerial photography can play an important role in monitoring the scale and severity of these destructive forces. There is however an urgent need to develop coherent policies for the preservation and management of archaeological sites and landscapes, both to safeguard the ever diminishing data base and also to conserve a vital element of the varied and distinctive landscapes of the British Isles for the education and enjoyment of present and future generations.

FURTHER READING

D. R. Wilson, *Air Photo Interpretation for Archaeologists*, London, 1982.

G. S. Maxwell (ed.), *The Impact of Aerial Reconnaissance on Archaeology*, London, 1983.

D. N. Riley, *Air Photography and Archaeology*, London, 1987.

R. Whimster, *The Emerging Past: Air Photography and the Buried Landscape*, London, 1989.

M. Jones, *England before Domesday*, London, 1986.

R. Bradley, *The Social Foundations of Prehistoric Britain: Themes and Variations in the Archaeology of Power*, London, 1984.

S. S. Frere and J. K. S. St Joseph, *Roman Britain from the Air*, Cambridge, 1983.

T. Darvill, *Ancient Monuments in the Countryside: An Archaeological Management Review*, London, 1987.

2 From Roman Britain to the Norman Conquest

INTRODUCTION

The centuries between the departure of the Roman legions and the Norman Conquest still remain very much a 'Dark Age' as far as our knowledge of the historical geography of Britain is concerned. Two main factors make it difficult to obtain a clear understanding of this formative period. Firstly, there is a comparative dearth of archaeological material surviving from the fifth to eleventh centuries. This has generally been interpreted in part as indicating a fall in the population of Britain between the fourth and sixth centuries, but there is clearly a danger of circularity of argument over this issue.[1] Secondly, the artefacts left behind by the Anglo-Saxons and Scandinavians, and particularly their wooden buildings, were of a type less permanent than the stone and brick constructions of their Roman predecessors. Consequently, Anglo-Saxon and Scandinavian archaeological features have proved less easy to identify from the air than equivalent remains from Roman and later medieval times.

The evidence that does survive for the Anglo-Saxon and Scandinavian period can be divided into five types: literary sources, archaeology, place-names, documents, and the landscape itself. Most early work by geographers on the Anglo-Saxons was based on the first type of evidence – the use of literary sources such as the Anglo-Saxon Chronicle, and the writings of Gildas (c.AD 550), Bede (AD 731) and Nennius (c.AD 800). These provide a broad chronology of change which concentrates mainly on political events and the spread of Christianity.[2] Archaeological evidence from the last 30 years has challenged aspects of this chronology and, in particular, the nature of the early Saxon contacts with Britain. Despite the increase in such evidence, however, Anglo-Saxon and Scandinavian archaeological investigations are still relatively undeveloped and leave unanswered many questions on key issues relating to agricultural change and rural settlement. To some extent, this lack has been made up for by research into the cultural significance of place-names derived from literary and documentary sources. Thus, -hām, -ingas and -tūn place-names have been used to trace a broad chronology of Anglo-Saxon settlement, which can be contrasted with Scandinavian settlements having -bȳ place-names. But considerable problems also surround the use of place-names as evidence. It now seems possible that in the past too much emphasis was placed on their overt significance and not enough attention paid to the complexities of their interpretation.[3]

A fourth tradition of research has concentrated on documentary evidence. For example, Hooke has demonstrated how the boundary clauses of Anglo-Saxon charters can provide a wealth of information concerning estate organisation and the landscape of the mid- and late-Anglo-Saxon period.[4] The most important of such documentary sources is found in the unique record of Domesday Book, and it is here that most work done by geographers on the Anglo-Scandinavian period begins.[5] Domesday Book records the final achievements of the Anglo-Saxon and Scandinavian immigrants to Britain through the eyes of a new ruling elite, and in a retrogressive approach it must provide one major starting point for an interpretation of these achievements. As with the evidence of place-names, though, it is essential that Domesday Book is continually reinterpreted in the light of new evidence from other sources.

Finally, to these archaeological, literary, documentary and place-name sources must be added the evidence of the landscape itself, and in particular the banks and ditches, crop marks and soil marks recorded by aerial photography. Compared with Roman and later medieval studies, the application of aerial photography to Anglo-Saxon and Scandinavian Britain has been limited. Of the 121 air photographs reproduced in Wilson's major work on *Air photo interpretation for archaeologists*, only four are devoted specifically to Anglo-Saxon material.[6]

There are several reasons for this. Firstly, if there was indeed a lower level of population between the fifth and ninth centuries this would have given rise to relatively fewer features than have survived from earlier and later periods. Secondly, the materials used by the Anglo-Saxon population, most notably wood, generally had a lower survival rate than did, for example, the bricks and stones used by the Roman and later medieval populations. More Roman than Anglo-Saxon features are likely to have survived and be revealed by air photographs. Thirdly, the types of feature produced in the Anglo-Saxon and Scandinavian period do not always show up readily on air photographs. The pattern of post holes associated with an Anglo-Saxon building is less readily identified and more easily destroyed than the walls of a Roman villa; the grid plan of a Roman town or fort is more self-evident than the unclear morphology of an Anglo-Saxon village. Finally, much Anglo-Scandinavian material probably lies under villages and towns surviving today, and in rural areas much will already have been destroyed by the plough. This means that the evidence which can be illustrated by air photographs is limited, and also that what has survived is often not particularly clear or dramatic. Despite such problems, air photographs have been used to identify several Anglo-Saxon sites for the first time, and they also have considerable use in illustrating features of the Anglo-Scandinavian landscape of Britain.

This chapter describes some of these features in a broadly thematic manner. It begins with a discussion of the evidence of post-Roman decay. The Anglo-Saxon immigration to Britain is then investigated in terms of boundaries, settlement, buildings, burials and fortification. The chapter concludes with an analysis of Scandinavian rural and urban settlement.

POST-ROMAN DECAY

> Came days of pestilence, on all sides men fell dead,
> death fetched off the flower of the people;
> where they stood to fight, waste places,
> and on the acropolis, ruins.
>   Hosts who would build again
> shrank to the earth. Therefore are these courts dreary
> and that red arch twisteth tiles,
> wryeth from roof-ridge, reacheth groundwards. . .
> Broken blocks. . .

(*The Ruin*, eighth century)

The traditional image of the *Adventus Saxonum*, as expounded for example by Darby,[7] saw the coming of the Angles, Saxons and Jutes as a new beginning in the history of England. The literary sources inform us that from AD 410 the authorities in Rome told the towns of Britain to look to their own defences, and that over the next half-century raids and then settlement by the Anglo-Saxons led to the collapse of Roman civil order and the cessation of urban life. Such an image is well captured in the fragment from the Anglo-Saxon poem quoted above, which almost certainly refers to the town of *Aquae Sulis*, modern Bath. However, it is salient to note that even this poem, written some three centuries after the departure of the Roman legions, illustrates that, at the time it was written, ruins of the old Roman town still existed in the landscape.

In recent years this image of destruction has been replaced by one of continuity, with increasing amounts of archaeological evidence revealing the presence of Anglo-Saxons in Britain before the fifth century, and several studies of estate boundaries suggesting that many early medieval estates were based on pre-Saxon territorial units.[8] However, much still remains uncertain about the historical geography of England in the fifth century, and the precise balance between cataclysm and continuity probably varied in different parts of the country.

The efflorescence of urban life in Britain under the Romans was one of the most visible results of their rule, with towns playing fundamentally important administrative and economic roles. In the medieval period the majority of these Roman towns, notably *Londinium* (London), the *coloniae* of *Eboracum* (York), *Lindum* (Lincoln), *Glevum* (Gloucester) and *Camulodunum* (Colchester), and a number of *civitas* capitals such as *Durovernum* (Canterbury) and *Venta* (Winchester), had re-emerged as important urban centres. Despite considerable archaeological investigation, however, there is still much debate as to the precise fortunes of many such urban settlements in the Anglo-Saxon period. In discussing the topography of Anglo-Scandinavian York, for example, Richard Hall has noted that

> excavation has shown that individual Roman buildings were upstanding for many centuries after the Roman withdrawal but, in the face of an almost total absence of excavated material of 5th, 6th or early 7th century date, there has been much speculation concerning the fate of the city as a whole in the immediate post-Roman centuries.[9]

Likewise, Tim Tatton-Brown has commented with respect to London that

> It now seems very clear that there is no continuity whatsoever between the Roman and medieval cities and that although sub-Roman occupation may have continued well into the fifth century, the city of London was probably a virtually empty shell, full of the decaying ruins of Roman buildings throughout the sixth century.[10]

Similar findings from elsewhere in the country indicate that although some form of occupation appears to have continued in many former Roman towns – their built fabric decaying only gradually – urban life as it had been prior to AD 400 ceased to exist during the early Anglo-Saxon period.

16 Silchester, Hampshire. This photograph shows the remains of the Roman town of *Calleva Atrebatum*, with the outlines of the forum clearly visible in the centre and the grid pattern of the streets filling the bounded area of the walls, which were probably built some time in the third century AD. Silchester is one of the few main Romano-British towns to have been completely deserted in the post-Roman period and not to be reoccupied in later centuries.

This stage of urban decline is well captured by a few towns such as *Viroconium Cornoviorum* (Wroxeter) and *Calleva Atrebatum* (Silchester) which were not redeveloped as urban centres in the succeeding centuries. The view of Silchester from the air (photo 16) thus clearly illustrates the Roman street plan, the forum and basilica complex, the wooded amphitheatre outside the eastern gate, and the outlines of houses scattered throughout the area within the town walls.[11] Here, it is easily possible to imagine the gradual decay of the great stone buildings and massive walls, which the Anglo-Saxon author of *The Ruin* referred to as being the 'work of giants'.[12] Without a tradition of building in stone and brick, the Anglo-Saxons failed to repair the crumbling fabric of the town, which was in any case no longer required to support its former administrative and economic

functions. Unlike towns which were later rebuilt, Silchester captures the ghost-like essence of urban life in England at the end of the fifth century.

The fate of rural areas in the immediate post-Roman period is also but poorly understood. A number of scholars, including Jones, Bonney and Hooke have suggested that territorial units and estates may have survived largely intact from Roman times well into the Anglo-Saxon period, but remarkably little is known about changes in the agrarian activity that may have taken place within this framework.[13] The use of air photographs has revealed a considerable amount of material concerning Iron Age and Romano-British field systems, as well as much information on later medieval ridge and furrow, but so far very little evidence concerning Anglo-Saxon agriculture has been forthcoming, despite Fowler's suggestion that a systematic examination of the evidence should reveal traces of whole landscapes laid out before ridge and furrow came to dominate the scene.[14]

In cases where attempts have been made to relate traces of Romano-British and prehistoric field systems to the later medieval landscape conflicting results have emerged, suggesting that a number of different processes may have been giving rise to a variety of distinct regional landscapes in Anglo-Saxon Britain. One good example of an apparent discrepancy between the territorial organisation of Roman and medieval times is provided by Riley's work on the pattern of probable Roman fields in southern Yorkshire and northern Nottinghamshire.[15] Here, on the basis of air photographs, Riley has identified a series of long parallel ditches which divide the landscape into a series of strips averaging about 100 metres in width. These are in turn subdivided by a number of short cross ditches creating a brickwork pattern of fields mostly averaging between 0.5 and 2.8 hectares in area. Photo 17 illustrates a small part of this extensive pattern of fields on the border between the townships of Harworth and Styrrup in Nottinghamshire. The significant feature to note here is that the township and parish boundary, expressed in the landscape by the hedge running approximately east to west across the centre of the photograph, cuts directly across the pattern of earlier fields. This lack of coincidence between the Roman field system and the medieval township and parish boundaries is found throughout the area and suggests both that these boundaries are relatively recent, and also that there was probably a discontinuity in land use between the Roman and medieval periods.[16] Elsewhere in Britain, though, it is possible to place a different interpretation on the relationship between early field systems and medieval boundaries. For example, on the basis of evidence concerning the relationship between Roman roads and field boundaries in East Anglia and Essex, Williamson has suggested 'that while parish or township units might not themselves pre-date the early medieval period, the areas within which they were located might, nevertheless, have been continuously settled and exploited throughout the post-Roman period'.[17]

While much remains uncertain about the nature of fields, boundaries and rural settlements in the fifth century, air photographs are beginning to provide some answers to questions concerning continuity between the Roman and medieval periods. As with the collapse of urban life, the growing economic crisis in rural areas early in the fifth century seems to have been associated with the departure of the legions. While the subsistence economy of many small Romano-British settlements may have continued relatively unchanged, the great villa estates producing grain for the market economy probably encountered severe difficulties. The breaking of links with Rome almost certainly resulted in a reduction in demand for grain, with there no longer being a need for the provisioning of the legions stationed in Britain. It is perhaps here, in the collapse of the grain market, that it is possible to identify the beginnings of the disintegration of the links between town and countryside that had enabled both the small market towns and the great villa estates to exist in a reciprocal relationship over the previous centuries of Roman rule.

By the early seventh century, the Anglo-Saxon conquest of lowland England was complete, with victories having been won over the British at Dyrham in AD 577, *Catraeth* (Catterick) *c.*AD 600 and Chester in AD 613. It is mainly from this period onwards that evidence on air photographs concerning Anglo-Saxon boundaries and settlements begins to occur in any abundance.

ANGLO-SAXON KINGDOMS AND BOUNDARIES

There was in Mercia in recent times a certain valiant king called Offa, who was feared by all the kings and kingdoms around, and who ordered a great dyke to be built from sea to sea between Britain and Mercia.

(Asser, *Life of King Alfred*, AD 893)

17 Harworth, Nottinghamshire. Here a brickwork pattern of fields of probable Roman or earlier date is seen underlying the more recent patterns of field boundaries and roads. The township and parish boundary between Harworth and Styrrup is represented by the hedge running approximately east to west across the upper centre of the photograph. A smaller rectangular enclosure lies astride this boundary, and two possible trackways, one running south-east from the bottom centre of the photograph and the other running north-east from the top right-hand corner, are also visible.

According to Bede, 44 years after the *Adventus Saxonum* the British won a famous victory against the Anglo-Saxons at Mount Badon.[18] This delayed the Anglo-Saxon advance and it was only from about AD 550 that they again began to push westwards, creating as they did so the future historic kingdoms of England. The literary sources, such as the Anglo-Saxon Chronicle, make it clear that the Anglo-Saxons were far from united, and it is apparent that the various kingdoms were involved not only in waging war against the British but also in frequent conflicts with each other. These power struggles have given rise to some of the most impressive remains from the Anglo-Saxon period still visible in the landscape today in the form of the defensive banks and ditches of Wansdyke and Offa's Dyke, as well as other shorter defensive works found elsewhere in the country such as the Devil's Dyke and the Fleam Ditch between Cambridge and Newmarket.

Considerable debate still rages over the precise dating and purpose of these defensive boundaries, particularly with respect to Wansdyke. Photo 18 shows a part of this great defensive work, named after the Anglo-Saxon god Woden, as it crosses Tan Hill in Wiltshire, with its bank and ditch facing to the north apparently designed to protect the lands lying to the south. This forms part of the 20-kilometre eastern section of Wansdyke, which is separated by some 30 kilometres from the western 14-kilometre section in Somerset. After excavations in the late 1950s Sir Cyril and Lady Fox argued that these were in reality two

18 Tan Hill, All Cannings, Wiltshire. One of the best preserved parts of the eastern section of Wansdyke as it crosses the downs south of Avebury. People from the north would have had first of all to negotiate the ditch and then the impressive bank on its southern side. A small cross-ditch is visible just before the kink in Wansdyke and the remains of several tumuli can also just be detected.

19 Llanfair, Waterdine, Shropshire. A well-preserved section of Offa's Dyke as it crosses Llanfair Hill, with its ditch on the western side of the bank. At the southern end of the photograph the bank is followed by a line of trees, but these then leave the Dyke which continues to the north-west to be crossed after a short distance by a track from the trees to the east.

separate earthworks, with the eastern section most likely to have been a West Saxon construction built using British labour by Ceawlin after his defeat at Fethansleag in AD 584 to protect the lands to the south from the Saxons of the middle Thames valley.[19] In contrast, they saw West Wansdyke as probably having been constructed by Cynegils on a line imposed by Penda of Mercia some time after AD 628, with its main purpose being to control traffic and incursions southwards from the Cotswolds and the lower Avon valley. Arguing against this, Myres preferred to see both sections of Wansdyke as having been part of a single defensive work which could have been constructed on one of three different occasions: by the Britons at the end of the fifth century to protect themselves from Saxon

inroads along the Thames valley; by the Cerdicings of the Salisbury area in the mid-sixth century during their assaults on the Thames valley; or as a defensive barrier against an anticipated southwards attack by Ceawlin in the second half of the sixth century.[20] Whatever the origins of Wansdyke, though, it stands as an impressive memorial to the power struggles of the early Saxon kingdoms of southern England, and its dominance of the landscape is brought out very clearly in photo 18.

With Offas's Dyke, first mentioned in the quotation from Asser's *Life of King Alfred* cited above and illustrated in photo 19, we are on much firmer ground, although several questions still remain concerning its purpose and construction. About 130 kilometres of this great earthwork survive along the 240-kilometre frontier stretching from just east of the river Wye's junction with the Severn estuary in the south to its northern end near Treuddyn in south Flintshire. Associated with Offa's Dyke are several smaller dykes to the west, and in the north the 70-kilometre long Wat's Dyke which lies to its east running from Basinwerk-on-Dee to Morda Brook in Shropshire. Offa's Dyke was first surveyed by Sir Cyril Fox who saw Wat's Dyke and the smaller western dykes as being early defensive works built by the Anglo-Saxons to protect themselves from Welsh attacks. He then saw a discontinuous Offa's Dyke being constructed in the late eighth century as an agreed frontier boundary between the Mercians and the Britons of Wales, with the gaps being in areas of dense woodland which were left unguarded. More recent archaeological work, however, has shown that the gaps were not original and that in several places the ditch can be traced beneath the present level farmland.[21] In addition, it appears from Welsh sources that there was almost continual war between the Britons and the Anglo-Saxons at this time, and it therefore seems likely that Offa built his ditch and bank not as the result of a peaceful agreement, but rather as a necessary defensive barrier to prevent British attacks on Mercia.

Wansdyke and Offa's Dyke, although broadly similar in form, are thus probably separated by about two centuries, representing very different stages in the Anglo-Saxon conquest of Britain. They are not, however, unique features, and the closest parallel to Offa's Dyke is the *Danevirke* in Denmark which was constructed around AD 737 and which formed a major defensive barrier across the southern end of the Jutland peninsula. Features such as these reflect the formal establishment of territorial frontiers, the strong centralised power of the kings who ordered their construction, and also the ability of Anglo-Saxon government to co-ordinate and organise considerable numbers of people to build them.

ANGLO-SAXON RURAL SETTLEMENT

It is a well known fact that the people of Germany never live in cities... Their villages are not laid out in the Roman style, with buildings adjacent and connected. Every man leaves an open space around his house, perhaps as a precaution against the risk of fire, perhaps because they are inexpert builders. They do not even make use of stones or wall-tiles; for all purposes they employ rough-hewn timbers... They also have the habit of hollowing out underground caves, which they cover with masses of manure and use both as refuges from the winter and as storehouses for produce.

(Tacitus, *Germania*, AD 98)

Behind the constantly fluctuating, but westward and northward moving, frontier between the Anglo-Saxons and the Britons a new pattern of rural settlement was emerging. There is still considerable debate about the extent of continuity between Roman and Anglo-Saxon estates, but it does now seem to have been the case that many Anglo-Saxon settlements were probably established on new sites. It is also apparent that the nucleated villages of medieval England were not introduced in the early stages of settlement but emerged from a dispersed pattern of farmsteads as a result of a later reorganisation of fields and settlements. Air photographs have helped to identify a considerable number of Anglo-Saxon rural settlements, but subsequent archaeological investigation has usually revealed them to be of far greater complexity than the photographs alone suggest. Thus, Jones and Jones referring to the site at Mucking in Essex have noted that 'Most outstanding of all, discrete crop marks within one enclosure turned out to be the graves of a Romano-British cemetery, while elsewhere they proved to be a veritable rash of Saxon sunken huts in a quantity and extent quite unknown in England'.[22]

Two particular kinds of small Anglo-Saxon building are readily identifiable from air photographs: the *Grubenhaus* or 'sunken hut', and the rectangular timber hall with entrances opposite each other on the longer sides. The forerunners of both types of building can perhaps be seen mentioned in the quotation from Tacitus cited at the beginning of this section, even though it was written over three centuries before the Anglo-Saxon migrations to Britain. Examples of each of these types of building are illustrated in photos 20, 21 and 22.

Photo 20 shows, before excavation, part of the largest excavated crop mark site in England, that at Mucking in Essex, with the small dark rounded oblong marks representing a few of the 213 Saxon 'sunken huts' scattered over the site.[23] This photograph also indicates Bronze Age, Iron Age and Roman material, thus suggesting that the gravel terrace on which the site lies was used from the prehistoric period right through to medieval times. However, the overlapping of features and the problems associated with the analysis of hut fills make it difficult to argue with certainty that there was close continuity of settlement occupation throughout the period. Excavation has revealed that the Saxon huts themselves date from the early fifth century to the early seventh. The floors were dug out from between 30 cm to 1 m below the ground surface, and in size they range from about 3 m by 2.5 m to approximately 6 m by 4 m. Each hut had two main posts which would have supported a ridge pole and roof, with the walls of the longer sides being made from turf. From the material found within these huts it is possible to get a good idea of the economy practised by the Saxon inhabitants of Mucking. Thus, animal bones indicate that there were horses, oxen, sheep, pigs, deer, dogs and cats; seed impressions on potsherds reveal that barley, wheat and oats were cultivated; loomweights give evidence of cloth production; and there are also some indications of metal working. Comprehensive excavation of this site has revealed many features not apparent from air photographs, and two Saxon cemeteries dating from the same period as the huts have also been identified, one of which lies near the field boundary in the lower centre of photo 20.

The second main type of Anglo-Saxon building which can be identified by air photography is the small rectangular timber hall, normally between 8 m and

12 m in length, and illustrated in photos 21 and 22. Photo 21 shows amongst other linear and circular features the apparent remains of six such buildings, one much bigger than the others, at Drayton in Berkshire. Without detailed archaeological work it is not possible to attribute all such features to the Anglo-Saxon period on the basis of their plans alone, although the presence of doors lying opposite each other in the centres of the longer sides is strongly indicative of an Anglo-Saxon origin. Excavation of such sites has revealed that the history of their occupation was often much more complex than might appear to have been the case. At Chalton in Hampshire, for example, excavations have revealed four different types of wooden house dating from the sixth and seventh centuries,

with the post-hole outlines of these buildings being clearly visible in photo 22.[24] The earliest buildings seem to have been small, square or oblong post-built structures with only one doorway. A second phase is represented by longer, post-built structures with their two doors set opposite each other in the long sides, and the third phase consisted of houses built of posts set in continuous trenches, with internal subdivisions dividing them into several rooms. A final type of building, a good example of which is clearly visible in the middle of photo 22, consisted of a central building with rows of either buttresses or 'verandah-posts' on either side of its two long sides.

Chalton is an example of a small nucleated settlement, but Cunliffe has argued that in the surrounding area there were also many isolated farmsteads some of which may have originated in the Roman period. In the ninth century Chalton seems to have been deserted as part of a general shift in the area from hilltop settlements to new villages in the valley bottoms. It thus illustrates one example of a much more widespread characteristic of Anglo-Saxon settlement, namely its impermanence. Indeed, increasing evidence from many different parts of the country suggests that one of the most important features of rural settlement change at this period was the gradual shift that took place from a pattern of dispersed farmsteads to one of nucleated villages.[25]

21 Drayton, Berkshire. A wide range of linear and circular features is visible on this photograph. The important Anglo-Saxon features are what seem to be six rectangular wooden halls. Three of these are to be seen to the right of the largest circular feature. The largest hall overlies a smaller circular feature further up, with another smaller hall lying just below it. A sixth apparent hall lies at the top centre of the photograph above the road running across the area.

22 Chalton, Hampshire. A vertical photograph of the excavated Anglo-Saxon settlement at Chalton, showing the post-hole outlines of a number of different types of rectangular timber building. These are attributable to at least four phases, probably dating from the sixth to the seventh centuries. Chalton is important as an example of an area where there was considerable settlement change in the late Anglo-Saxon period, with this site becoming deserted in the ninth century. It was then replaced by the villages of Blendworth and Chalton which are recorded in Domesday Book.

23 Sprouston, Roxburghshire. The Saxon cemetery is clearly visible in the centre of this photograph, with the graves lying packed together on a broadly south-west to north-east alignment. To the north of these lies a double ditched oval enclosure somewhat similar to the Great Enclosure at Yeavering. Elsewhere five Anglo-Saxon halls are also visible. The largest of these, furthest to the north-west, is represented by clearly identifiable individual post-holes. To the south is another hall, this time with narrow extensions on both of its short sides, and there are three other smaller and simpler rectangular halls to the south-west.

ANGLO-SAXON BURIALS

> Upon the headland the Geats erected a broad, high tumulus, plainly visible to distant seamen. In ten days they completed the building of the hero's beacon. Round his ashes they built the finest vault that their most skilful men could devise. Within the barrow they placed collars, brooches, and all the trappings which they had plundered from the treasure-hoard. They buried the gold and left that princely treasure to the keeping of the earth. . .
>
> (*Beowulf*, eighth century)

The Anglo-Saxons used both cremation and inhumation burials, and their graves have been found singly, in cemeteries and under impressive barrows. While cremation pits rarely produce crop marks, and individual inhumation burials are unlikely often to be detected from the air, the larger cemeteries and barrows do show up well on air photographs. Photo 23 thus illustrates the Saxon cemetery and settlement at Sprouston, and photo 24 the barrows surrounding the magnificent seventh-century ship burial at Sutton Hoo. Prior to their conversion to Christianity, which began with Augustine's mission to Kent in AD 597, the pagan Anglo-Saxons buried grave goods with their dead, or in the case of cremations buried the ashes in decorated pots. It is from these artefacts that much of our knowledge about the lifestyles of their former owners have been gained. In addition, by mapping the distribution of pagan burials it is also possible to gain an impression of the areas which had been settled by the Anglo-Saxons prior to the early seventh century. In her survey of these early burials, Meaney was able to identify regional differences in burial customs within England.[26] Thus, in the southern Jutish and Saxon kingdoms she suggests that cremation was only used in the very earliest period, and that it was then rapidly replaced by inhumation. In most of the Anglian areas cremation was used throughout the pagan period, although some inhumations are found during the latter sixth century, and in central and western England there appears to have been a mixture of inhumations and cremations from an early period. Meaney also notes that it was only towards the end of the heathen period that barrows came into use, and that in later Anglo-Saxon times many of the burials with the richest grave goods were in fact Christian.

Sprouston, in Roxburghshire, is a fine example of a site first brought to light by air reconnaissance, and it has been analysed in detail by St Joseph.[27] Here, unlike at Chalton, Mucking and Drayton, air photographs reveal a cemetery in close juxtaposition to the buildings of the settlement (photo 23). In an area of about 50 m by 30 m a large number of graves can be seen packed closely together in rows lying in a broadly south-west to north-east direction. At least six rectangular buildings can also be identified, two of which are on a much larger scale than any of the buildings discussed in the previous section, and one of these has narrow extensions to both of its short sides.

The ship burial at Sutton Hoo (photo 24) is perhaps the most famous example of an Anglo-Saxon grave in England, and from the artefacts found within it a wealth of information has been obtained concerning both the attributes thought necessary to accompany a king on his journey to the next world, and the economic and political links between England and continental Europe in the seventh century. The cemetery occupies at least 4 ha and contains 15 barrows, with recent work revealing three further inhumations without grave goods to the east of the nearest known barrows. Bruce-Mitford has argued that the burial was probably that of Raedwald, the only East Anglian king to have become Bretwalda or high king. Raedwald had been converted to Christianity in Kent but had apparently relapsed to pagan beliefs well before his death in AD 624 or 625. The nature of the burial, and the designs of the helmet and shield found within it, suggest close links between Sweden and eastern Suffolk at this time, and the presence of Merovingian coins from France, Belgium, the Rhine area and Switzerland, together with other artefacts such as the silver dish from Byzantium and the bronze bowl from Alexandria, all indicate wide contacts between England and continental Europe in the seventh century.[28]

ROYAL PALACES

Indeed, so great was the fervour of faith and desire for baptism among the Northumbrian people that Paulinus is said to have accompanied the king and queen to the royal residence at Ad-Gefrin and remained there thirty-six days constantly occupied in instructing and baptizing.

(Bede, *A History of the English Church and People*, AD 731)

The large halls noted at Sprouston (photo 23) are but one example of features increasingly being recognised by archaeologists as Saxon royal palaces, with other examples including the halls at Northampton and Cheddar. Excavations at Northampton have thus revealed a large mid eighth-century wooden hall which was replaced early in the ninth century by a rectangular stone hall, and at Cheddar a series of similar large halls have been traced from the ninth century through to the fourteenth century.[29] However, the first of these palaces to undergo extensive excavation was that at Yeavering (photo 25), which was first noticed from the air in 1949. This complex series of crop marks has been identified as the

24 Sutton Hoo, Suffolk. This general view of the Sutton Hoo site shows how it stands on a gentle hill overlooking the river Deben, with the town of Woodbridge in the background. The famous ship burial is within the excavated area at the western edge of the mound field. Parallel anti-glider ditches cross the site from south-east to north-west, and a shallow medieval hollow way runs from the ship burial to the north-east corner of the site. The mound at the northern edge of the site has also revealed a boat-shaped pit under the barrow.

25 Yeavering, Northumberland. Dominating this photograph on the left is the Great Enclosure. To the right of this can be seen the complex series of Anglo-Saxon palaces built between the end of the sixth century and the second half of the seventh century. Slightly lower, and to the right of the palaces is the faint outline of the triangular assembly structure, looking like part of a Roman amphitheatre. Just within the Great Enclosure and almost on a line with the palaces can be detected the church, probably built after the enclosure had gone out of use.

royal residence of Ad-Gefrin, mentioned by Bede in the quotation which introduces this section.[30] When the Anglo-Saxons first arrived at Yeavering the site already had a long prehistoric past, having been used as a cremation cemetery since about 2000 BC. In the Roman Iron Age cremations were still taking place and a palisaded enclosure was built. This large circular feature now known as the Great Enclosure is clearly visible in photo 25 and appears in its earliest form to have probably been a defended cattle corral. However, it then became an important cult centre and ceremonial meeting place, continuing in use as such into the seventh century. Between the end of the sixth century and the second half of the seventh century, a series of seven, or possibly eight, rectangular wooden halls was built, with the largest of these being over 25 m long and 13 m wide. It seems likely that this great hall was that of Edwin, and it was also probably he who enlarged the triangular assembly structure that had been built earlier, possibly under Aethelfrith, on the other side of the halls from the Great Enclosure. Yeavering was twice deliberately destroyed by fire, almost certainly by the Mercians, and by the time Bede was writing in the eighth century it was already deserted, with a new palace having been built nearby at Milfield (*Maelmin*). Following the first fire a small church was built within the bounds of the former Great Enclosure. This illustrates a more widespread process by which minster churches were established at the sites of important royal settlements throughout England, giving rise eventually to the familiar parish structure which emerged fully fledged in later medieval times.

Yeavering was undoubtedly the centre of an important royal estate in the kingdom of Bernicia, and Campbell has argued that

> with its long history as a centre for the assembly, rule and, doubtless, exploitation of the hillmen of the Cheviots, [Yeavering] is almost conclusive proof for substantial continuity between the Anglian regime and its British predecessors. There is good reason to suppose that here, and in other areas in the north, the system of local organisation and government was not so much created by the Anglo-Saxons as taken over by them from the British.[31]

Jones has argued that many other large estates elsewhere in Britain, as at Aberffraw, Aucklandshire, Wakefield and Malling, represented a degree of continuity between British and Anglo-Saxon administration, with the essential features of these 'multiple estates', as he calls them, being that they contained 'a hierarchy of settlements, settlements which were in part functionally differentiated and whose occupants, supervised by a ministerial aristocracy, owed rents and services for the support of a lord'.[32] While the archaeological record, as at Yeavering, and the documentary evidence used by Jones from elsewhere, indicate that in parts of England there certainly appears to have been some degree of continuity of estate organisation, it is probable that in some areas of the country the Anglo-Saxons introduced new patterns of settlement and territorial structure.

URBAN RENEWAL: POLITICAL AND ECONOMIC INFLUENCES

> If during the course of these royal admonitions, the commands were not fulfilled because of the people's laziness, or else (having been begun too late in

a time of necessity) were not finished in time to be of use to those working on them (I am speaking here of fortifications commanded by the king which have not yet been begun, or else, having been begun late in the day, have not yet been brought to completion) and enemy forces burst in by land and sea (or, as frequently happens, by both!) then those who had opposed the royal commands were humiliated.

(Asser, *Life of King Alfred*, AD 893)

By the seventh century the political and economic instability consequent upon the collapse of Roman authority and the early Anglo-Saxon settlement had subsided. Trade was again possible, and indeed necessary if the aspirations to luxury as represented by the finds from Sutton Hoo were to be fulfilled. Until recently little was known about the nature of this Anglo-Saxon trade, but a number of excavations at, for example, London, Southampton and York, have revealed the presence of important trading centres in these towns. These market centres, known from their characteristic place-name element as *wics*, have so far clearly been identified at Dover (Wyke), Dunwich, Fordwich (near Canterbury), Hamwic (Southampton), Ipswich, Lincoln (Wigford), London (Aldwych), Norwich, Sandwich, and York (Eoforwic); they may also have existed at Harwich and Swanage. All were in areas that were settled early by the Anglo-Saxons, and many were situated close to old Roman walled towns but outside the walls and on sheltered estuaries and seashores. As has been noted,

> The significance of all of these sites is that they had a good protected foreshore on which boats and ships could be pulled up, and above which trading with the indigenous population (and each other) could take place. Temporary sites (perhaps of the sixth century) would soon become semi-permanent and, until the arrival of the Vikings in the ninth century, they were the only major trading or proto-urban centres in north-west Europe.[33]

Following excavation, Hamwic, or Saxon Southampton, is one of the best known of such *wic* settlements. It was founded by the early eighth century on a new site some 500 m south-west of a Roman fort, and flourished throughout the eighth and ninth centuries, growing to a maximum size of about 37 ha. Hamwic 'was possibly the largest and most densely populated town in 8th century England'.[34] It appears to have been a planned and centrally maintained settlement, trading particularly with the Carolingian empire as indicated by imported pottery from the Meuse region, the Pas-de-Calais, and the Ardennes. Industrial activity on the site included bone working, textiles, glasswork, metalwork and carpentry.[35] By the end of the ninth century, the increasing Viking disruption of trade in the North Sea region appears to have brought an end to Hamwic, as it did to many of the other *wic* settlements of England, and in most cases when renewed pressures for urban development were later felt they found their physical expression on different sites, often reverting to the areas within the walls of old Roman towns.

Haslam draws attention to another aspect of urban development at this time when he asserts that

a common feature of the landscape of much if not most of southern England (as indeed of Midland England as well) was a series of small multi-functional settlements which developed around royal (and occasionally monastic) central places as a direct result of their essentially non-agricultural roles. These places must have developed such characteristics at a period well before *c*.800 AD, and there is good reason for supposing that they would have acted as true market centres, albeit under royal control and possible jurisdiction.[36]

One possible, although later, such settlement can be seen at Old Windsor in Berkshire (photo 26). Here, a large stone building and a mill were built in the eighth and ninth centuries near an earlier Saxon settlement by the church. This upheaval was probably associated with the conversion of the settlement to a palace. In the mid eleventh century Old Windsor is recorded as a royal residence with 25 *hagae* (enclosed plots) suggesting that it had some pretensions to urban status, and Astill has suggested that 'it is this type of increased exploitation of resources on royal sites which has been regarded as a preliminary to the establishment of a small market'.[37] Old Windsor did not, however, survive as an urban settlement, and when the Normans came to this part of the Thames valley they moved the settlement focus nearer to their newly fortified castle at the present site of Windsor.

If settlement changes, such as occurred at Old Windsor, can in some ways be seen as organic in nature, the next major impetus to urban development was caused by external influences and came with the Viking raids on England during the ninth century and the consequent construction by Alfred of a system of defensive *burhs* across the south of the country. In Loyn's succinct summary, 'some of these were based on Roman defences, as at Chichester, Portchester, Winchester, Bath and Exeter, while others were no more than emergency forts set up on the site of iron-age hill-forts. Some developed into important permanent urban settlements, while others faded away into complete obscurity.'[38] These *burhs* were particularly significant as far as the history of government and administration is concerned because the responsibility for their defence and maintenance was laid on the surrounding countryside. Thus, from each 16 hides of land 16 soldiers were to be sent for the defence of 22 yards of wall.

Two contrasting examples of *burhs* established during the wars between the Saxons and Scandinavians are provided by South Cadbury and Malmesbury. The air photograph of South Cadbury (photo 27) shows the hillfort standing proud above the low-lying surrounding fields of southern Somerset, with its banks and ditches forming an impressive defensive system. Archaeological work at South Cadbury has revealed that the site was occupied as far back as the Neolithic period.[39] There were apparently no defences in the Bronze Age, but in the early Iron Age ramparts were built and a number of houses have been excavated within their bounds. The hillfort, with its series of four ramparts, was taken by the Romans, and in the relatively peaceful years that followed it lost its military function. With the unrest of the fifth and sixth centuries it again became an important defensive site, with legend equating it with Arthur's Camelot. Whatever legend might say, archaeological evidence indicates that the defences were renewed at this time and a feasting hall constructed in the interior. Other finds reveal the presence of imported bowls and amphorae. It then seems to have gone out of use again until the late Anglo-Saxon period. Alfred did not choose it as one of his *burhs*, and it was only the renewed conflicts against the Vikings in Ethelred's reign that led to its final efflorescence. Ethelred founded the new *burh* of *Cadanbyrig* on the site of the old Iron Age hillfort probably about AD 1010, and excavation has revealed the remains of a mortared wall of stone slabs backed by a rubble core and a bank of earth, rubble and stone. The wall itself was over a metre thick which, together with the bank, makes the width of the whole defence almost 7 m. It crowned the top of the hill, running for some 1,200 m around its circumference, and the old south-western gate was renewed and con-

26 Old Windsor, Berkshire. Remains of the Saxon settlement of Windsor have been traced around the church on the left of the photograph. Archaeological excavations can be seen in the field to its right, and here the remains of a sophisticated mill with three vertical waterwheels served by a channel 20 feet wide have been found, as well as a stone building with glazed windows and a tiled roof. The earliest Saxon settlement seems to have been inhabited from about AD 600, and the developments indicated by the mill and stone building to have dated from between AD 750 and 850. Crop marks indicating former field boundaries can be seen in the light-coloured field on the right, and a further crop mark of a ditch can just be seen running diagonally across the two fields below the church.

siderably strengthened. There is some evidence that an attempt was made to build a church within the interior, but apart from this the archaeological record has provided little that would suggest a truly urban function. Nevertheless, it is apparent that a mint was established on the site, with coins bearing the name *Cadanbyrig* being known from elsewhere, and its seems possible that other urban activities may have taken place on the site. By AD 1020, however, the moneyers had left and South Cadbury had lost any claim it might have had to urban status.

South Cadbury is therefore a good example of a site which served mainly a political and military function, and which was used for defensive purposes as and when necessary. If such defensive attributes were also associated with features which made a site of economic importance, then it was likely that a *burh* foundation would develop into a fully fledged urban settlement, as at Wallingford in Oxfordshire or Cricklade in Wiltshire.[40] The town of Malmesbury, also in Wiltshire, provides another good example of a site with a number of urban attributes which was given an additional impetus through its creation into a *burh* (photo 28). It is possible that Malmesbury was once an Iron Age hillfort, which like South Cadbury, became a British military centre in the fifth or sixth centuries.[41] In the mid seventh century, the Irish monk Maeldulph then founded a monastery on the site in close proximity to the royal manor of Brokenborough. This provides another good illustration of the way in which the emergence of Anglo-Saxon ecclesiastical administration was closely linked to the organisation of royal estates. It seems likely that once established, the abbey attracted a number of craftsmen and merchants to its gates, and that the settlement of Malmesbury thus gradually began to take on certain urban characteristics.

Nevertheless, it was with Alfred's choice of the site as the location for one of his *burhs* in the late-ninth century that the development of the town really began. As may be clearly seen from the air (photo 28), Malmesbury forms an excellent defensive site, being on a hill surrounded on three sides by water, with only a narrow neck of land to the north-west requiring major additional protection. The basic street pattern, with roads entering from the north-west and the north-east to join the high street running along the spine of the hill, may have existed prior to Malmesbury's transformation into a *burh*, but it seems likely that the laying out of regular property divisions within the defended area was part of a conscious policy to turn the settlement into both a military fortress and an economically functioning town. Unlike South Cadbury, however, Malmesbury grew, and became an important mint during the reign of Edgar. This growth was undoubtedly largely associated with the importance of the abbey, with Athelstan being buried there in AD 939. Malmesbury thus provides a fine example of the way in which a multiplicity of functions was important for the success of an urban settlement if it was to flourish in the succeeding centuries.

SCANDINAVIAN RURAL SETTLEMENT

After that Thorfinn started back home and arrived safe and well in his own earldom. By now he was finished with piracy and devoted all his time to the government of his people and country and to the making of new laws.

27 South Cadbury, Somerset. The dominant features of this photograph are the four banks and ditches of the Iron Age hillfort, but surmounting these are the remains of the Anglo-Saxon bank constructed around AD 1010 when Ethelred designated the hill as a *burh*. The hill itself is an oolitic limestone outlier to the west of the Jurassic limestone escarpment, and it clearly dominates the low-lying area of southern Somerset to its north and west. Traces of former cultivation terraces can be seen in the bottom left corner of the photograph.

28 Malmesbury, Wiltshire. The excellent defensive site upon which Alfred's *burh* of Malmesbury is situated, lying on a peninsula between the two branches of the Avon, is well illustrated here. The abbey founded in the mid seventh century lies on the highest ground in the narrow neck of land at the top of the photograph, and the burgage plots on either side of the High Street can be seen regularly laid out to the south.

He had his permanent residence at Birsay, where he built and dedicated to Christ a fine minster, the seat of the first bishop of Orkney.

(*Orkneyinga Saga*, c.AD 1200)

Although the Anglo-Saxon Chronicle notes that the first Viking raids on England occurred following the year AD 787, it was only in the 850s that the Scandinavians first wintered here and in the 870s that they began to settle and cultivate the soil. Unfortunately it has proved to be exceedingly difficult to differentiate between Viking rural settlements and Anglo-Saxon farms and villages on the basis of archaeological evidence alone. In rural settlements the artefacts most likely to be found are the basic requirements of everyday life, and these seem to have varied little between the Danes and the Anglo-Saxons. It is likewise impossible to identify specifically Scandinavian rural settlements simply from air photographs.

For these reasons historical geographers have turned principally to the evidence of place-names for an understanding of the distribution of Viking settlements in England, and have in particular looked at the distribution of place-names ending in -*bȳ*, the standard Scandinavian word for a settlement. Such an analysis reveals that almost all such -*bȳ* place-names are found in the Danelaw to the northeast of the boundary established following the agreement between Alfred and Guthrum in AD 886. Place-names in which the first element is a Scandinavian personal-name and the second element is the Old English -*tūn*, meaning a farmstead or village, such as Flixton or Gamston, have also been used to identify settlements where it seems probable that previous Anglo-Saxon villages were taken over by the victorious Danes of the Great Army.[42] Place-names studies are fraught with difficulty, but they do provide a broad indication of areas of Scandinavian settlement, and when studied alongside literary sources which give some chronological sequence of events, such as the Anglo-Saxon Chronicle, they enable us to gain a general impression of the ebb and flow of Scandinavian influence over different parts of the country.

Most of the Anglo-Saxon literary sources dealing with the ninth and tenth centuries refer to the conflicts between Vikings and Anglo-Saxons in lowland England. However, it is clear from a study of place-names and other literary sources, such as the Norse sagas, that there was also extensive Scandinavian settlement elsewhere in Britain, with Norwegians settling in north-western England, the Isle of Man, the Hebrides, Orkney and Shetland. In the case of Orkney and Shetland it would appear that not many of the former inhabitants survived, since there are very few pre-Scandinavian place-names remaining today, and indeed the whole language of the islands was replaced by a Scandinavian language known later as Norn. In addition to the saga evidence, major excavations at Jarlshof, Aikerness and Brough of Birsay have now added considerably to our knowledge of the Viking occupation of these islands.[43] One basic difficulty in interpreting such sites, however, is that they often represent a series of successive building stages, from the prehistoric to the medieval. Thus, despite the numerous remains found for example at Jarlshof, it appears that in the Viking period there were probably never more than three families living at the site at any one time.

29 Brough of Birsay, Orkney. The Norse church and churchyard, which may possibly be the remains of Thorfinn's minster, lie at the centre of this photograph. In the area to the east, Viking Age buildings replaced earlier structures, and the buildings to the north appear to be contemporaneous with the construction of the church, indicating the elevation of the site to that of a higher status settlement.

At Brough of Birsay (photo 29) there is clear evidence of Viking period buildings replacing earlier structures in the area to the east of the chapel.[44] In the early Viking period it seems that Brough of Birsay was a secular settlement, but the construction of larger buildings and then the erection of a church, clearly visible in photo 29, indicate a transition to a high status and then religious site. Unlike in lowland England, the plentiful supply of flagstones has enabled us to gain a good impression of the nature of these Viking buildings from the archaeological record alone. Nevertheless, it is also evident that there was frequent rebuilding on the site and several changes in the orientation of the buildings have been noted. From the *Orkneyinga Saga* we know that Birsay was the seat of the Earls

of Orkney, and it seems that we have here a settlement of comparable status to, for example, the earlier royal palace at Yeavering. The church remains, which stand out so visibly at Brough of Birsay, have been the subject of much debate, and it is uncertain whether they are indeed Thorfinn's minster of Christ Church. They nevertheless reflect a considerable expenditure of energy and wealth, and they illustrate both the political power of the earls and also the particular blend of war and religion that played such an important part in the lives of the Viking inhabitants of these islands such as Thorfinn and Rognvald. Little is known about the economy of the Viking settlers of Orkney and Shetland, but the archaeological record goes some way to supporting the image of a hard and difficult farming lifestyle portrayed in the *Orkneyinga Saga*. It seems that bere (barley) and oats were the most important cereals, and some flax was also grown. Animal husbandry, dominated by sheep, was fundamental, and fishing also seems to have been significant. However, the impression given by the saga of an economy partly supported by the undertaking of regular raids into more prosperous areas, seems undoubtedly also to have been true.

SCANDINAVIAN URBAN SETTLEMENT

867. In this year the army went from East Anglia to Northumbria, across the Humber estuary to the city of York. And there was great civil strife going on in that people, and they had deposed their king Osbert and taken a king with no hereditary right, Ælla. And not until late in the year did they unite sufficiently to proceed to fight the raiding army; and nevertheless they collected a large army and attacked the enemy in York, and broke into the city; and some of them got inside, and an immense slaughter was made of the Northumbrians, some inside and some outside, and both kings were killed, and the survivors made peace with the enemy.

(*Anglo-Saxon Chronicle*, AD 867)

If the initial Scandinavian forays into England were carried out as raids, it is evident that by the mid ninth century settlement and trade had assumed greater significance, and this is nowhere better illustrated than in the city of York whose capture by the Vikings is recorded in the above extract from the *Anglo-Saxon Chronicle*. The city became the capital of the Viking kingdom of York and it was ruled by Danish and Norwegian kings until its incorporation into the united kingdom of England in AD 954. York had been one of the most important towns of Roman Britain, and remains of the fortress can easily be traced on photo 30 around the minster on the north side of the River Ouse, with the walled outline of the *colonia* also being clearly visible to the south of the river. Following the departure of the Sixth Legion around AD 400, both the written and archaeological records concerning York dry up almost completely until AD 627 when Edwin was baptised at York and established it as the see of his teacher and bishop, Paulinus.[45]

The Anglian town of York was then known as Eoforwic, but there is remarkably little archaeological evidence to testify to its undoubted ecclesiastical import-

Plan of York illustrating photograph 30. (After S. S. Frere and J. K. S. St Joseph, *Roman Britain from the Air*, Cambridge, 1983.)

30 York, Yorkshire. The Roman and medieval features of the city of York are still clearly visible from the air, despite the subsequent imposition of the railway sidings and twentieth-century housing estates. To the north-east and north-west of the Minster, located just above and left of the centre of the photograph, the outlines of the walls of the legionary fortress can be seen as a vertical and horizontal line. Likewise, the walls of the *colonia* can be traced to the south of the river Ouse (near the bottom of the photograph) as straight lines going south from the right-most bridge, then west until they head north again to join the river at the next but one bridge upstream. The main source of Anglian finds has been from the area around the confluence of the rivers Fosse and Ouse, to the east of the Roman fortress and the mound of the Norman castle, and it would seem that here lay the main trading focus of Eoforwic.

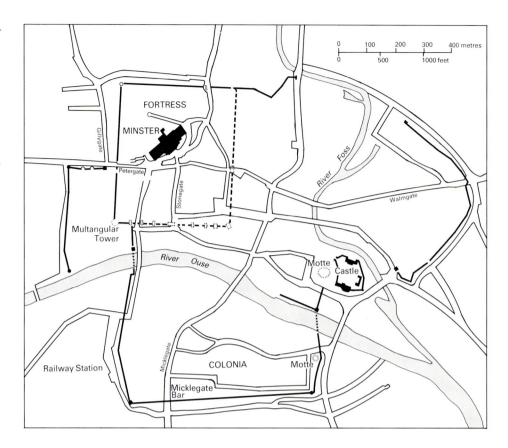

ance at this time. It seems as though the remains of the former Roman headquarters building were incorporated into a palace complex with the cathedral nearby, but little else is known about the city. The main economic activity at this period would appear to have taken place well outside the remains of the Roman fortress, at Fishergate to the east of the river Fosse at its confluence with the Ouse. Here the evidence of buildings and roads used between the seventh and ninth centuries, together with the remains of imported pottery and evidence of manufacturing industry, indicates the existence of a typical *wic* trading settlement, with its shelving foreshore being ideally suited for the pulling up of boats.

It was not, however, until the capture of York by the Vikings in AD 866/7 that it began to develop further and take on a vibrant urban character. By the tenth century Jorvik, as it had become, was a thriving town with contacts throughout the Scandinavian world; the excavations at Coppergate, to the north-west of the castle mound, have revealed a wealth of information about the daily lives and commercial activity of its inhabitants. At some date around AD 910 a major reorganisation seems to have taken place in Jorvik, with new tenement boundaries in the form of post and withy fences being laid out in association with buildings along the street now called Coppergate.[46] By the end of the tenth century the only larger and wealthier city in England was London, and the buildings in Coppergate had been rebuilt once again, with semi-basements being dug beneath the previous floor level and the lower parts of the walls being constructed of oak planks and posts. Elsewhere in York there is also considerable evidence of Viking activity during the late ninth and tenth centuries, with many of the

roads of the medieval city first being laid out in this period. Nevertheless, the precise extent of the Viking city of Jorvik is not yet known. That Jorvik was both a commercial and industrial centre of major importance is attested by a wealth of archaeological material. Commercial links with Scandinavia and elsewhere are reflected in finds of steatite, Mayen lava quernstones, honestones, pottery, ivory and silk, while the manufacturing industries for which evidence survives included the production of amber and jet ornaments, glasswork, metalwork, bone and antlerwork, stonemasonry, leather, textiles, pottery, carpentry, and an important mint.[47]

If York was the most impressive testimony to the impetus given to urban development by the Scandinavians, it was not the only example. Returning to the military influence on urban development to which reference has already been made, it is evident from entries in the *Anglo-Saxon Chronicle* that once they had decided to remain in England the Danes fortified their encampments. Thus in AD 868 the *Anglo Saxon Chronicle* records that Burgred, Ethelred and Alfred 'went with the army of the West Saxons into Mercia to Nottingham, and came upon the enemy in that fortress and besieged them there'.[48] Other Danish fortified settlements were constructed at Derby, Leicester, Lincoln and Stamford, and these can be seen as having acted as further foci for urban development in a similar way to the later Saxon *burhs* of Alfred.

CONCLUSION

Much remains uncertain about this elusive period in the historical geography of Britain. Aerial photography has identified key sites, such as Sprouston and Yeavering, which when excavated have yielded a wealth of information about Anglo-Saxon settlement and society. Air photographs also provide an opportunity to envisage the scale and grandeur of major earthworks such as Offa's Dyke and Wansdyke, and to capture at a glance the complex pattern of buildings found on sites such as Birsay. However, to obtain a broader insight into the economic, social and political changes that took place between the departure of the Romans and the Norman conquest it is essential to combine the evidence of air photographs and archaeology with that of the literary and documentary sources.

Many questions nevertheless still remain unanswered. In particular, we must recognise that there may have been important regional differences within Britain at this time, and that processes operating in the uplands of Northumbria may have been very different from those taking place say in Kent. Detailed multidisciplinary studies need to be undertaken on the settlements and early field systems used by the Anglo-Saxons and on how changes in agrarian structure were related to changes in settlement pattern.[49] To gain a true understanding of the relative balance between cataclysm and continuity in the years between the departure of the Romans and the Norman Conquest we need to understand the important relationships that existed between boundaries, settlements and fields, and we must relate changes in these surface features to underlying economic, social and political changes that took place between the fourth and eleventh centuries.

FURTHER READING

J. Campbell (ed.), *The Anglo-Saxons*, Oxford, 1982.

M. Gelling, *Place-names in the Landscape*, London, 1984.

D. Hill, *An Atlas of Anglo-Saxon England*, Oxford, 1981.

D. Hooke (ed.), *Anglo-Saxon Settlements*, Oxford, 1988.

G. R. J. Jones, 'Celts, Saxons and Scandinavians', in R. A. Dodgson and R. A. Butlin (eds.), *An Historical Geography of England and Wales*, second edn, London, 1990, pp. 45–68.

D. Whitelock *et al.*, *The Anglo-Saxon Chronicle: a Revised Translation*, London, 1961.

3   The early Middle Ages: 1066–1348

In the two centuries after 1066, population increased, settlements grew in size and number, more land was brought under cultivation and trade expanded. There has been much debate as to why this was such a period of growth in Britain as it was also on the continent. Population seems to have increased steadily when it might be expected that numbers would have been held in check by poor living standards, endemic diseases and periodic food shortages. Steady growth may, however, have been possible because the period was free from major epidemics of plague such as were later to sweep through the country in the second half of the fourteenth century. As there is no evidence at this period of any mass immigration into the country the inescapable conclusions are first, that in most years birth rate exceeded death rate and, secondly, that enough food was produced to sustain population growth in all but years of poor harvest. The increasing supply of labour must have contributed to rising aggregate production which in turn generated surpluses which could be marketed both at home and abroad. As a result, the period was one of increasing commercialism within the context of the feudal system.

How far these trends continued or were reversed between the end of the thirteenth century and the Black Death of 1348–9 is debatable. M. M. Postan's thesis of a crisis in the relationship between population and resources at the end of the thirteenth century,[1] although still widely supported, is coming under increasing scrutiny. Studies of different parts of the country have led to varying and sometimes conflicting conclusions. Much hinges upon the situation in the years between 1315 and 1322 when, throughout Europe, there was a sequence of bad harvests and consequent famines.

Undoubtedly the demographic and economic tide was beginning to turn. As E. Miller expressed it some years ago 'the first half of the fourteenth century was a time of waiting for the blow to fall'.[2] This was said with an historian's hindsight; those living at the time could have had no inkling that the 'blow' above all others was to be the Black Death, an outbreak of disease on a scale that Europe had never known before.

Politically, the Normans had consolidated their hold on England by 1100. In the 1070s William ruthlessly put down resistance, especially in the north and by the time of his departure for the continent late in 1086 almost all the country was directly in his hands or held for him by Norman lords under what has come to be known as the feudal system. Despite internal strife England emerged as the dominant political entity within Britain in the twelfth and thirteenth centuries with relatively strong government and centralised institutions. By contrast the situation in Scotland and Wales was more fragmented. While, under the aegis of Scottish kings, Anglo-Norman feudalism penetrated lowland Scotland, the uplands of the north-west remained a core region of Celtic culture. The same was true in Wales where although Anglo-Normans took effective control of most of the east and south the uplands remained the territory of Welsh princes until their conquest by Edward I in 1282–4. Geographically, therefore, the impact of the Normans and their institutions in the late twelfth century varied greatly; in general terms the hallmarks of the new order – castles, cathedrals, monastic houses and new boroughs – were commonly found in the agriculturally productive lowlands whereas the uplands show greater continuity with earlier cultures.

Through the administration of church and state the Normans generated new documentation of which, fortunately, much has survived. By far the most valuable single survey from which to reconstruct aspects of the geography of late eleventh-century England is King William's 'descriptio' of 1085–6 which by the late twelfth century was already called the Domesday. There has been much debate among historians as to the exact purpose of the survey and opinion remains divided. Some have seen it essentially as a survey of landholding following the redistribution of Saxon estates to Norman lords; others incline to the view that it was mainly an assessment of wealth and resources as a prelude to taxation. A recent and challenging view is that the survey might have been directly related to the court held at Salisbury in 1086 when William received homage and fealty from his landholders, an event sometimes described as the 'Salisbury Oath'. J. C. Holt has revived this view and suggested that in return for their loyalty William's chief tenants received recognition and confirmation of their holdings from the King; Domesday Book, he argues, was, from their point of view, in effect 'a vast land book which put a final seal on the Norman occupation'.[3]

Whatever its exact purpose the details recorded in Domesday Book make it into what has been described as 'probably the most remarkable statistical document in the history of Europe'.[4] There is nothing comparable to it for that period on the continent, and historians and geographers of medieval England who have this unique source at their disposal are the envy of their colleagues elsewhere in the British Isles and on the continent. For historical geographers the survey comes at an opportune moment in that it may be used both to reconstruct the geography of late eleventh-century England and to act as a 'baseline' against which to measure the changes of the later Middle Ages. For all its merits, however, Domesday is not without its drawbacks and complications. The northern counties of England – Durham, Northumberland, Cumberland and Westmorland – were not included in the survey and as there is nothing similar for Wales and Scotland a reconstruction of the geography of the whole of Britain in 1086 is not possible. Despite this, the information for much of England is of the utmost importance, especially for what it tells us of the distribution of population and resources.

While there are many problems in unravelling and understanding the Domesday information it can be stated with confidence that the densities of population were much higher on the more fertile lowlands of the south and east of England than they were in the more broken upland of the west and north. At that time the number of people was closely related to the carrying capacity of the land and in particular to those areas best suited to basic cereal crops. Yet even in the most populous parts of the country such as Norfolk, Suffolk and the Sussex coastal plain the recorded Domesday population seldom exceeded 20 per square mile. As those recorded were almost certainly only the heads of households the total number of people would have been much higher, perhaps in the order of 100 per square mile. Such high densities were, however, exceptions; the recorded population over most of the south-east was seldom above 15 per square mile and over most of England it was under 10. Some areas appear to have been extremely thinly settled; they included the Weald, the Breckland, most of the Fenland and much of the south-west and the north of England.[5]

In the absence of similar information for Scotland and Wales we can only surmise that the population was also higher in the lowlands than in the uplands. Total numbers are a matter of speculation: estimates for England in 1086 based on different interpretations of the accuracy and completeness of the survey range between about 1.5 and 2.5 million. For Britain as a whole it seems unlikely that there could have been a population of more than 4 million in the late eleventh century. Today the population is around 56 million and the comparison is here made to emphasize just how thinly populated the country was at that time.

Nevertheless, bearing in mind that relatively few people now live in rural areas, a few parts of the countryside may have had as many people in 1086 as they do now. The same, however, could not be said of the towns which, in the late eleventh century, were very small by modern standards; only a few could have had more than 2,000 people and most were no bigger than large villages are today.

That the population of England grew rapidly in the two centuries after Domesday is not in doubt but by how much it is impossible to say. In the absence of censuses, historians have had to make use of other indicators to show that population increased; there has been remarkable agreement over the trend even if there is continuing disagreement over absolute numbers. Most are satisfied that the total population doubled between the Norman Conquest and 1300; in some areas the increase may have been greater. It seems likely that the populations of Scotland and Wales also increased during this period but by how much it is impossible to say. Everywhere there must have been periodic checks to growth by famine and disease but the period is free from catastrophic epidemics and the evidence suggests that in general food production managed to keep pace with population growth at least until the middle of the thirteenth century. It may indeed have stimulated it. Not until the second half of the thirteenth century are there signs that in some areas numbers were beginning to outstrip food supplies and that a critical relationship between population and food resources was developing. Local 'subsistence crises' as they have been called, became more frequent in the late thirteenth century and intensified in the period 1315–22 when a series of bad harvests caused widespread famine and distress in Britain as they did on the continent. Some historians see this short period of the 'Great European Famine' as the real end to expansion and growth in the medieval period. The impact of famine and disease no doubt varied from one area to another and only now are such regional differences being more fully explored. With only limited sources available we are unlikely ever to see the complete picture.

As population grew in the twelfth and thirteenth centuries so also did the number of dwellings, whether as farms or in hamlets, villages and towns. The

limited documentary evidence for the increase in the number and size of settlements may be supplemented by evidence from archaeological excavation and from those features of the medieval period which are still to be seen in the present landscape. In this respect aerial photography has a particularly important role to play both by revealing features that may not be visible at ground level and by bringing different perspectives to surviving features of the medieval landscape be they monastic houses, churches, field patterns, hamlets or villages.[6]

AGRICULTURE AND THE LANDSCAPE

Population growth in the Middle Ages could have been achieved only if people were reasonably well fed and famine kept at bay in all but years of bad harvest. Evidence suggests that at least until the second half of the thirteenth century food supplies kept pace with demand. Much of the increased production was achieved by bringing more marginal land under the plough (photo 31). This was easier than increasing yields from existing arable land. Agricultural progress was held back for a variety of reasons which included a low level of technology, a lack of scientific knowledge, a limited range of crops, soil exhaustion and low levels of investment. Despite this, recent research has shown that some parts of the country were much more progressive than others and that yields were being increased by better farming practices which included more effective rotations (with increased use of legumes), less annual fallow, more manuring, and the use of horses rather than oxen for ploughing. In other words there was more intensification of production especially in areas where there was little marginal land still left to reclaim. One such area was north-east Norfolk where, as B. M. S. Campbell has shown, medieval agriculture was more advanced than has hitherto been thought.[7] Whether this was due to relatively good soils, to the availability of labour, to good management, to the stimulus given to production by nearby Norwich, or to a combinaton of these factors is now a matter of debate. What is certain is that both processes, intensification and extensification, went on together between *c*.1100 and *c*.1300 and that their relative importance in increasing food supplies varied from one area to another.

Evidence for the expansion of the cultivated area is not hard to find. Twelfth and thirteenth-century sources include many references to 'assarts' or clearings whereby arable land was won from woodland and 'waste' (unimproved pasture and scrubland). Locally this was the usual way of adding new acres to the existing agricultural land of a township. While peasants may have added an acre or two, lords made large additions to their demesnes and used their extra acres either for cultivation or sometimes, as was the increasing fashion, for deer parks. As woodland and waste were used up what remained became more precious both to lords and commoners; the conflict of interests is evident by 1235 when the Statute of Merton permitted lords to enclose woodland so long as adequate amounts were left for their freeholders. In those parts of the country which were still well wooded, reclamation was accompanied by new settlements as for example in the Arden of Warwickshire and the Weald of Kent and Sussex.

Increasing pressure of population on available agricultural resources is usually indicated both by the reclamation of new land and by the more intensive use

31 This photograph of an abandoned settlement at Hound Tor, Devon was taken in 1971 after the clearance of vegetation and the partial excavation of the site. The outlines of the buildings therefore show up clearly; on a recent visit they were partially overgrown again and would now be less clear from the air.

Excavations showed that in the thirteenth century this hamlet consisted of four long-houses, four smaller houses and three buildings with internal corn-drying kilns. This was one of several small clusters of farms around the moorland edge occupied during the expansion phase of medieval population and agriculture. Excavation revealed that the granite-walled houses were the successors of earlier sunken huts and turf-walled buildings; it seems likely that the site was occupied, not necessarily continuously, from the late Saxon period.

of areas already under cultivation. Such was the case in the twelfth and thirteenth centuries, a period when it became increasingly necessary to ration the better land and to regulate its use. In Britain this was achieved by widespread use of communal field systems, most of them under manorial control, especially in the English Midlands. While doubt has recently been cast on the view that there was a widespread transition from two to three field systems during this period[8] there is little doubt that relatively diminishing resources led to more complicated systems of landholding and cultivation. The more that medieval field arrangements are studied the more varied and complicated they appear to have been. Many different systems were in operation depending on terrain, soils and social organisation.[9] In very general terms infield-outfield systems (in which there was intensive cultivation of land close to the main settlement and periodic cultivation of land further away) were characteristic of upland Britain and of areas of dispersed settlement, while open-field systems (where most of the land of the township was divided into large common fields) were to be found in areas where the characteristic forms of settlement were large hamlets and villages, notably in the English Midlands.

Remnants of what H. L. Gray called the 'Midland System' (which was certainly in place by the thirteenth century and probably had its origins in the late Saxon period) have, for a number of reasons, been more readily identified than have remnants of infield-outfield systems. Not only are Midland field arrangements better documented in the medieval period but they survived, albeit in modified forms, in hundreds of midland parishes until the period of Parliamentary Enclosure between *c.*1750 and *c.*1850. Before enclosure many common fields were surveyed and mapped in great detail and, where they survive, the maps facilitate comparisons between what now remains on the ground (so often seen very effectively from the air) and what was there before the replanning of the landscape by the Enclosure Commissioners.[10]

One characteristic of Midland fields was that their internal subdivisions or 'furlongs' were usually ploughed in a series of parallel, slightly curved ridges usually showing the form of a shallow reversed S (photo 32). There has been much discussion as to why the ridges and the furrows between them were ploughed in this way rather than in straight lines. The most convincing explanations to date are technical and concern the nature of the plough and the difficulties of manoeuvering large plough teams of oxen.[11] These fail to explain, however, why so-called ridge-and-furrow does not seem to have been characteristic of some parts of the British Isles, such as Ireland, where oxen were also used for ploughing. Many questions remain unanswered. Whatever the reasons, many areas of ridge-and-furrow survive under present grassland most notably on heavier soils in English Midland counties such as Leicestershire and Northamptonshire. When of reversed S form, the ridge-and-furrow is almost certainly of medieval origin; however, it must be stressed that it resulted from continuous ploughing on the same lines over long periods and that it is rarely possible to date it with any precision either from documents or excavation. In all probability most of the sinuous ridges that are well seen from the air (photo 32) are the fossilised remnants of medieval plough strips which were in use until the arable land was converted to pasture at a time of enclosure. It needs to be stressed that ridges were ploughing

32 This oblique photograph of English Midland countryside near Lowesby, Leicestershire under a light covering of snow shows the considerable but uneven survival of ridge-and-furrow in pasture fields and its faint traces where it has been ploughed out. Of reversed S form, these ridges, the remains of medieval plough strips, are almost certainly medieval in date. This piece of country is typical of much of the Midland landscape which experienced conversion of arable land to pasture in the later Middle Ages. In this particular view no villages are to be seen; Lowesby, which gave its name to the parish in the foreground, is deserted, its site within woods and parkland in the middle distance. The modern field pattern with its hedgerows and standard trees dates from the period of Parliamentary Enclosure after 1750 as may the farm in the foreground.

33 A landscape of well-preserved terraces for cultivation (lynchets) on the chalk Downs near Mere in Wiltshire. Ploughed along the contours the lynchets are presumed to be medieval in date but could be of earlier origin. They survive here because much of this land has been open sheep walk since the end of the Middle Ages.

units; without proof they should not be equated with tenurial strip holdings in the open field although at some time many of them may well have been.

Much ridge-and-furrow has been ploughed out in the last 50 years especially in the arable areas of the east. When cross-ploughed by modern machinery all traces disappear within a few years. Headlands, the substantial earthen banks at the ends of the ridges on which the plough-teams were turned, may survive longer although much reduced from their original size. In some parishes the mapping of surviving headlands offers the best, and sometimes the only, opportunity of reconstructing the framework of the common fields.[12]

Steep slopes were sometimes ploughed along the contours producing a series of wide terraces which survive as lynchets; there are particularly good examples in Wiltshire and Dorset (photo 33). Again they are difficult to date but they are generally thought to be from the expansion phase of the medieval period.

WOODLAND AND FOREST

The Domesday record leaves little doubt that while most of the English lowlands were cleared and settled by the end of the Anglo-Saxon period considerable areas of woodland still remained, especially on less attractive soils; they were important both in the medieval economy and the landscape. That woodland survived at all in the twelfth and thirteenth centuries was in part due to the Norman introduction of Forest Law whereby large areas were set aside for the King's hunting of deer and protected by officials appointed by the crown. Many woodlands and areas of open grazing which would otherwise have been reclaimed for agriculture were thereby preserved. In fact, the existence of Forest Law and its enforcement may in part be seen as a contemporary awareness of the already diminishing habitats for game, especially for deer and wild boar.

In England the total area under Forest Law probably reached its maximum extent in the mid twelfth century; even a century later perhaps as much as a fifth of the country was still designated as Forest. While by no means all this land was tree-covered there were many large tracts of crown forest in southern England, for example – in Essex (Waltham, Hainault, and Hatfield), Hampshire (the New Forest, Alice Holt and several others), Berkshire (Windsor), Wiltshire (Savernake, Melksham, Clarendon and others), Staffordshire (Kinver and Cannock), Gloucestershire (Dean) and Nottinghamshire (Sherwood). In the north there were large areas under Forest Law in Yorkshire (Pickering and Galtres), north Derbyshire, north Lancashire and Cumberland (Inglewood). Oliver Rackham estimates that just before Magna Carta in 1216 (after which no new forests were created in England), there were at least 142 forests in England.[13] In Scotland, where forests continued to be created after this date, there were probably about 180 forests in the Middle Ages, most of them in the southern uplands, along the eastern edge of the Highlands and in the central lowlands and Aberdeenshire. About half belonged to the Scottish crown and half were in private hands. In Wales almost all the 100 or so forests were in the south where they had been created by Anglo-Norman lords in imitation of those of the English crown.[14]

Not all these forests were tree-covered; many lowland forests included open land (on which deer were protected) and many in Wales and Scotland were no doubt on moorland. While it is difficult to determine the exact nature of the vegetation cover in the medieval period even with modern scientific methods, it seems certain that many areas of upland were as open in character then as they are today, as for example in the Peak, Dartmoor and the Scottish Highlands. Some lowland forests included open heathland as for example the New Forest, a piece of country set aside for hunting by William soon after the Conquest and, as Domesday records, cleared of many of its existing settlements. In some forests settlements survived, not just around the fringes but in the central area, as in the Wirral of Cheshire. Medieval kings, in need of revenue and recognising the demand both for timber and for land, frequently granted rights to graze, collect wood and fell trees to individuals and to institutions. Foremost among the recipients of such privileges were monastic houses, many of which held rights by charter in nearby forests and depended upon them for supplies of oak and other building timber, underwood for firewood and charcoal, and bark for tanning. Whereas not all forest was woodland the converse was equally true; the medieval landscape was dotted with patches of woodland which were carefully managed for timber trees (for building) and for underwood (mainly for fuel). That such woodland was a valued resource is seen by the importance given to it in the Domesday survey. The replies to the commissioners question '*Quantum*

Silvae'? was given in a number of ways; sometimes the size of a wood was given by measurement (linear or acreage) and sometimes by the number of swine it could support. Maps of the returns give a very clear impression of the remarkable nature of the record in a way that the document itself cannot do.[15] In 1086 the distribution of surviving woodland in England was already very uneven. In parts of the country woodland is recorded for almost all communities, as for example in the area around London, in north Warwickshire and east Somerset, whereas there appears to have been very little wood left in the Fens, the Breckland, the Yorkshire Wolds, south Warwickshire and several parts of the Midlands. In some areas wood-pasture was important; trees were pollarded for wood and livestock grazed the undergrowth and grass. In the twelfth century, mainly as a result of the Norman introduction of fallow deer, the making of parks became more common. By 1300 there were probably over 2,000 parks in Britain, the overwhelming majority of them in England. Their distribution corresponds with that of woodland as the fallow deer, the commonest animal of the parks and kept for its venison, was regarded as a woodland animal. Each park would have been surrounded by a high pale, usually of cleft oak stakes; many were internally divided by banks and fences to allow for coppicing and to prevent the animals from eating the new growth. Wood and timber were valuable assets in a park and supplies could only be maintained by careful management of both the trees and the livestock.[16]

RURAL SETTLEMENT

Over 13,000 place-names are to be found in the Domesday folios, almost all of them of Anglo-Saxon type. While this record has been invaluable for the study of the evolution of English place-names, it has also raised interesting questions as to what the names represented on the ground. Unfortunately for historical geographers the survey did not record the number of houses or the size and shape of settlements. It should be stressed that the Domesday place-names refer to feudal holdings which, in all probability, took their names from existing places. Thus we can read for example in the Cambridgeshire folios of the manor of Elsworth without knowing how many settlements were contained within the manor. In giving its name to the manor it seems reasonable to assume that Elsworth was already the most important place in the area but was it the only place or was it one among several? Was Elsworth then a large hamlet within a pattern of single farms and other hamlets or had the place which carried the name in 1086 already become the nucleated village that it is today? (photo 34)

As almost all the Domesday place-names are of Anglo-Saxon type and because so many can be equated with present-day villages of the same name (even if the modern name has a later form) there has been a tendency in the past to assume that nucleated villages, now to be found in many parts of the English lowlands, were of early Anglo-Saxon origin and already in existence in the form that we know them today by 1086. In recent years both these assumptions have been challenged. Current research suggests that many settlements have their ultimate origins in the Romano-British or prehistoric periods and that nucleated villages are of comparatively 'late' date, i.e. between the late Saxon period and the

34 Elsworth, Cambridgeshire is a village at the centre of a parish of almost 4,000 acres; this vertical photograph shows it surrounded by its agricultural land. Despite Parliamentary Enclosure, here just after 1800, there has been hardly any development of outlying farms; the land is still cultivated from farms on the edge of the village. Almost all the ridge-and-furrow of the former open fields has been ploughed away; it survives only in a few of the smaller closes near to the village, now used for grazing. In the large fields created by enclosure it has been replaced by the regular lines of modern arable cultivation.

In Domesday Elsworth was a large manor of the Abbot of Ramsey. In all likelihood there was already a village here in 1086, nucleated near the church but very much smaller than it is today. Signs of a medieval planned component with regular house plots along both sides of the stream and street may be seen west of the church.

thirteenth century. While some villages may have been large and nucleated by 1086 (and Elsworth may well have been one) others were still only very small settlements. This is not surprising when one considers the relatively small total size of the eleventh-century population. Only a few manorial holdings recorded in Domesday could have had more than 150 people living in 30 or so households. In some areas the houses may already have been grouped together in small settlements at the centre of their cultivated land; with population increase in the twelfth and thirteenth centuries such places grew in size eventually to become the lowland villages with which we are familiar today. In other areas, however, the population at the time of Domesday was probably dispersed in farms and hamlets and it was only later that villages evolved, either through a coalescence of hamlets or by the deliberate replanning of settlements and their associated fields.

Pioneer work on these issues has been done by C. C. Taylor in the course of detailed parish surveys for the Royal Commission on Historical Monuments

in several English counties. One of his Cambridgeshire examples, Bottisham, now a large village and with an Anglo-Saxon name, is listed in Domesday as a manor held by Walter Giffard; 51 people are recorded there. As Taylor says, 'there seems every reason to assume that it has always been a single large village', yet his detailed documentary and field studies show that Bottisham as we know it today has evolved from two or perhaps three separate settlements a quarter of a mile or more distant from each other. Moreover, within the medieval parish there were at least five other small settlements by the thirteenth century; when they originated is problematic but at least three of them are likely to have been there (but unrecorded) in 1086.[17]

Complexity of a different kind has been revealed by the excavation of the deserted medieval village of Wharram Percy on the Yorkshire Wolds. When

excavation started there in 1950 the expectation was that an early Anglo-Saxon village would be located under the earthworks of medieval houses abandoned at the end of the Middle Ages. For years nothing Saxon showed up; the medieval houses were built directly on the underlying chalk. On the other hand, some Saxon features turned up unexpectedly beneath a sunken road and under a boundary bank and there was a scatter of Saxon pottery from elsewhere on the site. The accumulated evidence after 40 seasons of excavation suggests that by the seventh and eighth centuries there were at least six small areas of Saxon settlement at Wharram Percy, similar in number to those of the Romano-British period. The general picture that emerges is one of scattered farms. Even such intensive and prolonged excavation has failed to answer conclusively when and why the village of Wharram Percy came into existence. The earthworks show that there was a planned lay-out at some point in time but whether this was before or after the Conquest still remains unresolved.[18]

Elsewhere in the north of England there are many examples of villages which appear to have been laid out along regular lines, rather than having gradually evolved from farms and hamlets. Many villages seem to have been planned additions to the existing settlement pattern and, in much the same way as new towns, to have been used by their promoters to attract population and to develop the local agricultural economy. It may be that many new villages were laid out in conjunction with new common field arrangements.

The best evidence for 'new' villages lies in the regularity of their plan (photo 35); these may often be masked by later expansion of the village and only unravelled by detailed studies of old maps and new aerial photographs. (Such was the case for example at Wharram Percy where, despite the boldness of the remaining earthworks, colour aerial photographs taken for the Royal Commission on Historical Monuments in 1979 revealed a series of tofts and crofts which had not been seen before.) Surprisingly few villages are documented. The regular shape of many settlements has, of course, long been recognised if inadequately explained (photo 36). In 1949 H. Thorpe drew attention to the large number in County Durham, many of them with village greens; as 88 per cent of them have Anglo-Saxon names he raised the possibility that the tradition of laying out greens dated to Anglian and Scandinavian times.[19] The total number and extent of village greens in England and Wales was first recorded in the report of the Royal Commission on Common Land in 1958. Among the Commissioners were W. G. Hoskins and L. Dudley Stamp who was later to publish a paper on the common lands and village greens of England and Wales.[20] The recognition of the number surviving and the published distribution map widened the debate as to their origin. Despite the great amount of work that has been done since then most of the questions posed by the unevenness of the distribution are still unanswered and remain a challenge to future workers.

In the north of England, particularly in Yorkshire and Durham, most villages of planned form seem to originate at a time of population increase probably in the twelfth, thirteenth and early fourteenth centuries. In a few cases this view can be supported by documentary evidence as for example at East Witton, Yorkshire, where the long village green was probably established for a village market in 1307 as part of estate organisation.[21] Such precise dating is exceptional. In

35 In contrast to Elsworth (photo 34) Braunston, Northamptonshire is a village laid out along a single main street which follows the spine of a low ridge. Church and manor house are at the west (far) end. In this oblique view from the north-east the houses and plots on the north side of the street are clearly seen as is the back lane which still divides the settlement from its fields. Long, hedged enclosures overlie earlier ridge-and-furrow; they follow the 'grain' of the earlier plough strips without strictly adhering to them.

Beyond the village is the Grand Union Canal and beyond that a main road and railway. Between the canal and the railway embankment (upper right on photograph) may be detected the faint earthworks of the nearby settlement of Braunstonberry which appears to have been deserted sometime in the Middle Ages. Whether it predates Braunston in origin or whether it was a secondary, manorial settlement within the parish will only be fully answered by excavation.

most cases it can only be presumed that a village was laid out sometime in the late Saxon period or later. In Somerset, for example, where similar planned villages have been recognised, M. Aston has argued that it was a long process. He suggests that on the Glastonbury estates the plantation of new villages was probably completed before the Norman Conquest, but that in other parts of the county villages were not laid out until the twelfth and thirteenth centuries.[22] On the other side of England, in Suffolk, where the patterns of rural settlement are unusually complex, the origins of green-side settlements are associated with post-Conquest population growth and the development of new tenements.[23]

We cannot yet say whether the 'planned village' was a concept which originated in a particular part of the country and diffused to other areas. However, it can be said with increasing confidence that villages were a comparatively late addition to the medieval rural settlement pattern. In many parts of the country, especially in the pastoral uplands, dispersed settlement continued to be the norm and villages the exception throughout the Middle Ages.

CASTLES

The most enduring symbols of the feudal order in medieval Britain are castles. On account of their size they usually show up well from the air and photographs not only bring new perspectives to the surviving structures but frequently reveal traces of outworks long since removed and no longer visible at ground level. Aerial photography is therefore of particular value in adding to knowledge of medieval castle design. As castles have already been the subject of another Cambridge Air Survey volume,[24] only a brief account is included here.

In the early years of the Norman Conquest earthen fortifications (which survive as mottes) were built to secure newly-acquired territory; their erection signified the Norman take-over of land and property beginning in the 1060s and 1070s. Some fortifications were built on the orders of the Conqueror himself, as at Cambridge in 1068, while others were built by his tenants-in-chief. Usually situated on high points or at strategic river crossings they follow a common ground plan even though details may vary from site to site according to terrain. Common to them all was a circular mound of earth built from the upcast of a surrounding ditch (photo 37); beyond the ditch was usually one or more enclosures (baileys) which were in turn surrounded by outer banks and ditches. The whole complex

36 Eltisley, Cambridgeshire, seen here from the south and before it was bypassed, is a village laid out around a triangular green. The church (with the rare dedication to St Pandionia, daughter of a Scottish king) is situated at the west end of the green and presumably pre-dates it although the earliest surviving parts of the fabric are dated to *c.*1200. The planned shape of the green and the deliberate arrangement of the village houses around it raise questions, as yet unanswered, about its date and origin. Eltisley, a place-name with the characteristic *-ley* suffix that might indicate its Anglo-Saxon origin from a clearing in the woodland, is recorded in Domesday but there is not, as usual, any indication of its morphology at that date. In the medieval period there was a second, smaller green at Caxton End and five moated sites within the parish.

37 At Castle Hill, Hallaton, Leicestershire are the near-perfect remains of a Norman earth castle mainly constructed of the material upcast from the surrounding defensive ditches. This oblique view from the north shows the circular motte (on which there may have been a wooden tower) and an adjacent crescentic bailey; there are hints of other earthworks. Situated on higher ground above a shallow valley the castle appears unaltered since its abandonment. Nor has any settlement grown nearby; the village of Hallaton is half a mile to the east and remnants of the plough strips of its common fields may be seen underlying the more modern field pattern.

would have been surmounted by wooden palisades and, in the early years, there would have been a wooden tower on top of the motte. Although none of these timber features survives, their traces may sometimes be found from excavation; in some cases the pattern revealed by the vestiges of post-holes is enough for conjectural reconstructions to be made of the timber buildings, as for example was possible for the motte at Abinger in Surrey.[25]

Even though many mottes have been destroyed or have been replaced by later stone castles, large numbers survive and indicate their widespread use in the late eleventh and twelfth centuries. It has been a matter of lively debate whether mottes were to be found in this country in the late Anglo-Saxon period or whether they were a Norman introduction. A few, particularly in Herefordshire, were built by Norman and French lords who were already here before the Conquest. Certainly they were the preferred type of fortification for the early Normans in Britain and Ireland as was first convincingly established by Ella Armitage in her remarkable book of 1912.[26] The use of this form of fortification, quickly built, no doubt by impressed labour, spread rapidly and was in common use, the more so in areas of territorial dispute such as the Welsh March and lowland Scotland. Motte-and-baileys were not however the only form of fortification; on the evidence available some great castles – for example, London, Dover and Rochester – originated as banked-and-ditched enclosures without a motte.

Stone was used for castle building from an early stage of the Conquest especially in royal castles. As the more powerful Norman lords got a grip on their newly-acquired lands and consolidated their positions, so stone castles began to replace motte-and-baileys often on the same ground plan. Stone donjons, now called keeps, were built into or on mottes and curtain walls of stone replaced wooden palisades. The continuity of plan can clearly be seen in castles such as Arundel and Windsor. At some castles where there has been subsequent destruction of the outer fortifications, only the keep survives; one of the best examples is at Orford, Suffolk, where the remarkably elaborate royal keep built for Henry II between 1165 and 1173 towers over the surrounding earthworks (photo 38).

Henry's tower at Orford is an example of a keep which had become more than simply a fortification; it had a basement, two residential floors, a kitchen and small rooms within the thickness of the walls – in short a temporary residence fit for a king.

Throughout the late twelfth and the thirteenth centuries, castles became the residences of the most powerful feudal lords and the administrative centres of their lordships. Architecture changed to meet these new needs. Defence was still necessary and usually took the form of high, massive surrounding stone walls with mural towers. There was increasing emphasis on the fortification of the corners and the entrances (the most vulnerable points) and less on the internal buildings. Gate-houses became particularly massive and well-defended. By the later years of the thirteenth century some new castles were built without a central strongpoint and with all the emphasis on the surrounding curtain wall and gatehouses (photo 39). There are particularly good examples of this type in north Wales where medieval military architecture in Britain reached its zenith in the wake of the English conquest of the 1280s. Beaumaris is illustrated here (photo 40). A similar plan was used at about the same date at Roscommon in Ireland,

38 The small coastal town of Orford, Suffolk is dominated by a tower keep, all that survives of Henry II's new castle built between 1165 and 1173. The tower is of a sophisticated polygonal design with three buttress towers and a forebuilding clasping a circular interior; the residential accommodation within is suitably royal in scale. That the surrounding bailey was defended by a stone curtain is known from, among other sources, a view by John Norden at the beginning of the seventeenth century; the foundations no doubt lie beneath the extensive earthworks which surround the keep.

The town of Orford, on a grid plan, predates the keep and its origins are unclear. It was not named in Domesday and seems likely to date from the early twelfth century. Its relative importance as a port has declined with the southward advance of Orford Ness, the shingle spit lying to the east beyond the coastal marshes.

39 Caerlaverock, a Scottish
castle situated near the shore of
the Solway Firth is of unusual
triangular design. Although
much altered in later times it
dates from the thirteenth century and is an interesting
example of a small castle where
protection was provided not
by a central keep, as it might
have been earlier, but by
strong perimeter walls, corner
towers and a moat. The
strongest element, a twin-
towered gatehouse on the land-
ward side, protects the castle at
its most vulnerable point
where there was no doubt a
drawbridge entry across the
moat. The design reflects the
changing role of castles in the
thirteenth century from post-
Conquest fortifications to residential centres of feudal
administration.

40 Beaumaris Castle, Anglesey
was the last of Edward I's
castles in north Wales and was
begun after the re-conquest of
Anglesey from the Welsh in
1295. It is the ultimate in concentric design (permitted by its
low-lying site) and, although
never finished, is nevertheless
one of the great achievements
of medieval military architecture. There was no central
keep; instead, the inner ward
was defended by two gate-
houses, four cylindrical corner
towers and two D-shaped
towers. This was surrounded
in turn by a towered outer
curtain and a moat. Despite
huge sums expended on this
royal castle it was never
finished; abandoned by the
sixteenth century its fabric
survived remarkably intact, a
monument to the skills of its
builders, particularly Master
James of St George, master
mason to the King.

another area where surviving mottes are indicative of the early years of Norman activity (in this case after 1169) and where stone castles mark the more permanent presence of feudal overlords.[27]

Only the richest and most powerful feudal lords could afford the building and upkeep of stone castles. Most manorial lords had to be content with surrounding their modest residences of stone and timber with moats or earthen enclosures. Moats were particularly effective in lowland country where they could be fed from nearby streams and where the water table remained relatively high. In the thirteenth century moated residences became the fashion and large numbers were built, especially on areas of heavy soil. Although more easily destroyed than castles (especially in recent years by bulldozers) moats survive (photo 41) in large numbers and at various levels of sophistication ranging from single moated enclosures to complex sites with associated buildings (usually of later date), fishponds and other water courses.

THE CHURCH

It cannot be doubted that the church in Britain received an immense boost from the arrival of the Normans who, in the wake of their military success, made every effort to ensure that God continued to be on their side. As William's claim to the throne had papal backing there was little resistance from the Anglo-Saxon church in England which bore the brunt of the initial changes. In 1069 the Archbishop of Canterbury, Stigand, was removed and replaced by Lanfranc. Within ten years all the bishoprics except for Worcester were held by new men, most of them Normans. The power, wealth and influence of the church was increased and it took its place alongside the secular feudal order in the new administration and government of the country. Episcopal sees were recognised, the parish system was completed and great impetus was given to monastic life by grants of land and property to Benedictines and to the new orders. This period was a most formative one in the history of the church both organisationally and architecturally.

The so-called Norman style of architecture (a variation on the continental Romanesque) rapidly became the fashion as new knowledge brought from the continent was added to the existing skills of Anglo-Saxon masons. The style had already been introduced to England before the Conquest by Edward the Confessor in his abbey church at Westminster where, ironically, William was crowned king on Christmas Day 1066. Within a few years the new bishops began to rebuild their cathedrals; in the 1070s and 1080s work began at, among other places, Canterbury, Durham, Lincoln, St Albans and Rochester. Even the Anglo-Saxon bishop Wulfstan, who had somehow survived at Worcester, was caught up in the architectural upheaval.

At the parish level the Normans intensified the already established late Saxon practice of building churches in stone. Today Norman parish churches may look small and of simple construction compared to later medieval churches but in their day they were an architectural advance on what had gone before. Not only were they generally larger than Anglo-Saxon churches but their very thick walls were stronger and more durable. Ornamentation gradually increased with more elaborate stone-carving on doorways, capitals, arches and fonts.

Norman churches were invariably built upon the sites of earlier churches as is evidenced from the increasing frequency with which, in England, the foundations of earlier churches of wood or stone are found directly beneath later medieval churches. On the evidence of some excavated examples it seems likely that the walls of the new church were built outside the pre-existing church while it was still in use and that the older church was only demolished when the shell of the new one was in place. If an Anglo-Saxon church was of stone then some of the better masonry and carving might be incorporated in its successor; if it was of wood then all traces have usually disappeared and will only be found by excavation. A number of late Saxon churches continued to be used either because they were in some way special or because they were built of stone and were large enough to serve the new order and a growing population. An outstanding example of a large Anglo-Saxon church which has survived almost intact is that at Brixworth, Northamptonshire, a county in which there are several other fine examples of Anglo-Saxon stonework including the towers at Barnack, Brigstock and Earls Barton. Such survivals are, however, exceptional. The majority of Anglo-Saxon parish churches, like the Norman ones which succeeded them, were replaced by larger churches in the late twelfth and thirteenth centuries partly it would seem to meet the needs of an evolving liturgy and partly to accommodate larger congregations. The Norman style gave way to the so-called Transitional style and it, in turn, to Early English; by the fourteenth century the Decorated style had arrived, characterised by the ogee curve and more flamboyant window tracery. This period of elaborate curvilinear tracery was short-lived: by the later fourteenth century the fashion was for upright panel tracery, the hallmark of what became known as the Perpendicular style. In architectural terms the early Middle Ages in England were far from static; the succession of new styles reflected greater understanding of load-bearing, of stress and of architectural form. Pointed arches replaced semi-circular, and as roofs were supported on taller and more graceful columns so walls could be made higher and thinner thereby providing more space for windows. While such developments may be seen in most medieval parish churches they reached their finest expression in the cathedral and abbey churches.

In Wales the church was quickly caught up in the new scheme of things but it was only in the east and the south that the Normans had a lasting impact. Everywhere they had to protect themselves with castles; their manorial villages with churches were new additions to a landscape dominated by dispersed farms and hamlets. In Scotland, where Anglo-Norman institutions were encouraged by David I, King of Scots (1124–53) new bishoprics were created and cathedrals built even as far north as the Norse Kingdom of Orkney where the cathedral of St Magnus remains the finest example of Norman architecture in Scotland. In Orkney also, at Orphir, is a fragment of one of the few examples in Britain of a round church inspired by the Church of the Holy Sepulchre in Jerusalem. As in England a few Norman parish churches survive almost in their entirety but most were replaced at a later date and only some features of the earlier work survive.

At the same time as the episcopal and parish structures were evolving so the monastic church was increasing in importance through growth in the number of Benedictine houses and the arrival of new orders. The Benedictines continued

41 Many hundreds of moated enclosures survive in the landscape and this photograph of one at Whissendine, Rutland (now Leicestershire) is representative of many photographed by the Cambridge Unit. The large moat is almost square with sides measuring just over one hundred metres. It was probably fed from the nearby stream. Upcast from digging the moat has been used to make banks on its inner and outer sides; originally these were probably palisaded. The original entrance appears, as is usually the case, to have been midway along one side, in this instance on the south (far left) where the moat appears to be partially filled. There are adjacent earthworks which appear to be included within an outer enclosure, an unusual survival. Traces of buildings are visible on the central enclosure; almost certainly they are those of a manorial complex, perhaps of the thirteenth century. To determine the exact status and date of this impressive site the aerial photograph must be used in conjunction with documents, ground survey and archaeology.

42 The fragmentary remains shown in this photograph are all that survive of the first Cistercian house in Britain at Waverley in Surrey. Founded in 1128 from L'Aumône in Normandy, Waverley, never a wealthy house, was, with the Yorkshire houses of Rievaulx and Fountains, among the most influential of the Cistercian houses not just because it was the first but because it was from here that monks and lay brothers moved on to establish new houses elsewhere. They included Brightley in Devon (which later moved to Forde in Dorset), Combe in Warwickshire, Garendon in Leicestershire, Grace Dieu in Monmouth and Otley in Oxfordshire (which moved shortly afterwards to Thame).

43 This panoramic view in mid-Wales conveys an impression of the sort of upland country acquired and used by the Cistercian monastic order in the twelfth and thirteenth centuries. In their search for isolation most of the order's abbeys were founded in upland valleys; on the adjacent uplands, and through a network of outlying farms or granges, the order ran large sheep flocks and specialised in the production of wool. In this view of the upper Teifi valley about fourteen miles south-east of Aberystwyth, the cluster of farm buildings on the lower, cultivated fields surrounds Strata Florida abbey, of which little remains except the excavated foundations. The abbey was founded on this site about 1200 after the abandonment of the original foundation of 1164 about two miles to the south-west.

to acquire land and property by gift and to use the income from their estates to expand their older houses and to build new ones. The post-Conquest additions began in Sussex with William's new foundation of St Martin de Bello at Senlac (soon to be known as Battle Abbey) as a thanksgiving for his victory over Harold. There followed many new foundations including Colchester, Chester and Shrewsbury in England, Brecon, Cardigan and Kidwelly in Wales and Dunfermline in Scotland.[28]

Of the new monastic orders which came into the country in the twelfth and thirteenth centuries the Cistercians had by far the greatest impact on the rural landscape and the economy. Their first house was at Waverley in Surrey in 1128 (photo 42) but ultimately of more importance were their two Yorkshire houses at Rievaulx and Fountains, founded in 1132. From then on the white monks, valuing isolation, invariably built their abbeys in remote valleys in northern and western Britain. Their houses included Byland, Jervaulx and Kirkstall on the Pennine flanks: Furness, Holmcultram and Calder in Cumbria: Strata Florida (photo 43), Valle Crucis, Cymmer and Margam in Wales: Tintern, Abbey Dore and Buildwas on the Welsh borders: Melrose, Newbattle, Glenluce, Sweetheart (photo 44) and Dundrennan in southern Scotland and in the north-east, Kinloss and Deer.

From these houses and others, and using large numbers of lay-brothers as labour on their home farms and granges, the Cistercians improved the use of upland pasture for cattle and sheep. They thereby became among the greatest producers and suppliers of the country's main export commodity, wool.

TOWNS

With both population and trade increasing the period between the Conquest and *c*.1300 was a favourable one for the continued growth of existing towns and the foundation of new ones. As the Normans added impetus to church building, so too did they boost urbanism. Their priorities, however, in the years immediately following 1066, were conquest and subjugation. Castles, initially in the form of mottes, were added to almost all the towns taken over from the Anglo-Saxons; in the most important of them stone castles soon replaced mottes and became the centres of shire administration as for example at Norwich, Lincoln, Warwick and York. As the new regime settled in and as trade and commerce flourished so the improving economic climate favoured an increase in commercial centres. On the coast, particularly of the south and east, local and continental trade led to the growth of old ports and to the creation of new ones. Inland, increases in production and commerce generated markets, often in association with new urban centres. These developments took place within the context of the feudal system in which capitalistic attitudes became increasingly evident during the Middle Ages. The crown and other major landholders, secular and ecclesiastic, were alive to opportunities to increase their income; rents from urban property were seen as important supplements to income from taxation and from manorial dues and services. Where the crown led others followed.

Most late Saxon towns increased their population in the post-Conquest period. Of the 112 places named as boroughs in Domesday the large majority continued to have an important place in the urban network of medieval England. This was particularly so of the shire towns of southern and eastern England, for example Canterbury, Chichester, Ipswich, Norwich, Cambridge, Leicester, Northampton and Oxford. Unfortunately there are no means of calculating natural demographic increase nor rates of migration from the countryside. Some examples of urban growth are well documented, however, and the layouts of some medieval towns are particularly well illustrated by aerial photography.[29]

Within a few years of William's foundation of the abbey of St Martin de Bello a new town was taking shape outside the abbey gatehouse, no doubt to cater for, and take advantage of, the large numbers of travellers who stopped at Battle either on route for London or for the coast at Hastings. With the market outside the abbey gate the new town of Battle (photo 45) was laid out along a single street with burgage plots on either side, a practical layout which was frequently used for new towns of the period.

Whereas Battle was an entirely new town, the new borough outside the much older monastic house at Bury St Edmunds was an extension to the existing town. In the 1070s the new Norman abbot, Baldwin, laid out a new borough west of the abbey precinct and by 1086, as recorded in remarkable detail in Domesday Book, 342 houses stood on land which had been under the plough at the time

44 Over a century separated the foundation of Waverley, Surrey (photo 42) from that of Sweetheart, the last Cistercian house in Scotland founded in 1273 near the estuary of the Nith on the Solway Firth and colonised by monks from Dundrennan. The name derives from the embalmed heart of John Balliol, kept by his widow Devorgilla the foundress of the abbey, and buried with her in the abbey church. The church survives to roof level and despite the loss of most of the buildings around the cloister there are enough foundations left to confirm that Sweetheart followed the long-established Cistercian ground plan.

of King Edmund. A new market was included within the plan and the Domesday description leaves little doubt that commerce was already flourishing.[30]

Like Baldwin, other prominent ecclesiastics who saw towns as a means of increasing their revenues, were to play a major role in the creation of new urban centres in the two centuries which followed. In 1219, for example, the bishop of Salisbury initiated changes which led to the creation of New Sarum (Salisbury) (photo 46) on part of his manor alongside the Avon. Within the town his new cathedral replaced the Norman cathedral which had been built within the defences of the Iron Age hillfort of Old Sarum, two miles away. Like the Norman cathedral the borough of Old Sarum was also abandoned; it can never have been very flourishing and there has even been uncertainty over its exact site. New Sarum, on the other hand, rapidly became among the most important towns of central southern England. Laid out in a series of parallel streets (still visible today) it became an important centre of the cloth industry and, to judge from its tax contribution in the early fourteenth century, it was then among the wealthiest of English towns.

45 Battle, Sussex is one of the best surviving examples of a town promoted by a religious house, in this case the Benedictine abbey of St Martin founded by William the Conqueror in 1067 as a thanksgiving for his victory over Harold. The abbey precinct, seen in the foreground of this oblique view from the south-east, is separated from the town by its great gatehouse. As at Bury St Edmunds, Suffolk, the town is a remarkable survival of a late twelfth-century layout by a monastic order. At Bury there is a grid plan; here at Battle the town is aligned along a single street with houses and plots on both sides. Markets are still held on the triangular space outside the abbey gate.

46 Salisbury, Wiltshire has its origins in the early thirteenth century, when the bishop of Salisbury was finally authorised by a papal bull (of 1219) to abandon Old Sarum and to build a new cathedral and market town on the flatter, more accessible (and, as it turned out, more commercially viable) land of his manor alongside the Avon. Work on the new cathedral commenced immediately and within fifty years it was finished: this remarkable building achievement, in what was later to be known as the Early English style, has survived in its entirety and left us with the most unified of all English cathedrals. With its remarkable spire it is seen here together with cloister and chapter house in an oblique photograph from the south-west. Beyond the spire and despite post-medieval changes, the original grid layout of the new town is still visible. As the hill-top site of Old Sarum declined, so New Sarum flourished. The cloth industry took root here; within a few hundred years Salisbury was among the wealthiest towns of medieval England.

47 Crail, Fife is one of many burghs founded in Scotland at a time of rapid urban expansion in the twelfth and thirteenth centuries. While there may already have been a small settlement around an inlet of the Firth of Forth (now the harbour, upper left on photograph) the regular layout of the town as seen in this view from the north-east indicates a planned addition of medieval date. Two near-parallel streets link the parish church (foreground) with the castle and harbour; both are lined with burgages and are unusually wide, no doubt to accommodate market activity. Crail's early prosperity was linked to fishing; there are records of large quantities of herring being supplied for the royal household in the medieval period.

48 There was no need of a moat at Pembroke, south-west Wales, where the castle, seen here from the west, was built within the natural defences of tidal inlets of Milford Haven. The castle, not the first on the site, is dominated by the impressive circular keep, probably built about 1200 when William Marshal had become earl of Pembroke. It has residential floors above a basement. Within the inner ward (of which the foundations of the gatehouse may be seen just to the right of the keep) are additional residential halls which jut out beyond the line of the curtain wall. In the outer ward a massive gatehouse commands the entrance from the town. The castle was the centre of the lordship until the end of the Middle Ages. As at Battle (photo 45) the town was aligned along a single street; here it follows the spine of the narrow peninsula and the burgage plots slope down from the street to the town walls (of which fragments remain) and the creeks. The burgage pattern, probably from the early twelfth century, is remarkably well preserved.

New urban foundations and changes of site almost always involved an element of planning. This is expressed in the frequent use of rectilinear layouts derived ultimately from Greek examples. Such plans imply carefully considered regulation of space and the use of regular plot sizes to which standard burgage rents could be applied. It was rarely possible to use perfect rectilinear layouts due to the constraints of the site or of pre-existing rural settlements. Moreover, the need to make new towns defensible and/or commercially viable meant that they were seldom laid out on absolutely flat lowland sites. No surviving town in Britain is as geometrically perfect as some of those on the north Italian plain or in south-western France. Nevertheless, as at Salisbury, there are many English towns where a planned element of medieval date may still be detected in the street pattern and in the regularity of the burgage plots. Winchelsea in Sussex is one. It is one of many examples listed and illustrated by Maurice Beresford in his book *New Towns of the Middle Ages* (1967), still the most authoritative survey of the new urbanism of the twelfth and thirteenth centuries. Like England, Scotland and Wales were similarly caught up in the European-wide movement towards urbanism and town foundation in the twelfth and thirteenth centuries.[31] Many of Scotland's 'burghs' – a title first conferred by King David I (1124–53) – were created at this time, frequently at places with earlier origins (photo 47). In Wales, Norman castle-building and town foundation went hand-in-hand. Initially the towns were small but they included the vital elements of a market place and street lined with

burgages; among the earliest were Abergavenny, Brecon, Cardiff, Carmarthen, Kidwelly and Pembroke (photo 48). While urban growth continued in the late twelfth century it was the thirteenth century which was most formative in Wales. There were new foundations in the south, among them Trelech, Cowbridge and Caerphilly, and along the March at Knighton, New Radnor and Montgomery. In the north there was a flurry of castle and town building in the wake of the Edwardian conquest. Over 20 new castle-boroughs were established, among them Flint, Caernarvon, Conway and the new Rhuddlan. In these English-planted towns, the castle was the dominent element; the streets were laid out nearby usually on a rectilinear grid and within the protection of the castle. In Welsh boroughs, which frequently grew out of earlier settlements, the church tended to be more of a focus, as at Bangor, Llantwit Major and Llanrwst.

Most of these many towns in Britain were sufficiently established by the end of the thirteenth century to withstand the crises of the fourteenth. A small number however, over-optimistically established in poor locations, remained very small and lost their urban functions in the later Middle Ages. Some even disappeared almost without trace in the two very different centuries which were to follow.

Over a century ago J. E. Thorold Rogers in pioneer studies of work and wages put forward the view that the population of England began to decline sometime in the early-to-mid fourteenth century. Subsequent research, most notably by M. M. Postan has on the whole supported this view. Additional evidence suggests that some land was going out of cultivation and that many small communities were struggling to survive. The Black Death, long thought of as the initiator of change, is now seen as an accelerator of trends which had already appeared well before 1348.

FURTHER READING

G. Astill and A. Grant (eds.), *The Countryside of Medieval England*, Oxford, 1988.

M. W. Beresford, *New Towns of the Middle Ages*, London, 1967.

M. W. Beresford and J. K. S. St Joseph, *Medieval England: An Aerial Survey*, 2nd edn, Cambridge, 1979.

H. C. Darby (ed.), *A New Historical Geography of England before 1600*, Cambridge, 1976.

R. Morris, *Churches in the Landscape*, London, 1989.

T. Rowley, *The Norman Heritage, 1066–1200*, London, 1983.

R. Allen Brown, *Castles from the Air*, Cambridge, 1989.

E. Miller and J. Hatcher, *Medieval England: Rural Society and Economic Change 1086–1348*, London, 1978.

4 The later Middle Ages: 1348–*c*.1540

Any discussion of the two centuries after 1350, conventionally labelled the later Middle Ages, must be grounded on the social and economic changes which followed on from the Black Death. As the most catastrophic demographic event of the medieval period, the plague had profound effects on both life and landscape; some were immediate and short-term, others protracted and fundamental to the gradual demise of feudalism.

In the first outbreak of the plague, 1348–9, people died in very large numbers and at rates hitherto unknown to a society already used to death rates which were very high by modern standards. Contemporary chronicles leave no doubt as to the scale of the disaster but precise figures for mortality are impossible to determine. The best available evidence, from ecclesiastical records, suggests that between 35 and 50 per cent of beneficed clergy died and that deaths in the monastic orders were at a similar level. Most historians believe that this level of mortality can be extended to the population as a whole, at least for England. In absolute terms this probably meant the death of well over a million people. The plague seems to have hit young and old, male and female, landlord and tenant. Except perhaps for the clergy who through their ministrations were unduly exposed to the disease, it cannot be yet asserted with any confidence that the Black Death attacked specific groups more virulently than it did others. It is thought, however, that people living more closely together in the insanitary conditions of towns were more vulnerable. While likely, it cannot be demonstrated conclusively as the incomplete sources do not allow this level of analysis.

Where figures have been calculated the effects of the Black Death vary even within small areas. For example, on the Cambridgeshire estates of Crowland Abbey, 20 out of 42 land-holding tenants died at Dry Drayton (47 per cent), 33 out of 58 at Cottenham (57 per cent) and 35 out of 50 at Oakington (70 per cent).[1] On the Hampshire manor of Bishop's Waltham, 65 per cent of the customary tenants died[2] and on 22 manors of Glastonbury Abbey the average was about 54 per cent, with the figures ranging between 33 per cent and 69 per cent.[3] At Halesowen in Worcestershire, a community studied in great detail by Zvi Razi, at least 88 peasants (43 per cent) died in the plague, a number four times greater than in the famine of 1317 and eighteen times higher than the annual average number of deaths recorded between 1340 and 1348.[4] These figures are not exceptional. At Alvechurch, only eight miles from Halesowen, C. Dyer has estimated that 43 per cent of the tenants may have died in the Black Death.[5] At Alrewas, Staffordshire, at the height of the epidemic sixty people died in May 1349, seventy in June and fifty in July compared to the usual figure of two or three a month.[6]

While some of the details of the above records and calculations might be queried, the general level of mortality revealed can be supported by many other examples. However, the overall sample is still small and there is still much work to be done on this important question. The trend of recent studies has been to support the view of those who have argued for the great severity of the Black Death and to refute the small number of scholars who think that it has been exaggerated. J. Hatcher's judicious estimate of a national death rate of between 30 and 45 per cent for England[7] continues to win support. The impact of the Black Death in Scotland and Wales, particularly upon the dispersed communities of the uplands, is unknown. It may never have reached many of them.

In England, such high levels of mortality caused widespread social dislocation; the numbers of widows, widowers and orphaned children increased dramatically. On the limited evidence available society appears to have acted quickly to remedy this situation; where court roll evidence has been examined, as for example at Halesowen, marriage rates increased very greatly in the years following the plague. Presumably this was followed by an increase in the birth rate.

For those who survived the Black Death the next decade was a time of readjustment. Local food shortages aggravated by scarcity of labour were offset by the fact that there were fewer mouths to feed. There was no immediate famine. The able-bodied took advantage of local labour shortages to demand higher wages, a move countered immediately by the commons in Parliament who brought in new legislation to restrict mobility and to set maximum wage levels. An ordinance of 1349 but more specifically the Statute of Labourers of 1351 pegged wages at pre-Plague levels by forbidding landlords to pay, and labourers to receive, more than the customary rates. Despite initial attempts at enforcement the intentions of the Statute were soon defeated not only by labourers who, knowing that they could command more, refused to accept the conditions, but also by landlords who found that the legislation hampered them in the competition for labour.

By the mid 1350s things had apparently begun to settle down again but at a much reduced level of population. The catastrophe had accelerated change in the fundamental relationship between population and resources. No longer was it necessary to win new agricultural land from woodland and waste nor to intensify production on existing fields. Landlords had to adjust to new circumstances and in particular to a reduced supply of labourers to whom they had to pay higher wages. Despite this, demesne agriculture seems to have remained relatively buoyant in the 1350s with livestock farming becoming an increasingly viable alternative to arable crop production.

By 1360, ten years after the plague, we must presume that everyone, while looking back with terror on their experience, was making the most of the new opportunities which had come their way. They were not to know that the plague was to break out again in 1361–2 (the *pestis secunda*), and again in 1368–9 and 1375. In general terms these outbreaks appear to have been less serious than that of 1348–9 but contemporary chroniclers believed that the 1361 outbreak was particularly severe on infants and young children. If so, then there was high mortality among those born in the decade after the Black Death and this might help to explain why there are no signs of population recovery by the end of the century. The cumulative effects of these outbreaks appears to have been a further lowering of numbers well into the fifteenth century.

In south-east England the early 1370s were troubled times in other ways.

There were several very wet years when there was not only flooding but mildewed grain crops and ruined harvests. Additionally, there were severe outbreaks of disease among sheep and cattle. The French were hostile along the south coast and landlords and war recruiters competed for able-bodied men. Despite some bad years harvests improved in the second half of the decade; that of 1375, said by Bridbury to have been the best for twenty-six years,[8] brought down prices. This was good for the consumer but not for the producer, the more so as wage levels remained relatively high. Bridbury sees this year as the end of the 'Indian Summer' of demesne farming and the beginning of its very rapid contraction over the next half century; to him this was the year when the Black Death and the later outbreaks of plague really began to transform medieval agrarian society. His view has gained general support even if the timing of the onset of decline varies from one estate to another.

To add to the troubles of the 1370s there was a further flare-up between English and Scots in the Border country. Edward III, already stretched by the French, had to raise money for his army in the north and did it in part by the imposition of poll taxes in 1377, 1379 and 1381. These taxes were an additional burden upon an already suffering population and were a contributory cause of social unrest and, in particular, of the Peasants' Revolt of 1381. If the taxes were a burden for medieval peasants they have proved a blessing for medieval historians. For the first date after 1086 they provide a basis for a reasoned calculation of the population of the whole of England. For estimating total numbers the tax of 1377 is the most valuable. It was levied at the flat rate of a groat (4d.) per head on everyone over the age of 14 excepting the clergy, mendicants and beggars. The overall amounts collected from every shire were enrolled at the Exchequer and it is therefore simple to calculate how many tax-payers there were in every shire. It is much more difficult, however, to estimate the total population having regard to the problems of knowing what proportion of the population was under 14, how many were exempt and how many managed to avoid payment. Nevertheless, on the assumption that the effectiveness of the tax collection did not vary greatly from one shire to another, the returns for each shire are a useful guide to the relative distribution of population – as was appreciated as long ago as 1936 when R. A. Pelham produced a map of the 1377 returns in a chapter on fourteenth century England.[9] There have since been many reproductions of this map and new variants of it. They all show that the tax-paying population of England in 1377 was distributed in broadly the same way as the Domesday population, that is with the greatest densities on the more fertile lowlands. While the plagues lowered the population they apparently did not fundamentally alter its distribution. This is also likely to have been the case in Wales and Scotland.

Historians have much more confidence in the 1377 returns than they do in those for 1379 and 1381 when evasion appears to have been much more common. In any case these poll taxes were not at a flat rate and similar calculations to those for 1377 cannot therefore be made. Where the returns do survive, however, they are more detailed; tax payers are named and frequently their occupation is given, especially in 1381. The lists are therefore especially valuable in studying the social composition and occupational structure of particular communities, and especially of the towns for which the returns survive.[10]

J. C. Russell's estimate of *c.*2.2 million for the population of England in 1377[11] is now, for various reasons, regarded as on the low side. Hatcher believes 2.75–3 million to be more realistic.[12]

It is not until the 1520s that another reasoned estimate for the population of England is possible; again it is based mainly upon taxation returns and particularly those for 1524 and 1525. Using the evidence for selected counties J. Cornwall estimated the population of England in the 1520s to be in the order of 2.3 million.[13] While some think this too low others find it too high; B. M. S. Campbell has suggested that it might have been as low as 1.8 m[14] – a figure which is so low as to come as something of a shock. If this was the true figure then it implies that the population continued to drop steadily after 1377 and that, if recovery was already under way by 1520, it must have dropped to little more than a million sometime in the fifteenth century. Such a view lends weight to those who believe that population remained very low in the fifteenth century on the evidence of continuing low levels of grain prices, land values and rents, as well as the abandonment of land and the shrinkage and desertion of rural settlements. Why the population remained at such a low level and when and why it began to recover are subjects of lively and continuing debate.

AGRICULTURE AND RURAL SETTLEMENT

By the 1380s the cumulative effects of the Black Death and of later outbreaks of plague were increasingly being felt and many estates gave up their struggle to maintain the farming systems which they had known for two centuries. Faced with loss of income from vacant tenancies, poor returns from grain crops and high labour costs many lay and ecclesiastical landlords, particularly in the arable areas, gave up the direct cultivation of their demesnes and passed the responsibility on to tenants in return for money rents. The practice of leasing was not of course new; it had been done before but usually on a short-term basis. In the late fourteenth century it ceased to be a temporary expedient; from the 1380s the pace of change quickened and from one end of England to the other, from Kent and Sussex to Northumberland and Durham, demesnes were broken up and leased out to tenants. As longer leases replaced shorter ones so farmers (i.e. those paying a 'farm' or fixed payment for their land) replaced villeins. Manorial labour services were replaced by rent-paying tenants and by wage-earning labourers. In this way the social order underwent fundamental change; the fifteenth century saw the emergence of a rentier economy and the foundation of landlord-tenant farming as we know it today.

With this change in one of the fundamental relationships within the feudal system the fifteenth century was, for the majority, one of increasing freedom and individualism. In overall terms there was more land per head of population; for those who had managed to survive the numerous outbreaks of disease there were new opportunities for betterment. Whereas a century earlier it had been necessary to subdivide holdings which were already small it was now possible for the most go-ahead peasant families to increase the size of their holdings both by consolidation and acquisition. On the other hand, without the security of the old feudal relationship less fortunate individuals were deprived of land and sometimes became victims of the more acquisitive members of society, not always great landlords.

As more and more land was leased or sold, to illiterate or barely literate people, so the written records of the great medieval estates began to decline. As it is these records on which we depend for detailed knowledge of the workings of medieval agriculture, this is a serious loss for historians of the period. The fifteenth century is a 'dark age' in this respect compared to the thirteenth.

While arable farming continued (wheat and rye for bread, barley for ale) it was at a much reduced scale and the area under basic cereals contracted. Moreover, there is evidence to suggest that yields per acre declined, in part because of labour shortages. It might be expected that in these circumstances efforts would be made to overcome labour shortages by new inventions and techniques but to date there is no evidence to suggest that there were any major innovations in late medieval agriculture. Unlike their Dutch counterparts British farmers were more concerned with consolidating their holdings than with experimenting with the new crops (clover and turnips) which were later to have such an impact on agricultural production. All the signs are that this was a period of recession in cereal production with acreages and yields well below those of the thirteenth century. No doubt there were exceptions to this general picture but peasants did not keep records and there are no means of ascertaining the situation from one holding to another.

As the cereal acreage declined so the amount of land available for grazing, be it marginal 'waste' or lowland pasture, increased. This expansion in the acreage available for grazing represents the positive side of fifteenth-century farming. While there are no detectable improvements in stock-breeding the number of grazing animals, especially sheep, almost certainly increased over the period; by the early sixteenth century numbers were causing increasing concern to those who wished to reverse the trend and to promote tillage.[15]

Numbers of sheep would not have increased without a continuing demand for meat and wool. For the large producer wool was undoubtedly the more important of the two as the cloth industry appears to have been able to absorb all the raw wool which was produced. In the uplands the increasing demand could be met from larger flocks; the growth of the cloth industry ensured the continuance of pastoral farming in much of upland Wales, Scotland and northern England. Whereas there was continuity in the uplands there was change in the lowlands; this was especially so in midland England where livestock farming gained at the expense of arable as a more economic and profitable use of land.

Where change from tillage to pasture happened on a small scale it passed unrecorded but when the change was such that it undermined the social fabric of rural communities it invariably caused local concern. It was by the conversion of land to grass that sheep replaced people as the more important inhabitants of many a Midland parish (photo 49). When the sheep belonged to those who had previously cultivated the land there was less of a problem; if they belonged to wealthier men, sometimes outsiders, then there was invariably resentment. Such a case was at Burston in Buckinghamshire where in 1488–9 John Swafield enclosed 400 acres for pasture and evicted sixty tenants. By 1517 it was said that the entire hamlet and manor had been converted to pasture. Significantly the land value had trebled. Burston was not resettled; it remains a good example of a deserted settlement where the lines of streets and crofts show clearly in the grass that grew over them.[16] Burston is one of those places where radical change happened very quickly. In other places the changes were less dramatic and more prolonged. At Littlecote, in the same county, the process of conversion of arable to pasture apparently began in the fifteenth century but was not completed until early in the nineteenth.[17]

We know of the activities of John Swafield and of others like him from the surviving record of evidence given to Cardinal Wolsey's Commission of Enquiry which was set up in 1517 to look into problems of enclosure and depopulation since 1488. As so often happens this was a case where government set up an enquiry after much of the damage had already been done. Nevertheless, the evidence presented is of great value to historians; in some cases it provides

evidence of the date and circumstances when a piece of land or a community underwent radical, and often lasting change.

In defending themselves against accusations of enclosing land and pulling down houses in the Warwickshire villages of Burton Dassett and Wormleighton Sir Edward Belknap and John Spencer both contended that this had been done by previous owners. At Wormleighton it was said that William Cope, Cofferer to Henry VII, had converted 240 acres of arable land to pasture and thereby had taken away the livelihood of sixty tenants.[18] In 1506, Spencer, a local grazier who was building up his landholding in the area, bought the estate. He built a new manor house and claimed that the church was now in a better state of repair than it had been before. A new village grew up around the church and manor house; the 'new' Wormleighton looks down on the bold earthworks of the medieval village and the earlier manor house below.

Wormleighton was one of many Warwickshire villages to suffer some enclosure and depopulation in the second half of the fifteenth century and the early years of the sixteenth. John Rous, writing about 1486, listed sixty villages in the county which he claimed were victims of the greed of 'destroyers and mutilators' who had enclosed fields, made parks and expelled peasants. Modern studies have shown that much of his outrage was legitimate and well-founded although in many cases the villages in question had been in a state of decay over much of the previous century.

Taken together documents and earthworks provide convincing evidence of the abandonment of many villages in the late Middle Ages, especially in the English Midlands. The extent of this phenomenon was only recognised in the 1940s and 1950s when W. G. Hoskins and M. W. Beresford began their detailed studies of Leicestershire and Warwickshire respectively.[19] Their work and that of others who followed their lead has been greatly helped by aerial photography (photos 50, 51), most notably by the hundreds of photographs of deserted sites taken by J. K. S. St Joseph, then Curator of Aerial Photography in the University of Cambridge and by D. R. Wilson his successor. Not only did these photographs add new perspectives to what could be seen on the ground but they often revealed features hitherto unseen; in some cases they were the means whereby examples of desertion were discovered for the first time.

Such convincing evidence of depopulation has inevitably led to some overemphasis on deserted villages in the history of English rural settlement and it is important to keep this late medieval episode in perspective. Even in those counties of midland England where desertion was most common, e.g. in Leicestershire, Warwickshire and Northamptonshire, the number of villages depopulated relative to those which survived was relatively small – about one in five at the maximum. Put the other way, four out of every five medieval villages survived the demographic and economic crises of the fourteenth and fifteenth centuries and grew again when population numbers began to rise. Elsewhere the survival rate of villages and large hamlets was even higher and testifies to the ability of communities to weather demographic crises and to adapt to changing economic and social conditions. Many settlements may not now be as big as they once were; remains of houses and crofts visible on the ground and from the air show that they were once larger (photo 52). Such earthworks have been interpreted as

49 This panoramic view of a piece of rural Buckinghamshire near Hillesden was taken in 1963. In recording on film the landscape as it then appeared the photograph also captured the surviving pattern of rectangular fields produced by Parliamentary Enclosure and beneath it, a 'fossilised' medieval landscape of earthworks and ridge-and-furrow. The only trees are those in the hedgerows; the original woodland cover has been entirely cleared and probably had been by the end of the thirteenth century. The landscape is typical of those parts of the English Midlands where arable land was converted to pasture for sheep and cattle at the end of the Middle Ages. When this photograph was taken much ridge-and-furrow of former arable fields still survived; by now much of it will almost certainly have been ploughed away.

50 *opposite* The earthworks of Hamilton, Leicestershire, adjacent to a stream and surrounded by the ridge-and-furrow of former arable fields, are among the best remaining of the many deserted settlement sites in the county. A hamlet of Barkby and only ever a small place, Hamilton's fields were enclosed and used for grazing cattle and sheep before the end of the fifteenth century. Today Hamilton is regarded as a fine example of a set of midland-type medieval earthworks in which the layout of the settlement can be clearly discerned both on the ground and, even more so, from the air. In this photograph the curved line of the main street may be seen continuing across the ploughed field beyond the site.

51 *above* Part of the deserted village of Gainsthorpe, Lincolnshire survives under a pasture field; the rest of the settlement has been ploughed away. The earthworks at Gainsthorpe are now among the most important of their kind in England; the lines of the streets and enclosures are very clear as are the stone foundations of the village houses. Once thought to be the remains of a Roman camp, the site was first photographed by O. G. S. Crawford in 1925. Crawford recognised it for what it was and linked it to a description of 1697 in the diary of Abraham de la Pryme in which he described seeing the foundations of buildings and, contrary to popular local belief that it had once been a den of thieves, rightly thought that the place had '. . . been eaten up with time, poverty and pasturage'.

'shrinkage' of a settlement but this raises problems. There is an increasing awareness now that communities were never static and that the abandonment of houses on one piece of land may have been matched by new buildings on another. Thus the population of a community may have increased despite the fact that earthwork evidence might suggest the opposite.

Only in a handful of instances do records suggest that abandonment was the immediate and catastrophic result of the Black Death as it appears to have been at Tilgarsley, Oxfordshire, where the tax collectors of 1359 reported to the Exchequer that they could not collect tax because nobody had lived there since 1350. Most abandonment seems to have been a long drawn out process. Old people died and their holdings were not taken up by others; younger ones moved away to other villages and nearby towns. It was probably short-distance movements that contributed to the survival of many settlements; it may be the underlying reason why, in the present landscape, flourishing villages may be found adjacent to near empty parishes which lost their nucleus at this time.

In a study of eleven deserted villages on the estate of the Bishopric of Worcester, C. Dyer has shown that most were either deserted or severely weakened over a long period of time both by death and by the voluntary departure of tenants as better opportunities presented themselves elsewhere.[20] Moreover, in general these villages were among those paying less tax — and were presumably therefore smaller and less prosperous — in the period before the Black Death. This confirms from a small sample what Beresford found in his country-wide survey of late medieval desertion.[21] It was more likely that small communities, which had become even smaller and socially disintegrated during the late fourteenth and fifteenth centuries, would be most vulnerable to enclosers and depopulators at the end of the Middle Ages. The sudden depopulation of larger and more flourishing communities was rare.

Because of their better documentation and in some cases their remarkable earthworks it is not surprising that English villages of Midland type have been the focus of attention in the debate on late medieval depopulation. A composite map of deserted villages confirms depopulation to be a characteristic of a broad swathe through England from Dorset and Hampshire in the south to Yorkshire and Northumberland in the north-east.[22] The map, however, may mislead. Many medieval villages were not deserted in the late Middle Ages but were casualties of the eighteenth century when the fashion for the creation of landscape parks led powerful landlords again to evict villagers and to remove their houses, as was vividly described in the 'Deserted Village' by Oliver Goldsmith who had seen it happening at Nuneham Courtenay in Oxfordshire.[23]

It is safe to assume that most deserted villages in England have now been identified and located; a few new dots will be added to the map but not many. In some parts of England and in most of Wales and Scotland there are none simply because large nucleated villages were not a characteristic form of settlement in the later Middle Ages. Over much of the country people lived either in hamlets or in isolated farms. Work on how these settlements fared in the late medieval population decline is only now getting under way. The task is difficult and daunting. Most small settlements were not specifically named in sources such as taxation returns and, if abandoned, their sites are hard to locate. Nevertheless this subject is now beginning to get the attention it deserves.

INDUSTRY

If the negative effect of the conversion of land from tillage to grass was sometimes social dislocation the positive side was the extension of grazing land for the production of wool. This may be seen as an early example of the modernisation of agriculture insomuch that it was a response to market forces. As the price paid for wool relative to grain continued to rise many landowners saw it as the best return from their land. Some men saw the economic advantages and pressed ahead irrespective of peasant rights; others were either blind to the opportunities or, for various reasons, did not take them.

The prosperity of the cloth industry is the most conspicuous exception to the otherwise rather bleak image of the fifteenth century. From its increasingly rapid progress in the late fourteenth century, when it was helped along by several measures of protection, cloth manufacture seems to have thrived throughout the fifteenth and early sixteenth centuries. Customs accounts show that, with the exception of a slump in the 1450s and 1460s, exports of finished cloth increased steadily throughout the period; conversely, after the 1370s, exports of raw wool which had been the backbone of the export trade of the thirteenth century decreased. The home industry began to absorb more and more of the wool that was produced in the uplands and created a new demand which stimulated increased production on the lowlands. As the industry became more capitalised clothiers emerged as powerful organisers of production; to those in control of manufacture and trade these were prosperous times. Wool and cloth were sold for cash; in the late fifteenth and early sixteenth centuries some of the wealthiest families in terms of money rather than land were those connected with the trade. Not only were individuals and fraternities involved in the endowment of schools and almshouses but, in an age when great store was set by charity, much money found its way into the church through offerings and bequests. In this sense the fleece rubbed off on the architecture, secular and ecclesiastical, of many villages and towns. In churches the contributions of the clothiers may be seen both in rebuilding and in details — stained glass, brasses, parcloses — and in additions — chantries, porches and towers. In the Cotswolds and in Suffolk there were many major additions to, and rebuildings of, churches between c.1450 and 1530, almost without exception in the fashionable Perpendicular style. Churches such as at Cirencester and Northleach, Lavenham and Long Melford, stand as monuments both to the wealth of the industry and to the beliefs of the time.

52 Knapwell, Cambridgeshire is the adjacent parish to Elsworth (photo 34); the lines of the parish boundaries suggest that it originated as a daughter settlement of Elsworth and that the parish was carved out of its larger neighbour. Seen from the air in this view from the north Knapwell is a very good example of a 'shrunken' village. Earthworks of the manor house may be seen in the field on this side of the church and in the foreground is a circular mound, probably the remains of a very small Norman motte. Along the main street running to the south (? a planned medieval extension) there are now only a few houses; most of the house plots are empty except for earthworks. The ends of the plots on the left side of the road as seen in the photograph are marked by a line of very old trees that stood between the plots and the arable field, now in pasture and covered with ridge-and-furrow. On the left of the photograph is Overhall Grove, a surviving strip of medieval woodland on the edge of Boxworth parish.

53 Kersey, Suffolk, seen here in a photograph taken in 1951, was one of several east Suffolk villages noted for its textile making in the later Middle Ages. Like Worsted in Norfolk it gave its name to a particular kind of cloth. The parish church of St Mary stands high above the south end of this picturesque village; its west tower was rebuilt, like so many in Suffolk, in the fifteenth century, presumably partly from the profits of cloth sales. Like all other cloth towns and villages in eastern England Kersey declined in importance when textile production was industrialised in the north of England in the eighteenth and nineteenth centuries.

Although such improvements were not entirely those of cloth manufacturers (the gentry, the clergy and other industries had their roles to play) they are best seen in those parts of the country where, for reasons that are still not fully understood, the cloth industry of the late Middle Ages was located. It is still a matter of debate why cloth manufacture developed in such disparate areas as Suffolk and Essex, the Cotswolds, west Yorkshire, Somerset and Devon. Why so little in Leicestershire, the west Midlands, or north Wales? The shift of the industry from towns to country has been variously attributed to the spread of the fulling mill (with its need for a regular supply of water power for a good part of the year) and to the restrictive practices of the town guilds. Neither of these explanations is adequate nor do they explain why the industry became concentrated in certain areas. Sheep were raised almost everywhere and were dominant on upland and marsh. Wool must have been gathered, spun and woven in almost every rural community yet cloth making became capitalised and organised as an industry only in some places and not in others. Significantly perhaps, these areas were outside the manorialised, open-field, arable belt of Midland England – just that area of, as we have seen, the most conspicuous examples of the conversion of land from tillage to pasture. Cloth manufacture emerged instead in what Joan Thirsk termed 'wood-pasture' areas[24] (for example north-west Essex, east Suffolk (photo 53), the Kentish Weald) and in some valleys near to good pasture

114

and with good water supplies (for example the Stroud Valley, the Lake District and west Yorkshire). While the advantage of available water for power cannot be denied this cannot be the complete answer. The debate over location now includes such issues as the need to supplement agricultural income from other activities, the availability of labour, social structures, degrees of freedom and individualism, and nearness to markets.

Notwithstanding the rise of the 'country' cloth industry several old established towns retained, with varying fortunes, their importance as places of cloth manufacture and trade; they included Coventry, Warwick, Salisbury, Norwich, York, Oxford, Lincoln and Stamford. For the export of cloth and raw wool London, Southampton, Yarmouth, Hull, Boston and Newcastle were pre-eminent.

The surviving evidence of the late medieval cloth industry is better seen on the ground than from the air for while cloth may have indirectly produced new churches it seldom altered the basic layout of towns and villages. Nor do many other industries of the medieval period leave vestiges that are visible from the air. Most traces of the English iron industry, principally located in the Weald, the Forest of Dean and Cleveland, have either been obliterated or are still concealed under woodland. So-called hammer ponds, some probably dating from the late fifteenth and early sixteenth centuries and linked to the spread of the blast furnaces and associated forges, are an exception (photo 54).

54 Following the introduction in the iron industry of the blast furnace and water-powered hammers, first recorded at Newbridge in Ashdown Forest in the 1490s, the Sussex Weald became the most important centre of iron production in the next half-century. The streams of many narrow valleys were dammed to provide reservoirs of water to drive bellows and hammers for much of the year. Hammer-ponds thereby became a characteristic, and lasting, landscape feature of the Weald. Furnace Pond, near Lower Beeding, West Sussex is a typical example; it remains surrounded by vestiges of woodland on which the industry depended for charcoal.

115

55 The field on the edge of the village of Barnack, Northamptonshire, known locally as the 'hills and holes', is all that remains of the quarries of one of the best-known building stones used in medieval England. Barnack limestone, Jurassic in age, coarse textured and very shelly, was quarried from here as early as the seventh century when it was used for the first abbey church at Medehamstede, now Peterborough. Today the remains of the pits are of considerable interest both as relict medieval quarries (and might one or two be re-excavated sometime?) and for their botanical communities.

Quarrying (photo 55) and mining activity do leave traces especially on the uplands. They usually take the form of spoil heaps associated with early workings. Where building stone, lead, coal and iron were near enough to the surface they were usually mined from pits dug into and along the seams. Examples of such remains may be seen and photographed from the air, often to dramatic effect (photo 56).[25]

TOWNS

As is to be expected, the foundation of new towns which had been such a vigorous movement in the twelfth and thirteenth centuries virtually ceased in the much changed demographic and economic conditions of the later Middle Ages. There was neither the population nor the trade to encourage and sustain them. In England one of the only exceptions was Queenborough in Kent (photo 57), founded in 1368 by Edward III and named after his queen, Philippa. For a decade the new port replaced Sandwich as the Port of the Staple on that stretch of the coast; customs duty on cloth was collected there until the privilege reverted to Sandwich in 1378.[26]

56 There are only a few other places in Britain where the signs of medieval iron mining survive as clearly as they do at Bentley Grange, Emley, north Yorkshire. In this photograph the circular mounds are the spoil heaps around shallow central shafts (now collapsed and colonised by bushes) which were dug down to the ore bed below. They form a regular pattern and interestingly appear to overlie ridge-and-furrow; this must mean that the land was under arable cultivation before the pits were dug. In the medieval period this area was farmed from Bentley, a grange of the Cistercian abbey of Byland almost fifty miles away.

117

57 Seen here from the east, with modern developments in the foreground, Queenborough on the Isle of Sheppey, Kent, founded in the reign of Edward III and named after his Queen, Philippa, is a rare example of a medieval town founded after the Black Death. The reason for it seems to have been a new castle (demolished in the seventeenth century) built as part of the coastal defences against the French. An arm of the sea gave shelter for ships and the opportunity was taken to promote a new port on the West Swale which flows into the Medway estuary seen here in the background with the Isle of Grain beyond.

Britain's stock of late medieval towns therefore consisted of those which had already come into existence before the Black Death. Those that were already flourishing by 1300 survived the next two centuries, often with fluctuating fortunes; those that had made little headway gradually dropped behind. Many boroughs created in the thirteenth century and still only small at the time of the onset of the fourteenth-century problems failed to become true urban centres. A number gradually assumed the character of villages; only their morphology, their legal status as boroughs and sometimes their names remind us of their origins. Typical of this type is Newtown, Isle of Wight (photo 58), founded by a bishop of Winchester in 1255–6 and acquired and chartered by Edward I in 1284.[27] By the end of the century over seventy burghal plots were occupied and in 1334 Newtown, still not fully-fledged in the eyes of the taxers and represented by the manorial name of Swainston paid £11.13.0 in tax compared to (now better-known) Newport's £7.5.0. Newtown gradually decayed in the later Middle Ages; by the seventeenth century only eleven houses were assessed for the hearth tax. Nevertheless, it clung to its status as a borough and, as the air photograph shows,

even to its original layout. Its patrons built a town hall (now owned by the National Trust) in its almost deserted streets. By 1831 when Newtown was still sending members to Parliament it was among the rottenest of 'rotten boroughs'; that it merits more discussion here than the more successful Newport is only because it is an extreme case of what happened to many a small borough in the later Middle Ages.

Sited at the head of a shallow creek and apparently unable to compete with the bigger ports on the mainland, Newtown attracted neither population nor trade. In this it was not alone; there were many other similar, if less dramatic, failures not only in England but in Wales and Scotland. Beresford has calculated that 23 English medieval boroughs and 18 Welsh ones have either disappeared entirely or dwindled to a handful of houses. For Wales this represents a 'failure rate' of almost a quarter. Some disappeared for ever because their founders did not reckon with the movements of the sea. Ravenserodd, unwisely set on a sandbank at the mouth of the Humber, had gone by the 1360s; overrun by the sea it suffered the same fate that Wavermouth and Skinburgh on the Cumberland

58 The layout of the medieval borough of Newtown, Isle of Wight, planted alongside a tidal creek in 1256 by the Bishop of Winchester, is seen to advantage in this vertical air photograph taken in 1968. The town's two main streets, Gold Street and High Street, are now mostly overgrown and only a few of the original house plots are now occupied. Many of the lines of the original layout survive as field boundaries.

coast had done sixty years earlier. Conversely where the sea deposited it was likely to leave new ports high and dry, as for example at New Romney, Kent, itself a replacement for the silted-up Old Romney.

While failures directly attributable to natural causes are small in number compared to those which failed for economic reasons it was often an unwise choice of site which put a town at a disadvantage relative to others. The same was true of rural markets. Many of the hundreds of markets granted by the crown between the mid twelfth and the mid fourteenth century were to lapse in the later Middle Ages. In Norfolk and Suffolk, for example, where there were intricate and competitive networks of markets before the Black Death[28] a large number had ceased trading by 1500. In Norfolk only about 35 remained out of a total of 140; in Suffolk over 50 had gone by the seventeenth century, many of them no doubt by the end of the later Middle Ages. Even with detailed local work it is usually difficult to determine the date of the final demise of a market; they tended to peter out without written record. The rediscovery of the site of a 'lost' market is sometimes the reward for a detailed study of local field names.

While some of the smaller boroughs decayed the majority of medieval towns struggled through the less favourable conditions of the late fourteenth and fifteenth centuries. Indeed there is some evidence to suggest that, in relative terms, the urban sector became increasingly important within the economy as a whole. In a comparison of the taxes paid by English towns in 1334 and 1524–5, A. R. Bridbury found that urban wealth constituted a larger proportion of total lay wealth in 1524 than it had done before the Black Death.[29] Only in Staffordshire was it less, and then only marginally. Everywhere else it was greater and some counties showed considerable percentage increases, for example, in Warwickshire urban taxes increased from 9.6 per cent in 1334 to 69.9 per cent in 1524, Norfolk from 6.0 per cent to 41.8 per cent, Surrey from 7.4 per cent to 38.6 per cent and Worcestershire from 2.9 per cent to 24.9 per cent. While these figures cannot be taken at face value (there are too many imponderables in both the sources and the calculations) they may be seen as indicative of a general trend.

It is generally assumed that, like rural manors, towns lost through plague between a third and a half of their inhabitants in the second half of the fourteenth century. While losses may have been partially offset by people moving in from the countryside there is little doubt that most towns were smaller in 1400 than they had been a century before. Nor is there any sign of population recovery in towns in the early fifteenth century. Most commentators see this period as one of continuing attrition and by the late fifteenth century there are numerous references to vacant tenements and to other forms of urban decay. There is, however, continuing debate on whether lower numbers made the economy of the towns more, or less, efficient. Bridbury has presented an optimistic view of the fifteenth-century economy while others have been more cautious. Generalisations are difficult because the fortunes of individual towns varied very greatly.

London continued to be pre-eminent. Whereas in 1334, according to its tax payment, it was five times wealthier than its nearest rival, Bristol, in 1524 it was almost ten times wealthier than Norwich which by then had overtaken Bristol and become the leading provincial city. At the hub of the road network (since Roman times) and ideally placed relative to the continent, London's prosperity rested upon its increasing role within administration and in the export and import trades; its merchants were making inroads into the transactions of provincial towns and ports, as at Southampton where London men with their better resources and international connections gradually surpassed local interests.

While Norwich was less favourably located than London and was moving up from a lower base (it was eighth in rank order in 1334), it was again favourably situated relative to the continent, was a regional centre within an area of relatively prosperous agriculture and, most importantly, it was a centre of cloth manufacture. Norwich remained the hub of the worsted industry; the wealth generated from this activity and from others is evident in the architecture of most of its fifty or so parish churches, especially in St Peter Mancroft rebuilt between 1430 and 1455 and a superb example of the Perpendicular style. In 1524 Norwich paid eight times the amount of tax that it had done in 1334. Interestingly this was much the same rate of increase as at Colchester, Bury St Edmunds and Hadleigh, all important centres of clothmaking and marketing. Surprisingly Ipswich paid only four times as much; nevertheless, its rank order among English provincial towns rose from 13th in 1334 to 6th in 1524–5.

Some other Suffolk towns, notable among them Clare, Long Melford and Lavenham also thrived on cloth-making as their magnificent rebuilt parish churches of the period bear out. Such prosperity could not last. At Lavenham in 1525, where the church tower was in the final stage of completion due in part to bequests from the clothier family of the Springs, the bells were rung out not in celebration but to rally around the country people to protest against the new tax and against unemployment in the industry.[30] The tide which had favoured Suffolk in the fifteenth century was on the ebb.

Some towns in south-west England also prospered in the fifteenth century, notably Exeter (where the export of cloth increased very rapidly in the last quarter) and Totnes (photo 59), a town which, like Lavenham, enjoyed a boom period and was among the twenty wealthiest provincial towns in 1524–5.

Evidence of prosperity can however be more than matched by evidence elsewhere of urban problems. C. Phythian-Adams has calculated that the population of Coventry decreased from about 10,000 in 1440 to around 7,500 in 1520[31] and there were associated problems in the textile and clothing industry. Lincoln also had its troubles; it was exempted from its tax payments several times in the mid-fifteenth century when there appear to have been severe mortality from disease and when several of its parish churches fell into a state of decay.[32] Over the course of the fifteenth century there appears to have been considerable falls in the relative prosperity of Yarmouth, Boston (associated with the decline in the export of raw wool), Shrewsbury and York among other places. It should be said, however, that because of a shortage of reliable sources the complete picture is very confused; decline in some towns seems to be balanced by evidence of growth in others.

In general this was not a period for the physical expansion of urban areas. A few towns had begun to outgrow their medieval boundaries as suburbs grew up outside the gates and along the main roads. They are still shown at this stage when they are first represented on town plans by various cartographers at the end of the sixteenth century and in the fifty or so town-views drawn by John

59 *opposite* Totnes in Devon, like Lavenham in Suffolk, was a town which thrived on cloth making in the later Middle Ages. This view of the town from the west, taken in 1950, is dominated by the Norman castle where the motte is crowned by a perfect example of a circular shell keep. Below it is the inner bailey, its defences obscured by trees. To the east of the castle the wall of the oval-shaped medieval town is clearly visible. The burgage plots on both sides of the main street retain their linear form although much infilled by buildings. At the top of the photograph is the east gate, the only remaining medieval gate of the town, severely damaged by fire on 4 September 1990 since this photograph was taken. On the inner side of the gate is the parish church of St Mary, wholly rebuilt in the fifteenth century as was the fashion in all the cloth-making towns.

Speed and included within his *Theatre of the Empire of Great Britain* of 1611–12. The plans serve to remind us of the very small size of most English towns at the end of the Middle Ages; most were still largely confined to their earlier medieval boundaries.

Scientific cartography was but one aspect of the influence of the Renaissance on British life and thought in the sixteenth century. While humanistic influences may be detected in the literature of the fourteenth century, notably in Chaucer, they did not spread rapidly in the fifteenth – a century which can hardly be assigned to the 'modern' period. There were few advances in science and agriculture; as a consequence the population remained very vulnerable to bad harvests, famine and disease. Communications were much as they had been in 1300; there were no major additions to the road network nor improvements in water transport. Architecturally the country developed an insular (but most successful) style, the Perpendicular, now seen by some as England's most notable contribution to the history of European architecture. Like all artistic movements architecture needed patronage which, as we have seen, came increasingly from merchant wealth.

Yet some strands of modernisation may be detected in the later Middle Ages. Feudalism, still strong in 1300 had fundamentally changed its nature by 1500. While power still rested with a small minority it was no longer exclusively in the hands of those of noble birth and with large landed estates. The feudal castle was in decline; by 1500 the country house was beginning to take its place even if, in the early years, it retained many of the defensive features of the medieval castle (photo 60). Merchants and craftsmen had increasing roles in the system,

60 *above* Having been favoured with property in Warwickshire by Henry VIII the Compton family rebuilt Compton Wynyates between *c.*1481 and 1530. Although built as a country house it retained vestiges of medieval fortification – towers, battlements and a moat. Built of brick with stone dressings it is irregular in its detail; nevertheless it is arranged around a courtyard, a plan in fashion at the time and echoed in colleges of the same period such as St John's, Cambridge. The house is situated on the site of the village of Compton which was depopulated to make way for it. It survived despite capture and use as a garrison by Parliamentarians in 1644. The formal garden stands out in sharp contrast to the informality of the landscape park worked upon by Capability Brown in the 1760s.

not least in local government and trade. Customary services had given way to wage labour. There was more spatial and social mobility. Men could move more freely; some were about to better themselves, others to become the urban and rural poor of the sixteenth-century. With the 'discovery' of America in 1492 the British Isles were no longer on the fringes of the known world; open to a new range of external influences, and with the population at last beginning to grow again, the Tudors acceded at an opportune time to lead the country into a new stage of its cultural evolution.

FURTHER READING

C. Platt, *Medieval England*, London, 1978.

C. Dyer, *Standards of Living in the Later Middle Ages*, Cambridge, 1989.

T. Rowley, *The High Middle Ages, 1200–1550*, London, 1986.

J. Hatcher, *Plague, Population and the English Economy, 1348–1530*, London, 1977.

A. R. Bridbury, *Economic Growth. England in the Later Middle Ages*, London, 1962.

J. L. Bolton, *The Medieval English Economy, 1150–1500*, London, 1980.

5 Late Tudor and Stuart Britain: *c.1540 – c.1714*

This period is an interesting one for historical geographers because many of the changes that transformed 'medieval England' into 'modern England' were initiated or accelerated during the sixteenth and seventeenth centuries. But the relationship between the restructuring of England's economic and social geography, and the changing English landscape – within which survive some artefacts to be photographed – is a complex one. Important integrative aspects of the space-economy (such as the organisation of household-based weavers into entrepreneurially controlled 'putting-out') produced little change in the landscape. Conversely, some major changes in the landscape's appearance owed little to changes in the geographical structuring of economic, social or cultural activity, but instead reflected chance or non-spatial factors (though their impact on patterns of human activity might thereafter be profound). Thus, we should not envisage a precise correspondence between the visibility of sixteenth- and seventeenth-century features in the landscape and their geographical importance: still less should we expect either visibility or geographical importance to co-vary with the survival of these features to the present day. Nevertheless, much remains that testifies vividly to the regional and local diversity of everyday life, and to the transformations which affected the lives of early modern English men and women.

In virtually all significant respects – economic, social, cultural – Britain, and especially England, in the early eighteenth century was a more integrated and less localised society than it had been two centuries earlier. This is not to imply that increasing integration was a concomitant of diminishing localism since in certain spheres (such as regional economic specialisation) integration into wider systems of exchange and distribution was frequently associated with regional economic differentiation. Nor is it to ignore that integration in terms of ascription to more widely shared cultural values could be highly specific to powerful minorities in local society and administration (as in the withdrawal upwards by local elites from popular culture, which was less and less a force for cultural homogeneity, more and more a residual and regulated culture of 'the poorer sort'[1]). Moreover, much of Wales, Scotland and Ireland remained very poorly integrated or entirely outside wider economic and social networks, despite the eventual political integration of these countries into the United Kingdom.

It is largely meaningless to apply a concept such as '*the* English space-economy' to early sixteenth-century England. While W. G. Hoskins certainly overstated his case in writing that the England of Henry VIII 'was medieval in every important respect',[2] most localities in early Tudor England only encountered extra-regional spheres through personal mobility, the Church and, less continuously, taxation, conscription, and the action of the King's justices. By the early eighteenth century we can recognise three components in a much more integrated space-economy, as shown in the figure below. First, some types of agricultural and industrial production were concentrated in relatively specialised regions. Modest but significant productivity gains had been achieved in many activities. Secondly, marketing had become more systematised. Quite extensive and well-integrated marketing systems existed at a wide variety of scales. The chief components of more efficiently integrated distributive systems were three-fold: improved technology in overland and river transport; the expansion of specialised occupations, institutions and premises involved in wholesale and retail trading outside open markets; and the appearance of financial institutions which had begun to provide channels for the movement of capital which were not dependent on face to face contact between lender and borrower. The importance of better overland transport extended beyond the movement of commodities and capital to embrace the movement of ideas, information, and – to a much lesser extent – the movement of labour. Indeed the sheer variety of forms of integration renders it dangerous to speak of *the* integration of the space-economy, since it collapses too many largely autonomous dimensions of social life into a single process.[3] Rather, several intertwined processes operated, sometimes at very different speeds. Finally, we can distinguish the substantial growth of commercially oriented attitudes and behaviour: more commercial attitudes to work and earning, and new attitudes towards consumption and spending.

Increasing economic and cultural integration prompted bases for social identification to become more strongly defined in terms of status within parishes or communities, although inter-regional and local rivalries were often added to rather than replaced. Broadly speaking, the geographical extent of cultural integration (through religious reformation and educational advance) affected social groups in proportion to their status in national, provincial and local life. Some aspects of cultural integration had pronounced impacts on the landscape through the creation of particular architectures or landscape features which combined both social-functional and symbolic components, especially in towns.

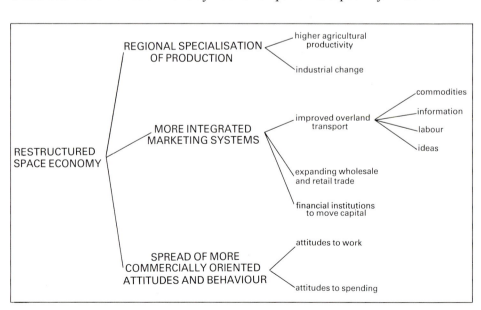

Components of spatial integration in early modern England.

The selection of integration, regionalisation, and social differentiation as central themes of early modern geographical change is obviously dependent on theoretical criteria, but is not itself controversial. However, it is clearly possible to interpret these developments in several ways. A number of broad frameworks play an important role in current interpretations. The most common, though not hegemonic, interpretation consists of a combination of economic and ecological components.[4] This interpretation stresses the slow commercialisation of an agriculture in the grip of a subsistence peasantry under the pressure of population growth. Agricultural output increased slowly, mainly by extension of the cultivated area rather than radical technical innovations before c.1640, and this enabled a slow growth of population from about 2.2 million to about 5.2 million by c.1650. The increase in agricultural output, however, was not enough to prevent substantial inflation, especially of food prices, which limited the scale of industrial growth. Thereafter, stable or declining population and agricultural improvements resulting in increased grain yields prompted the terms of trade to move in favour of the non-agricultural sector from mid-century. Consequently, the growing home market for consumer goods provided a secure base for growth in industrial and commercial sectors of the economy, which became progressively more important in terms of occupations and gross national product.[5] Through the working out of comparative economic advantage, regional specialisation increased sharply along with the volume of inter-regional trade.

Marxist and Marxian interpretations of the period would see most of these developments as themselves dependent on changing class relations and/or the form taken by capital accumulation in various branches of agriculture, industry and commerce.[6] Thus, regional specialisation reflected not the 'natural' process of adjustment to comparative advantage but the nature and degree of the control of capital over labour in particular types of commodity production and distribution, including the consolidation of private property rights over resources (especially arable land) hitherto exploited under some degree of cooperative control.

LANDOWNERSHIP AND SOCIAL CHANGE

The dissolution of the monasteries in the late 1530s and 1540s massively increased the wealth of the Crown through the confiscation of valuable goods and rents from confiscated monastic lands and spiritual possessions. The latter were fairly rapidly disposed of, occasionally by gift but usually by sale, to a relatively small number of gentry and Crown officials until by 1547 only 30 per cent of confiscated lands remained in the hands of the Crown. These large-scale changes in land ownership constituted a major redistribution of land, whose significance has long been debated. Although many parts of the country have not yet been studied in sufficient detail, analyses of the recipients of land from the Crown in the 1540s and 1550s indicate that the picture of church lands passing wholesale from conservative ecclesiastical lords into the hands of a new commercial class of agrarian capitalist landlords has been overdrawn.[7] Both the main types of beneficiaries – established families extending their estates, and 'rising' families often involved with the Tudor Court – usually seem to have followed orthodox land management strategies rather than radically new ones. Such changes as did occur can perhaps

61 Titchfield Abbey, Hampshire. Having been granted Titchfield Abbey by King Henry VIII in 1537, Sir Thomas Wriothesley dismantled most of the abbey buildings, and re-used materials in building a courtyard-focused house around the old monastic cloister. Although some of Wriothesley's buildings have in turn been removed, they vividly depict the transfer of landed wealth from ecclesiastical to lay hands, and the possibilities of upward social mobility among minor gentry supporters of the Tudor dynasty.

be more plausibly explained by more general changes in economic circumstances than by the landownership changes *per se*.

Predictably, when an estate was granted to a new owner many monasteries were dismantled. In some cases, former monastic buildings were adapted to the requirements of their new owner, as at Titchfield Abbey, Hampshire (photo 61). The Premonstratensian abbey of Titchfield was granted in 1537 to Thomas Wriothesley, later to become Earl of Southampton, who immediately began converting the buildings. As photo 61 clearly shows, in building his new house he dismantled most of the east end of the abbey church: the choir, presbytery and transepts, together with the west tower. However, he used the nave and the range of ancillary buildings to its north as the basis of a courtyard country house centred on the monastic cloister. In 1540 Leland observed that 'Mr. Wriothesley hath buildeth a right stately house embatelid, and having a goodely gate and a conduite castelid in the middle of the court of it'.[8] Much of Wriothesley's building no longer survives, but the 'goodely gate' does, and can be seen to be driven through the former nave. Perhaps nowhere else in England does the juxtaposition of monastic buildings and those that replaced them provide so clear a symbol of the changing relationship between Church and State.

128

Not all monastic sites found new uses. Many, especially the more isolated sites, were partially dismantled shortly after their dissolution, but were neither reoccupied nor completely demolished. A good example of such a site is Tintern Abbey, Gwent (photo 62). Tintern was an early-twelfth-century Cistercian house, set on a small plain in the wooded gorge of the lower Wye valley. Most of the surviving remains date from thirteenth-century rebuilding: by this time the abbey was the centre of a substantial estate based on pastoral farming. Like other Cistercian foundations, Tintern was remote from contemporary settlement, and so proved unattractive to those seeking to convert monastic buildings to private use. Its remoteness also protected the buildings from systematic dismantling for reusable cut stone, since its transport would have been very expensive. As it was, only the higher value items such as furnishings and lead were systematically removed. The roofless buildings were rented and used briefly as a wire-making works by the Elizabethan 'Mineral and Battery Company', but this produced little change in their appearance until their recognition as a fashionable scenic spot in the eighteenth century.[9]

Even without the dissolution of the monasteries and the regranting of monastic land, the dynastic succession of the Tudors (with its attendant opportunities for

62 Tintern Abbey, Gwent. The importance attached by the Cistercians to remote locations for the founding of their religious houses helps to explain why some of their monasteries are among the most fully preserved in Britain. At Tintern, far removed from major concentrations of population, and in an area of low capital, extensive pastoral agriculture, there was little 'demand' for salvaged building materials from the site.

63 Hatfield House, Hertfordshire. The Cecil family provide perhaps the most striking example of a minor family rising on the coat-tails of the Tudors to social eminence. Their building of Hatfield House from 1607 expressed their social status and aspirations, both through its great size, and its ornate brick-worked design. The formal gardens to the east of the house were remodelled in the nineteenth century, but have been restored since the late 1980s. They now provide a fine example of a formal Jacobean garden, with small plots for herbs and flowers separated by an intricate network of low box hedges.

their supporters), together with the prestige attached to conspicuous building and entertaining, ensured the construction of many large houses, both urban (especially in London) and in the countryside. The 'fruits of office' available at Court and through the centralised fiscal-judicial system enabled such building to attain lavish proportions. Hatfield House, in Hertfordshire (photo 63), built by Robert Cecil, first Earl of Salisbury, between 1607 and 1612 was one of the largest houses constructed during the early modern period. It survives very little altered from the original design, and the fortunes of the family that built it, and the history and appearance of the house itself in many ways epitomise major developments in society and landscape under the Tudor and Stuart monarchs.

The fortunes of the Cecil family were very closely linked to their relationship with the Crown. In the wake of Henry VII's triumph at the battle of Bosworth in 1485 many of his supporters, among them one David Cecil of Lincolnshire received grants of land, and minor posts at Court. Over the next two decades Cecil consolidated his position at Court and was able to obtain positions there for his son Richard Cecil including the prominent duty of Yeoman of the Wardrobe to Henry VIII. By Richard's death in 1553 the family's lands had greatly expanded, notably through his acquisition of grants of several former monastic properties.

His son William had by now become surveyor to the lands of Princess Elizabeth, and when she inherited the throne William Cecil entered the Privy Council as one of the Queen's two principal secretaries. Appointment to several lucrative posts followed, including the Mastership of the Court of Wards and Liveries from 1561. This post remained Cecil's until his death in 1598 when it passed to his second son Robert who held it, together with several monopoly licences, to his death in 1612. Stone has shown how the income deriving from these offices and monopolies ran to tens of thousands of pounds per annum, dwarfing the rent income from the family's ever-growing landed estate.[10]

With the continued prosperity of the family thus yoked to royal favour, prestige building projects – notably the huge palace of Theobalds at Cheshunt in Hertfordshire – were a major expenditure priority. Not without good reason did William write that Theobalds had been 'greatly increased by reason of her majesty often coming to it' between its inception in 1564 and its completion in the 1580s.[11] King James' regard for Theobalds was such that Robert Cecil offered the property to the Crown in 1607. In return he received the Hatfield estate a few miles to the north, which the Crown had held since its confiscation from the Abbot of Ely in 1540, together with land in nine other counties. Building commenced almost straightaway under the direction of Robert Lyminge and was largely complete within six years at a cost of about £40,000. In plan, the house was of a traditional design with a main range and two substantial wings, but very much larger than usual, with the main range almost 100 m long. As with an increasing number of country houses, the major building material was brick. The southern (winged) side faced the main approach drive from the London road and is much more ornate than the comparatively bare north front. The latter is now the 'front' of the house, approached by the long curving drive from the main road and railway station, past the now rarely-used cricket pitch. The new house was sited at the town edge of a park of about 530 acres. The major surviving features of this are the formal Jacobean gardens to the east of the house, and the former vineyard area to the north, at the end of the straight avenue of trees leading away from the north front. Although remodelled in the nineteenth century the gardens provide a good example of the relatively small scale, the formality, and the simplicity of many Jacobean gardens. As publications on, and aristocratic interest in, horticulture increased, such gardens contained growing numbers of new and imported plants, especially fruit. John Gerarde's *Herball*, for example, had been dedicated to Lord Burghley in its first edition of 1597.[12]

Once built, the house and estate provided an effective obstacle to further eastward development of the town and further urban building consequently occurred away from the town centre in other directions. This physical influence on the town was matched by the family's continued social influence, both on the day-to-day lives of Hatfield's inhabitants and in national political and social arenas.

AGRICULTURE

Economists have long recognised that much of the dramatic sixteenth-century increase in food prices reflected the difficulties involved in increasing agricultural output.[13] The food demands of a growing population before *c*.1650 were met mainly through the expansion of the cultivated area, both in hitherto marginal areas such as the Fens and the Somerset Levels, and by converting pasture to arable within established farming systems. Some degree of regional specialisation consequent upon improving inter-regional trade, and the extension of private property rights through enclosure also contributed to increasing output. Few technological innovations were widely adopted before the mid seventeenth century. These (including the floating of water meadows) were situated on the pastoral side of mixed farming systems. Major innovations in arable husbandry became much more frequent after *c*.1650 as farmers and landlords invested in attempts to protect their incomes as grain prices fell. Even by *c*.1700, there had been few comparable innovations in pastoral agriculture.

The most spectacular expansion of cultivation occurred in the Fens of Norfolk, Cambridgeshire and Lincolnshire, where medieval reclamation had been limited to silt areas north of the peat fens. A rising interest in fen drainage is evident as early as the 1570s among aristocratic and gentry landowners influenced both by general interests in agricultural improvements and by drainage schemes carried out in the Netherlands and France. By the time of Humphrey Bradley's proposals in 1589 the potential of successfully draining large areas of fen had been widely recognised. Such a scheme would, Bradley argued, be 'a regal conquest' capable of accommodating 200,000 families and more than 300,000 cattle, in addition to which he envisaged a substantial expansion of grain production resulting in lower domestic prices and large-scale exporting. The obstacles to improvement, he asserted, lay 'in men's minds' not in the physical landscape. The obstacles consisted of lack of capital, antagonism to the employment of foreigners, lack of coordination between landowners, and most important, conflict between landowners' interest in drainage and the interests of existing householders and smallholders reliant on the wide range of fenland resources (grazing, wildfowling, fishing, peat, reeds and sedge).[14] The overcoming of the third obstacle provided the key to the fourth, when in the late 1620s the Duke of Bedford agreed to drain his 20,000 acres of fen as the core of a major new scheme: the 'Bedford Level'.

The drainage of the Bedford Level simplified and straightened existing rivers to increase very slight gradients and accelerate water flow. The core of the system involved two elements: the Old Bedford River (1631) and the New Bedford River (1651); the first and last elements of the system to be completed (photo 64). From 1653 the New Bedford River formed the main channel for the river Ouse, but at high flows a system of sluices routed water through the Old Bedford River as well. The washlands between the two new channels provided an area which could be deliberately flooded to lower river levels when either channel approached bank-full. Further sluices at Denver, near Downham Market, regulated inflowing tides to prevent salt-water inundation.

If the draining of the Bedford Level largely solved some old problems it also created new ones. Chief amongst these were that the drainage network created ran against the natural movement of groundwater, and the failure to anticipate that drained peat would shrink thereby lowering the fen surface below the channels draining them. Hence, even to maintain the scheme required increasingly

64 Bedford Level, south of Denver, south-west Norfolk looking towards Cambridgeshire. Draining the East Anglian Fenlands in the seventeenth century constituted the largest single project of agricultural 'improvement' to that date. The draining of this extremely flat and low-lying area necessitated major artificial channels, and substantial embankments to prevent these channels overflowing and inundating new farmland. The unanticipated shrinkage of peat, and the lowering of the land surface that followed, subsequently exacerbated these problems.

From 1653, the New Bedford River (left) formed the main channel for the River Ouse, but at high flows a system of sluices routed water through the Old Bedford River as well. The washlands between the two new channels provided an area which could be deliberately flooded to lower river levels when either channel approached bank-full.

elaborate pumping arrangements, and flooding of drained lands recurred periodically. Even so, the Bedford Level and other smaller schemes made a significant contribution to increasing the cultivated area of Britain, particularly as many industrial and new agricultural crops were cultivated here: coleseed and rapeseed for oil; hemp for rope, sails and cables; flax; woad and other dye plants; new vegetables and grasses.[15]

One of the major limitations of sixteenth-century agriculture was that the arable and pastoral sectors of mixed farming were essentially competitive, in that an expansion of the output of either was largely dependent on a switch in land use away from the other. Many late-seventeenth-century agricultural innovations instead sought ways to improve arable or pastoral output through increased productivity rather than through substitution. In this respect the floating of water meadows was similar to other innovations such as the widespread introduction of new fodder crops, or of new fertilisers or horticultural techniques into arable farming. In other ways, such as expense and impact on the landscape, however, water meadows were less representative, since many innovations involved little capital and had little direct effect on the appearance of the landscape.

The purpose of constructing a water meadow was to remove the constraint of winter feed shortages from the sizes of flocks of sheep.[16] Sheep farmers needed to build up sufficient stocks of winter fodder to feed their flocks until sufficient spring growth of grass had occurred. Since water meadows brought forward the date at which spring fodder became available, they reduced the time for which flocks depended on stored fodder and hence enabled the over-wintering of larger flocks per unit area. They achieved this by ensuring that for much of the year meadowland was covered by a thin sheet of flowing water via elaborate systems of sluices and channels. The flowing water had three effects. First it maintained high levels of moisture at the soil surface; secondly it deposited silt directly onto the surface; and thirdly it offered protection against ground frosts in winter and spring since water temperatures were usually well above freezing point, thus nullifying an important check to grass growth. Moreover, the productivity of water meadows was considerably greater than that of ordinary meadows through the rest of the year so that they yielded more and heavier hay crops. The larger flocks so supported then provided an increased supply of dung and urine for the fertilisation of arable land.

By far the commonest location for these projects were the valleys of rivers in the chalklands of central and southern England, especially in Wiltshire, Dorset, Berkshire and Hampshire.[17] Photo 65 shows the elaborate network at Britford in the valley of the Wiltshire Avon, just south of Salisbury. By the end of the seventeenth century, similar schemes extended almost continuously from Salisbury southwards to Downton, close to the river's mouth. The river Avon is flowing towards the camera, and supplies the five major channels flowing at the tops of low ridges towards the bottom of the picture. These in turn discharge water to smaller channels set on much smaller ridges some 15 m apart, whence the water flows down the ridge sides to be collected in a second set of larger ditches and returned to the river. Clearly, the construction of the ridge and channel network was both time-consuming and expensive, depending on the lie of the land, and once built, required annual maintenance. Consequently, the dis-

65 Water meadow at Britford near Salisbury, Wiltshire. The River Avon is flowing towards the camera, and supplies the five major channels flowing at the tops of the low ridges towards the bottom of the picture. These in turn discharge water to smaller channels set on much smaller ridges some fifty feet apart, whence the water flows down the ridge sides to be collected in a second set of larger ditches and returned to the river.

66 Stanton, Gloucestershire. Today the village of Stanton provides a strong sense of the wealthier elements of seventeenth-century village landscapes, with substantial two- and three-storey farmhouses built in local limestones and slate. They exemplify how Tudor and early-Stuart yeoman farmers profited from booming prices for agricultural products, and improved their material standards of living.

tribution of water meadows remained fairly restricted, but the substantial rent rises associated with the floating of meadows leaves no doubt as to the magnitude of their impact on downland sheep-corn husbandry.

The prosperity of many farmers and artisans in early modern England was directly reflected in what W. G. Hoskins called 'the great rebuilding of rural England': the construction of tens of thousands of new houses, larger, and with a more sophisticated division of living space, than the houses of medieval peasants.[18] Historians now would place the chronological bounds of this phase rather wider than Hoskins' 1570–1640, and recognise that medieval peasant houses were sometimes more elaborate than Hoskins realised,[19] but there is no doubt that the form of many villages and hamlets was 'upgraded' with the prosperity of these social groups. For the first time, large sections of the rural population of England had both the means to erect relatively expensive buildings of permanent materials and the stability of tenure which made expensive operations worthwhile. In many villages an element of this persists in the present landscape.

Perhaps the finest surviving example is Stanton in Gloucestershire (photo 66). Virtually all the houses in the village's main streets were built during the seventeenth century (several buildings bear date inscriptions, ranging between 1614 and 1678), and the village as a whole has undergone only limited growth since then. Thus, most of the present buildings derive from a single, relatively short period of construction. The present day appearance of many of the buildings owes much to restoration work carried out between 1906 and 1937 at the instigation of the architect Sir Phillip Stott, who in 1906 bought the estate within which the village lies. Repairs and extensions to buildings were carried out in local materials (oolitic and lias limestone and slate) and seventeenth-century styles. Thus whilst the village landscape does reflect one man's ideas, it still conveys a strong impression of early modern Cotswold building styles. Although not 'undesigned', the buildings remain vernacular: the product of local building conventions rather than national or international fashions.[20]

INDUSTRY

As with agriculture, the extent of industrial progress in early modern England has been vigorously debated.[21] Consensus views emphasise the limitations that slowed the rate of expansion of industrial output and the lack of revolutionary technology, against earlier claims made by J. U. Nef and others. Few large centralised industrial enterprises were created (the nearest approach being the Naval dockyards) and these reflected the nature of production of large objects rather than production for large markets. Major technological innovations were rare (the exceptions were mainly in textile crafts, like Lee's knitting machine). A more typical development was increasing organisational complexity, best illustrated by 'putting-out', in which an entrepreneur coordinated and to some extent controlled the production of many outworkers. Even here, production remained dispersed. Also of considerable importance were developments which made the England of *c*.1700 self-sufficient in many industrial products that had only been available as imports in 1500, including armaments, paper, glass, and alum for dyeing. The Crown actively encouraged these developments with three aims: to replace imports on the growing home markets; to create new export markets and improve the balance of trade; and to create employment, especially in towns, as part of wider social policies. This last aim was shared by urban corporations and some landowners. Perhaps the most striking outcome of industrial growth was England's changing occupational structure. Wrigley has recently estimated that whereas fewer than one in four Englishmen was occupied in craft or trade pursuits in *c*.1520, about 40 per cent were so occupied in *c*.1670. The absolute number of craftsmen and tradesmen had increased by more than five-fold.[22]

In terms of volume of output, employment, and their impact on regional economies, textiles and mining remained England's most notable industries. The scale of individual workings for coal and ores remained fairly small, showing few signs of momentous eighteenth-century changes ahead. Individual workings were usually simple shafts and galleries, or surface diggings along outcrops and shallow veins. Almost all of these workings (especially coal workings) have been obliterated by subsequent workings, spoil or buildings.

The distribution of mining reflected three factors. First, most mineral resources were found in older geological strata and hence in the mainly sparsely populated areas of western, Pennine and northern England and in Wales and Scotland. Secondly, limited technology and capital restricted operations to small production units on accessible seams and veins. Thirdly, transporting the minerals produced was often difficult and expensive. Mines could serve extra-local markets only if they enjoyed easy access to transport networks (usually river or coastal shipping), or a link to such a network could be easily provided. Consequently many small mining areas supplied localised markets, protected by the high transport costs of importing coal or ore from further afield, even though it might have been produced much more cheaply. Conversely, large fields of inaccessible high quality resources remained undeveloped, despite being easy to work. A fine example of this is provided by the salt industry. The Tyneside salt industry, which obtained salt by boiling sea water, produced at four to five times the cost of the Cheshire industry, based on the digging and refining of rock salt. However, cheap coal for boiling was plentiful on Tyneside and access to coastal transport easy, whereas overland transport from the Cheshire workings to the Mersey was expensive and would require major capital outlays to make the Weaver navigable. Consequently, Tyneside supplied much of English salt requirements through the seventeenth century.[23]

Tyneside was also the dominant coalfield of early modern England, serving a very large supra-regional market.[24] By the early eighteenth century annual shipments from Newcastle and Tynemouth to London alone came to about half a million tons a year, about 20 per cent of total national output. Tyneside was also unusual in that some very large, deep pits were operating. Working depths of over 30 m were common, with depths three times these in the deepest pits. The centralisation of capital required to initiate mining and the development of specialised management expertise brought about a precocious three-way cleavage among owners, management and miners, but even on this heroic scale mining remained reliant on basic manual techniques.

Of other extractive industries the most important were lead mining (photo 67) and tin mining (photo 68). Their scale was small alongside coal production but, particularly for lead, had grown rapidly. At about 30,000 tons a year, lead production in Derbyshire, the north east, and the Mendips was second only to coal. The geographical pattern of the lead industry was increasingly shifting away from the last area. Although the Mendips had seen the introduction of several improvements in refining techniques, its production declined sharply after its peak period of *c*.1600–70, and few workings remained in use much beyond 1710. Thus, even in periods of relatively stable techniques and expanding output the pattern of regional production was dynamic, and the fortunes of industrial areas could change rapidly – for better or worse – with profound consequences for other aspects of local economies.

The tin industry, though smaller and growing more slowly than the lead industry, possessed two important characteristics. First it was highly concentrated in part of a single county, Cornwall, and thus dominated this regional economy

and landscape. Since much of its production in the early sixteenth century went to overseas markets, it was much more vulnerable to fluctuations in international markets and political disputes than most branches of mining. Secondly, its output was the basis for the production of pewter, one of the major consumer goods for which the early modern domestic market expanded dramatically.[25] This expansion compensated for increasingly difficult international trading conditions, and provided a more reliable demand for tin, until by *c.*1700 most Cornish tin (over 2,000 tons a year) was destined for pewterers.

Like mining, most branches of manufacturing did not involve employers or independent craftsmen in large capital investment, especially while even skilled labour remained cheap. Hence, units of both production and control in most industries were small. However, there were two great exceptions to the fragmented character of industrial organisation: metalworking and textiles, in which entrepreneurial merchants and merchant-producers played an increasingly central role.

67 Remains of lead mining at Chapelfell, near Forest, County Durham. It is in the nature of mining that large-scale activity destroys or obliterates the remains of earlier, and smaller-scale activities. Consequently, early remains are often best-preserved in areas whose importance faded at an early date. The remains of individual shafts at Chapelfell are difficult to date precisely, but variations in the degradation and clarity of the surviving mounds are evidence that some of the shafts and surrounding spoil heaps are much older than others.

Even the growth in mining employment was dwarfed by the workforce in the many branches of the textile industry. Cloth was England's main export (accounting for about three-quarters of English export earnings in the early seventeenth century) from an overwhelmingly domestic production system, involving scores of thousands of people at the start of the period and hundreds of thousands by the end. The form of domestic production units remained almost unchanged, but their organisational setting was transformed.[26] Cloth production moved away from being largely composed of independent weaving households towards more sophisticated forms in which part-time or full-time weavers working for entrepreneurs also existed in considerable numbers.

Historians have long recognised that a combination of economic, geographic, and social factors seems to have conferred significant advantages on cloth producers in certain areas. Neither economic nor geographic factors on their own can account for the industry's distribution. By the sixteenth century, some textile areas already imported most of the raw wool they used, and the better cloths were sufficiently valuable and prestigious to be able to absorb the transport costs from comparatively remote locations to mainly urban markets. Influential work by Thirsk has focused attention instead on the social context of successful textile industries. These were overwhelmingly rural, set in populous communities of small, usually pastoral farmers, who typically practised partible inheritance in areas where manorialism was relatively weak.[27]

The Gloucestershire cloth industry exemplifies these considerations (photo 69 and figure), developing during the later middle ages and expanding considerably during the sixteenth century. A unique occupational source permits a partial assessment of its scale. The Crown made county lieutenants responsible for compiling lists of adult males in their respective counties as part of the preparations for training a militia force to defend the realm in case of invasion. In 1608, John Smith, steward of Berkeley Hundred, on whom the task devolved in Gloucestershire, ensured that additional occupational information was collected about men in Gloucestershire.[28] The distribution of men in textile trade occupations is plotted on the map below. Of just over 17,000 men whose occupations were specified, over 2,600 were in the textile industry, with over 1,500 weavers. Within the county their distribution was highly concentrated on and immediately below the slopes of the Cotswold oolite scarp. The Frome valley around Stroud and Minchinhampton, the Cam valley around Dursley, and the Little Avon valley around Wootton-under-Edge all contained several parishes in which more than half the men listed were weavers or other clothworkers. In addition it is likely that men returned under other occupations may have been involved in weaving on a part time basis, in so-called 'dual economy' households.

Gloucestershire was only one among a number of major regional production systems in the textile industry. Elsewhere in the West Country, production was also expanding in Wiltshire and Somerset. In the West Riding, centred on Halifax, Wakefield and Leeds, woollen production was growing even faster.[29] Worsted production on a large scale was a feature of other parts of the West Riding and of Norfolk. Other production systems in older centres like Devon and southern East Anglia were becoming steadily more marginal, with widespread unemployment and economic distress in areas such as Suffolk and south-east Essex.

68 A landscape of tin mining at St Hilary, Cornwall. In Cornwall, as in many parts of the country, mining was combined with agricultural activities in so-called 'dual economy' households in which the availability of income from both farming and mining provided some protection against difficult economic conditions. The intermixture of fields and small mineshafts captures this close relationship between agriculture and industry.

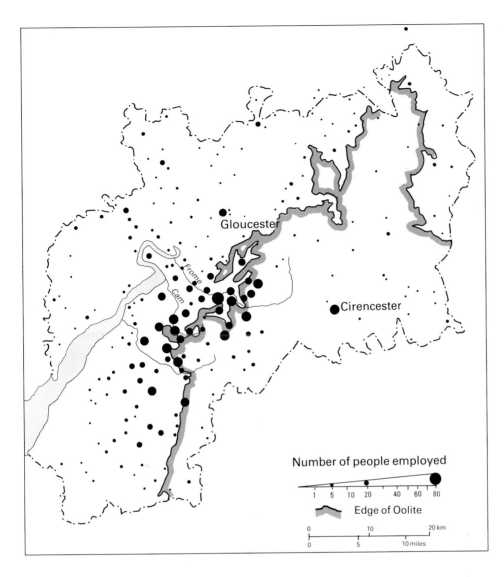

Gloucestershire, 1608: distribution of male textile workers. A rare insight into the degree of industrial reliance in early-modern industrial districts is provided by a survey of men in Gloucestershire in 1608. Over the county as a whole, about one man in six was ascribed an occupation in the textile industry, but these were unevenly distributed. In several settlements, the majority of men listed were weavers. These figures are relatively modest by comparison with the textile 'new towns' of the decades around 1800, in which three-quarters or more of men may have relied on a single occupation, but at this early date they testify to substantial inter-regional trade, not only in the industrial products, but in food to sustain the industrial workforce.
(After F. Emery, 'England circa 1600' in H. C. Darby, (ed), *A New Historical Geography of England*, Cambridge, 1973, p. 278.)

A number of writers have recognised similar organisational changes in industries other than textiles, especially in the metalworking trades in the west midlands,[30] south Yorkshire,[31] and London. Here too (as for that matter in mining) stress has been placed on the role of 'dual economy' households, and their changing relationships with entrepreneurs, and there are definite parallels in the organisational arrangements in these different trades. However it would be a grave mistake to assume that the 'dual economy' model provides an appropriate framework within which to analyse most types of non-agricultural activity. Most urban craftsmen and many rural ones were independent, specialist artisans rather than part-time outworkers.

INTERNAL TRADE

The increasing integration of the early modern English space-economy in terms of commodities, capital and information proceeded very unevenly. Even regional markets in many commodities (such as coal and salt) were still poorly integrated,

69 'Golden Valley', Minchinhampton, Gloucestershire. The focus of textile production in south-west England, reflecting a combination of environmental, economic and social factors. Environmental factors (high quality local wools, stream gradients offering water power for fulling, and water quality) were noteworthy, but not decisive. The flexibility of local agricultural systems, which accommodated part-time and, increasingly, full-time work, the inability of local landlords to control their tenants' activities, and easy access to distant markets via Gloucester, Bristol and London, were all critical.

70 Ddyle, north of Abbey-cwmhir, Powys (formerly Radnorshire); droveway. Even the most distant parts of the British Isles had become incorporated into the London-centred livestock trades by the end of the sixteenth century. These flows intensified as the capital grew extremely rapidly in the seventeenth century, and as other cities belatedly experienced their own population explosions. In the movement of livestock in large numbers, the availability of fodder along the journey was crucial, and drove routeways in open country took the form of wide braided tracks, permitting some degree of grazing on the hoof.

and would remain so until the technology of overland trade improved much further. One particularly well-integrated aspect of internal trade was that in livestock. Since livestock could walk to markets, long distance trade, especially in cattle was a well established feature of marketing. The scale of inter-regional trade in cattle and horses increased sharply during the sixteenth and seventeenth centuries. This reflected both rising demand for meat and haulage stemming from population growth, and developing regional production specialisms in upland Britain, and specialisation among markets in particular types of animals.[32]

The lack of documentation obscures all but the haziest outline of the dimensions of livestock trades, but the comments of contemporaries and the growing numbers of drovers and dealers appearing in market and toll books demonstrate its very considerable scale. In many parts of upland Britain it remains possible to trace the routes taken by convoys of cattle or horses on their journey from Ireland, Scotland, Wales or northern England to urban markets and the growing industrial areas such as the West Midlands. One such drove road is shown in photo 70. This is one of several similar roads which converge on the village of

Abbeycwmhir, Powys (formerly Radnorshire). The typically curving and braided network of intertwined tracks run across Upper Esgair Hill from Bwlch-y-sarnau towards Abbeycwmhir which lies just beyond the wooded spur towards the top of the picture. Cattle following this route originated from a wide area of central Wales as far west as Aberystwyth, and were destined for markets such as Worcester (and then Birmingham and the Black Country) or Hereford (and then London or elsewhere in southern England). By the later seventeenth century, contemporaries at Hereford estimated that some 10,000–20,000 cattle from mid-Wales passed through the town each year. As the trade grew and became more regularised, so the role of drovers as carriers of information, money, and credit notes became more important: they were thus participating in much more than merely the integration of livestock markets.

URBAN LANDSCAPES

By European standards, early modern England was peaceful and politically stable. Consequently, defensive or military factors were rarely important influences on the landscape, except in vulnerable border areas. Apart from the Civil War of the 1640s, the major stimuli to defensive constructions such as town defences were the prospects of Spanish or French invasion, especially when the latter were allied with the Scots during the reigns of the early Protestant monarchs: Henry VIII, Edward VI, and Elizabeth I.

Although many towns were provided with temporary fortifications or refurbished their surviving medieval walls during the Civil War, in only one place were major permanent fortifications constructed. This was at Berwick-upon-Tweed (photo 71) close to the border with Scotland. Berwick had changed hands during the middle ages, and although from 1482 it remained English it was perceived as both strategically important and highly vulnerable. Here as nowhere else, the military defence function of the town was paramount and this importance was reflected in Berwick's appearance. The Tudor defensive walls as shown in photo 71 differed markedly from medieval wall systems built prior to the general use of firearms.

Under Henry VIII the modernisation of the walls included the construction of new towers from which artillery could be deployed. Under Edward VI and again following the death of the Catholic Mary in 1558, the works were radically extended. Massive new building produced the high walls and corner bastions that survive today. These bastions supported gun platforms which provided covering fire for all points along the walls, and advanced artillery positions. Such designs were quite common on the continent but virtually unique (certainly in masonry) in England. During the Civil War, higher earthwork ramparts were built on top of the bastions but, as elsewhere in England, Civil War fortifications were of earth, turf and timber, leaving earlier walls and defences largely intact.

While Berwick's experience was clearly unique, it is not easy to identify 'typical' urban developments, because the fortunes of English towns were so diverse. At any given moment some towns were growing and others declining, for a wide variety of reasons.[33] Provided that this diversity is borne in mind, some general trends can be distinguished among the variety of particular urban

71 Berwick-upon-Tweed, Northumberland. By the sixteenth century, many English towns retained their medieval city walls, but their function became symbolic rather than military as weapons technology became more powerful and sophisticated. The only clear example surviving in England to rival fortifications constructed in less peaceful parts of the European continent is at Berwick, in its rather special situation of vulnerability to attack by the Scots, at least up to the unification of 1603.

histories. In the sixteenth century, most towns seem to have been relatively slow to share in economic and demographic expansion. Only after 1550 are there clear signs of urban economic vitality. Often, though, this was short-lived, with many towns struggling to cope with urban poverty and vagrancy by the 1590s (although it was perfectly possible for substantial private wealth and corporate poverty to coexist). The growth of urban populations can be approximately quantified as in the table below.

Distribution of English population (in thousands)*

	c.1520	*c.1600*	*c.1700*
London	55	200	575
Other major towns	122	165	275
Small markets & rural	2,223	3,745	4,210

*Taken from Wrigley 1984. In the absence of reliable population counts, they remain approximate.

146

In the sixteenth century the populations of the major towns (here defined as those whose populations exceeded 5,000 at some point during the period), failed to keep pace with national growth, and the overall increase in the proportion of population living in towns was due to London's rapid growth. In the seventeenth century, very different demographic circumstances prevailed in which population rose by less than a quarter in the century as a whole, and actually fell during the third quarter. Urban growth, however, continued apace. By 1700, London's dominance was unprecedented and the capital contained nearly one-eighth of English population.[34] But especially after 1670, other towns were also growing vigorously. New names on the urban map included Birmingham, Manchester, Liverpool and Leeds, reflecting the industrial developments in their respective hinterlands.[35] Contemporaries were acutely aware of this urban growth, especially in the case of London. In 1682, for example, the political arithmetician, Sir William Petty calculated that by *c.*1800 English population would have reached an equilibrium level of about 8 million, with half of these living in London. At this point, he averred, the higher death rates in the capital would exactly cancel out the surplus rural population migrating to London.[36]

London's role as a seemingly insatiable market for food, fuel and manufactures has been extensively discussed, but the many smaller towns – albeit on a smaller scale – were also important foci for marketing, migration and cultural pursuits. From the late seventeenth century in particular, provincial towns were pivotal in the development of a more culturally integrated nation, at least among 'polite' society.[37] This was true even of such small centres as Stamford in Lincolnshire (photo 72).

Stamford had long since declined from its medieval eminence based on religious institutions and an international centre for the cloth trade. Like nearby Boston, Grantham, Gainsborough and Louth, a revival in urban fortunes was slow to appear, and its population as late as the 1660s was well under 2,000. Between then and *c.*1700 however, the town's population grew by more than 50 per cent. There are two reasons for this. First, after decades of ineffectual planning, the river Welland was made navigable during the 1660s, which greatly facilitated the development of the malting industry, though the relationship between the navigation and malting was no doubt a two-way one, as in the earlier case of the Lea navigation in Hertfordshire. Hitherto, Stamford – though well-situated on the London highway – had been relatively unimportant beyond local markets. In addition improvements in overland transport and the growing volume of internal trade enabled the growth of victualling and innkeeping on a large scale. Defoe, for example, remarks on 'the abundance of very good inns, some of them fit to entertain persons of the greatest quality.'

The second element in Stamford's vigorous growth is largely cultural, though it had some important economic consequences, and epitomises wider developments in English urban society. New institutions and new amenities resulted in a very different type of town, and a very different urban landscape, though their creation ultimately depended on the new sources of wealth described above. The prosperity of trade stimulated the construction of public buildings and amenities, including assembly rooms, a library, a theatre, and a horse racing ground, as well as several large inns and many private houses. The latter in particular were

72 Stamford, Lincolnshire. Stamford exemplifies developments taking place very widely across the British urban hierarchy after 1660, with secular public buildings, private houses, inns, exchanges, and places of entertainment and recreation, coming to assume much greater importance in urban life.

increasingly being self-consciously designed, rather than merely 'built'. Some designing was prescribed, for example by building regulations which, after 1675, required new town houses to be slated or tiled instead of thatched, but much resulted from the diffusion of ideas derived from classical architecture. These replaced essentially localised vernacular styles and have been interpreted as the deliberate use of aesthetics to indicate social status.[38] By making appearance as important as function in design, buildings became increasingly intellectual in two ways. First, they consciously expressed aesthetic values which demonstrated participation in elite culture rather than provincialism, and secondly, they were the product of knowledge about theoretical rules governing proportion and other aspects of design. They thus provided an integrating cultural force at a national scale, at least for the upper levels of society. Parallel trends have been identified in a number of other areas of society: notably in leisure and the arts, education, and literary and political discussion. In all these areas the towns – even towns as small as Stamford – played a pivotal role.[39]

DIVERGENT REGIONAL EXPERIENCES

Several detailed studies have revealed the diversity of regional economic and social developments found even between neighbouring areas. In Cambridgeshire, for example, Margaret Spufford has demonstrated the contrasting fortunes of fen-edge, clayland and chalkland parishes.[40] In the clayland parish of Orwell (photo 73), population stagnated through the sixteenth century as most of the natural increase in population migrated out of the parish. The local economy was dominated by agriculture, and by the emergence of a small number of large commercial

73 Orwell, Cambridgeshire. In this clayland parish in southern Cambridgeshire, local economy and society continued to be dominated by a relatively small number of large farmers, who were able to keep their landholdings intact, or even growing.

farms in the late sixteenth and early seventeenth century. In this setting, access to land was restricted, and alternative livelihoods scarce. The situation in the fen-edge parish of Willingham (photo 74) could hardly have been more different. Here, the wide range of fen resources accommodated a large and growing number of small landholders, some of whom attained considerable prosperity on holdings that would have been too small to be viable in Orwell or Chippenham.

In Warwickshire, Skipp and Husbands have traced the economic divergence of different parts of the county in the early seventeenth century. In parishes in the Arden area to the south-east of Birmingham (photo 75), Skipp discovered a considerable shift in local economies towards cheaper grains, dairying and other pastoral husbandry, and industrial occupations in the wake of a series of harvest crises and food shortages in the 1610s.[41] He interpreted these developments as a 'positive response' to the chronic population–resource imbalance that had brought about the series of harvest failures and demographic setbacks. A few miles to the north-east (photo 76), the area around Nuneaton responded to similar demographic trends by moving in the opposite agrarian direction.[42] Here, there was a shift from a primarily stock-fattening economy to one geared to dairy produce and arable. Several contemporaries noted the shift towards arable production here. Blith in 1632 describes the expansion of crops to areas formerly dominated by livestock, and in the 1660s Gibson highlights the area's corn exports.

74 Willingham, Cambridgeshire. At Willingham, the diversity of resources around the fen-edge, and the near-absence of controls on immigrants resulted in rapid population growth through the sixteenth and seventeenth centuries. Smallholdings proliferated, producing a very different landscape from the large fields of Orwell. Whilst the fragmentation of plots in the late-twentieth-century landscape reflects market gardening, the general contrast between the appearance of these two areas only a few miles apart captures something of the long-term contrast between two very different ecological and socio-economic settings.

75 District of Knowle, Warwickshire. In the West Midlands, the growing integration of the English space-economy, and population growth, placed strains on local farming economies. One 'positive' pattern of response, to use Skipp's terminology, was to shift production to cheaper grains affordable by local populations, and to intensify small-scale labour-intensive employment: dairying, fattening, and industrial pursuits, especially metalworking.

76 District of Nuneaton, Warwickshire. The districts east of Birmingham were adopting an increasingly arable farming pattern. To some extent, these should be seen as complementary to the industrial districts, since by providing surplus food they released a constraint on the development of specialised industrial communities. The landscape here became substantially less-wooded during the first half of the seventeenth century, a characteristic it retains today.

Finally, many peripheral areas of Britain lay outside these various 'positive responses'. Society in the highlands and islands of Scotland, for example, was sinking into overpopulation (photo 77).[43] The combination of seemingly inexorable population growth and very limited arable resources posed deep structural problems. Settlement pushed into increasingly inhospitable settings. Holdings became fragmented, often through complicated chains of sub-letting, and in many areas scarce food was not so much an occasional hazard as a regular occurrence. With subsistence the major pre-occupation, few specialist craftsmen and tradesmen, and conservative agricultural practices through necessity, even small increases in exactions from outside local social systems could be impossible to meet, or liable to have a disastrously destabilising effect.

77 Two miles south of Port Ellen, Isle of Islay. The outward expansion of existing settlement into the surrounding waste, at both large and small scale, was the major feature in medieval and early-modern Scottish landscape change. However, on more ecologically-marginal land, only small amounts of arable cultivation were pursued, with the main emphasis on low-intensity grazing.

FURTHER READING

R. A. Dodgshon and R. A. Butlin (eds.), *An Historical Geography of England and Wales*, 2nd edn, London, 1990.

J. Thirsk, *The Rural Economy of England: Collected Essays*, London, 1984.

M. Girouard, *The English Town*, New Haven and London, 1990.

A. Everitt, 'Country, county and town: patterns of regional evolution in England', *Transactions of the Royal Historical Society*, 5th series, 29 (1979), pp. 79–108.

P. Hudson (ed.), *Regions and Industries: Perspectives on the Industrial Revolution in Britain*, Cambridge, 1989.

6 Georgian Britain: *c.*1714–1837

On 4 October 1784 James Sadler, a pioneer of British aeronautics, made an early morning ascent in a balloon (using the French Montgolfier method of heating the air by means of a stove in the gondola) from the physic garden in Oxford, and travelled a distance of six miles northwards to Islip before landing. He repeated the experience, this time with a hydrogen-filled balloon and in the direction of Aylesbury, on 12 November. These were probably the earliest occasions on which the landscape of a small area of Georgian Britain had actually been viewed from the air.[1] The view from a balloon, or the 'bird's-eye' view soon to be popular with cartographers, particularly in their representations of towns and cities, afforded a somewhat different perspective of a familiar, and normally highly parochial, landscape matrix: for the most part rural in aspect, though in certain places containing clear evidence of new urban and industrial growth, and a landscape which contained a regionally varied mixture of long-settled and managed agricultural land and newly 'manicured' landscaped estates, reflecting changing fashions of landscape taste and perception.

The recovery of an aerial perspective of Georgian Britain from the rare experiences of contemporary balloonists is, of course, nigh impossible, but the perspectives afforded by aerial photographs of the twentieth century are none the less invaluable for the extra dimension which they add to our understanding of the spatial and landscape perspectives of Georgian Britain, not the least to our knowledge of the way in which landscape modifications were planned by the rural and urban proprietors of the time. This advantage applies not simply to what might be termed the obvious material alterations to landscape, but also to the deeper structures, feelings, agencies and processes of which they are profoundly symbolic, including the progressive march of capitalist relations, the emergence of a class structure, the influences of growing concerns with property and property-rights (and their appropriation), and the changing bases of culture and taste. While the obvious direction to follow is essentially that of the changing fashion of landscape taste and the indicators of the social, cultural, economic, and material preferences and tendencies of the property-owning classes, what might be regarded as the other (or as it has been termed the 'dark') side of the landscape must not be forgotten, even though it has left far less overt landscape evidence, directly or in the form of paintings, for example. This other side of the landscape is that which symbolises the life-experiences of those who, during the course of the major transformations that took place in the eighteenth and early nineteenth centuries in the ownership, use- and access- rights of land, found themselves the casualties of a system of resource appropriation and allocation which tore them from their agrarian roots and rights and transformed them into an agricultural or an urban/industrial labour force, subject to the whims and vicissitudes of entrepreneurs and markets.

However characterised, Georgian Britain was at once a stable and rapidly changing entity, both politically and economically. Survivals from an essentially medieval economy and society were still marked on the landscape in the form of the communal arable management systems of the open fields of much of lowland England, Wales and Scotland, yet forces of change were at work during the course of the eighteenth century to effect major transformations of rural economy and landscape, principally though not entirely through the Parliamentary Enclosure movement in England and Wales and through more unilateral actions in Scotland. One of the reasons why such a transformation was possible was the relative political stability of Britain during the period whose end dates are marked by the change of monarchy from the House of Stuart to the House of Hanover, and which, more precisely, stretches from 1 August 1714, with the accession of George I to the throne, to 20 June 1837 with the death of William IV, and the beginning of the Victorian era.

By the time of the accession of George I, an important feature of British life was the existence and acceptance, thanks to the Revolution of 1688 and its aftermath, of a parliamentary monarchy, with the will of the nation expressed through parliament (dominated by land-owners). A social structure and hierarchy evolved whose hegemony represented an increasing accommodation between old-established estate-owning magnates and the rising entrepreneurs of the new capitalism, located in an economic context of expanding trade and increasing productivity, both normally sufficient to withstand the strains of localised disorders and protests. 'Improvement' became a key word in both economic and cultural contexts. Money was easily borrowable by governments seeking to finance a wide range of enterprises, including colonies and wars, while the inequitable distribution of wealth and the abuse of privilege, especially by government ministers, was partly accommodated by a powerful range of weapons of satire and by the increase in social mobility.

It is against this background of an increasingly confident and all-pervading nascent capitalism with its attendant social structures and relations of production that some of the major changes and features of landscape can be viewed. It must not be assumed, however, that the changes experienced in Georgian Britain everywhere took place at similar pace, nor that all the changes themselves were necessarily ubiquitous. In addition to the obvious and substantial variety of geographical conditions, both physical and social, there were great variations in political and cultural customs, traditions and inclinations, which conditioned the effects of the increasing range of innovative social and economic processes. To speak of 'Georgian Britain' is no more than a somewhat futile attempt to convey a geographical and historical fact, for it might well be imagined that the concept of 'Britain' meant very little to the majority of the populace, whose social and geographical horizons were more likely to be those of the parish or county boundary than the shores of this island itself. Some admittedly migrated to London as domestic servants and apprentices, some joined the army and the navy and saw service overseas, and a relatively small number of the populace actually emigrated to the colonies. The majority of the populace, however, did not, and although there were many local 'movers', the distances moved were short. Local customs of language dialect, feast-days, recreation and superstition were preserved into the nineteenth century, and these local and regional characteristics were in some senses enhanced by the difficulties of long-distance communication. There remained, however, at least outside the Gaelic and Welsh-speaking areas, a common language, a common system of law, and an increasing degree of economic integration, the primary forces being London as an engine of economic growth, and an increasing engagement with international market forces, both having strong influence for example on the price of grain and of industrial products. In essence, the period under consideration was in every sense a period of transition from early capitalism (with some remaining elements of late feudalism) to industrial capitalism, and the changing landscape in both positive and negative aspects reflects this very clearly. An important indicator of change was the increase in population which took place during the period under consideration.

Overall, the general sequence of population change in England was one of slow increase from the 1730s, from a base of about 5.2 million, which by 1751 had reached about 5.6 million. Thereafter, more rapid rates of increase were experienced. By 1801 the figure had reached 8.3 million, and by 1851 16.7 million. The rates of increase for each half-century are revealing: 5.2 per cent for 1700–51, 32.6 per cent for 1751–1801, and 110 per cent for 1801–51. Regional experiences of population growth differed: the highest rates in the second half of the eighteenth century were those of the North-West and of industrial Yorkshire, but during the first half of the nineteenth century expansion rates elsewhere, notably in the Midlands and the South-East, began to catch up. The population of Scotland, estimated at 6.9 million for 1701, rose to about 7.4 million in 1751, 10.5 million in 1801 and 20.8 million by 1851. The rates of increase were: 20.7 per cent for 1701–51, 27.1 per cent for 1751–1801, and 79.6 per cent for 1801–51. The corresponding figures for Wales are: 413,000 for 1701, 449,000 for 1751, 588,000 for 1801, and 1.1 million for 1851. The rates of increase were: 8.7 per cent for 1701–51, 34.9 per cent for 1751–1801, 98 per cent for 1801–51.[2]

THE CHANGING RURAL LANDSCAPE

The period from the late eighteenth to the early nineteenth century has frequently been characterised as an age of 'improvement', this word carrying the strong connotation of deliberate attempts, based on a forward-looking progressive type of entrepreneurial activity, to make better and more rational use of natural resources and of the power of labour (and later of machines). Such a 'linear' and 'progressive' view of the nature of social and economic development at the time can, notwithstanding its association with a period of Whig government (and a 'Whiggish' interpretation of history), overstate only one of several possible perspectives on the nature of change, and overemphasise not only the influence of 'heroic' individual entrepreneurs but also the perspective of those who owned land and land-use rights and whose parliamentary and legal influence enabled them to initiate change to their own advantage and often to the disadvantage of others. Much evidence of this sense of 'improvement' comes with the spate of agricultural treatises towards the end of the eighteenth century, especially the

General Views of agriculture in individual counties of England, Wales and Scotland which were produced for the Board of Agriculture. John Barrell has shown, in his study of changing literary notions of landscape of the time,[3] that the prevailing attitude to land and its improvement in such works was that of a rural professional class (of surveyors, commentators, and farmers), and that one of the characteristics of their general perspective was that enclosed rather than open-field landscapes were eminently more satifactory from both an aesthetic and functional point of view: an organised landscape was to be preferred to a wild, untamed landscape, though this moral order preference did pose some problems for the agricultural writers who had discovered the Picturesque.

Enclosure of open fields and commons had been a long-continuing process in England, Scotland and Wales, and there were many areas where enclosed fields had in all probability been the original basis of farming. The former widespread existence of open field farming systems in many parts of Britain is now a well-established fact, and a few examples of this ancient practice remain, including Laxton in Nottinghamshire. Laxton is in east Nottinghamshire, some 30 km north-east of Nottingham (photo 78). It lies on a sloping plateau of Keuper Marl, and comprises some 4,000 acres of relatively heavy but productive soil. Laxton is mentioned in Domesday Book, and by the twelfth century is known to have had at least two open fields, Mill Field and West Field, to which a third (South Field) was later added. There was also, until its enclosure in the present century, a fourth field, East Field, which may have acted as a separate unit in the past, but which by the middle of the seventeenth century was managed as a unit with the West Field. A survey of 1635 illustrates a vast complex of open arable fields, meadow and pasture land, already bearing some of the marks of agricultural change, including closes within the open fields and also areas of grassland, indicating the advent of a newer ley grass husbandry within an essentially medieval system. The major part of the open fields was subdivided into strips and bundles of strips (furlongs) demarcated by balks and headlands, and the land of individual farmers was scattered between the different fields. The cropping scheme was a three-course rotation. Although, unlike many open-field parishes in the East Midlands, Laxton was never totally enclosed, the process of consolidation of holdings over a long period of time and more restricted attempts at partial enclosure have effected changes in the layout of the fields. This is particularly true at the end of the nineteenth century, when almost all the estate passed into the hands of Earl Manvers, and much consolidation took place. Though enclosure was considered, its potential profitability was thought to be too low. A major reorganisation took place in the period 1903–13, with the East Field and areas of each of the other three common fields being enclosed. The management of the cropping of the communal lands and their use for grazing continues to be the responsibility of the Court Leet. In 1952 the estate was purchased by the Ministry of Agriculture, and in 1981 was bought by the Crown Estate Commissioners, who undertook to continue the traditional system of cultivation.

The essential elements of the open fields were the open arable fields themselves, of varying size from perhaps 200 acres or more in the lowland areas to perhaps 50 or fewer in upland areas. The fields were subdivided into physical and tenurial strips, bundles of strips being given different names in different

parts of the island, such as furlong, or shott. The holdings within the open fields of the members of the farming community were generally widely scattered, and in some instances periodically reallocated by lot. The rotations associated with them varied very widely, but generally incorporated a period of fallow of one of the fields. Rights of grazing over the fallow and the cropped fields also varied, including jealously guarded rights of fold-course for sheep, especially important in East Anglia. The open arable fields, which were fenced off at times when crops were growing, formed part of a wider complex of land use, which included meadow and superior pasture land, and poorer quality 'waste' land, together in many cases with woodland and other types of common land, including turbaries. Most open field communities also had areas of enclosed land within their boundaries.

ENCLOSURE

The process of the consolidation and enclosure of the scattered holdings within the open arable fields and the enclosure and sub-division into smaller holdings of large areas of common pasture and waste had accelerated during the course of the late sixteenth and the seventeenth centuries, generally by means of a process called enclosure by agreement, and there is some claim that the extent of enclosure in England in that period actually exceeded in area enclosed the amount of land enclosed in the eighteenth and nineteenth centuries by the process known as Parliamentary Enclosure. Parliamentary Enclosure was largely confined to England and to the southern parts of Wales. The appropriation of rights of common use and access to land in Scotland generally followed a different form and a different chronology.

From the middle of the eighteenth century, however, the main means of enclosure – that is, the appropriation of use-rights of land to individuals and the physical and permanent demarcation of that land by fences, hedges, ditches and walls – was generally effected by private act of Parliament and implemented by a group of enclosure commissioners locally appointed for the purpose. The employment of parliamentary acts reflects in part the increasing control and influence of the landed classes in Parliament, and their desire to use parliamentary enactments to remove the legal powers of the common law and the law of equity which hitherto dominated the management and regulation of common land. There was a gradual acceleration, and later a peaking, of the use of Acts of Enclosure during the course of the eighteenth and the early nineteenth centuries. In England there were 78 enclosure acts in the first half of the century to 1750 and a further 1,992 acts by the end of the century. The period from 1800–39 witnessed 2,000 enclosure acts, some under the more general authority of the General Enclosure Act of 1836.

The periodicity of waves of enclosure and the historical geography of the types of areas enclosed is an important matter. In general terms two main peaks of enclosure have been identified in the period under consideration, the first from 1755 to 1780, the second from 1790 to 1835.[4] The first wave mainly affected the heavy clay lands of the Midlands and the lighter clays of east Yorkshire and of Lincolnshire. The second wave was also influential on the remaining clays

78 South Field, Laxton, Nottinghamshire. Laxton is one of the few remaining examples in England of the formerly widespread open-field system, and has three open fields, South Field, West Field and Mill Field. The open fields have been modified by consolidation of the formerly widely scattered strips and by enclosure in the past. South Field was affected by consolidation of holdings and by a partial enclosure in 1905. At the bottom of the picture, to the left of the farmstead, is the remnant of East Moor Common and between it and the common field is an area of common grassland or 'syke', the Whitemoor Syke. The shape of the furlongs are indicative of the effects of traditional ploughing (aratral, reversed-S shaped curves). Near the centre of the photograph is a hedged enclosure.

79 Parliamentary enclosures and relict features of ridge-and-furrow ploughing north-east of Padbury, Buckinghamshire. The village of Padbury had three open fields before enclosure: Hedge Field (lower half of photograph), East Field (left centre), and West Field beyond the village. The pre-enclosure strips are marked by the patterns of ridge-and-furrow, which discordantly underlie the later field boundaries produced by the enclosure surveyors in 1796, implementing the enclosure act of 1795. Before enclosure almost all of the land in the parish was under arable. The new lines of parliamentary enclosure include the two roads in the foreground, which replaced older access ways, some reduced to footpaths and some stopped off altogether by enclosure.

of these regions, but to which were added the lighter lands of East Anglia, east Yorkshire, and Lincolnshire, the light-land heaths of the south of England and many of the marginal lands of the Pennines. A sub-division into enclosure of arable and other types of land is not easy, but the general difference is that about twice the amount of arable land was enclosed than other types of common land and waste, and that the main period of enclosure of wasteland (comprising in total about one-fifth of the total area of England at the beginning of the eighteenth century) came in the late eighteenth and early nineteenth century, especially during the French wars when much marginal land was used for the growing of cereals, though some of the more remote upland wastes awaited the cheaper enclosure method provided by the later General Enclosure Acts. In all it has been estimated that in the period 1730–1884, there were 3,093 enclosure acts primarily concerned with open-field arable, affecting 4.5 million acres, and 2,172 acts primarily concerned with common and waste land, affecting 2.3 million acres.

An interesting example of parliamentary enclosure and its effect on the changing rural landscape is provided by the parish of Padbury, in Buckinghamshire (photo 79). This was a community which the records show as having had three common arable fields. A survey of 1591 shows that to the two older arable fields, East and West Fields, there had been added by improvement of the waste land of the village a third open field – Hedge Field, to the east of the East Field. The open fields and commons were enclosed by Act of Parliament of 1795, but the ridge-and-furrow patterns of the old system of cultivation are still present in the landscape, and show an interesting and revealing contrast with the newer square and rectangular fields which result from the enclosure survey carried out by Richard Davis and Michael Russell for the enclosure commissioners' award.

The extent and nature of Parliamentary Enclosure in Wales is, not surprisingly, different from that experienced in England. The best estimates[5] indicate a later incidence, with only 12 acts before 1790, a peak during the Napoleonic wars, and a second peak after 1845. The first Enclosure Act was in 1733, with 35,000 acres enclosed before 1793, and 213,000 acres additionally enclosed before the end of the Napoleonic wars in 1815. The counties most affected were those with the largest amounts of unenclosed upland, namely Breconshire, Cardigan, Radnor and Denbigh, the largest single area enclosed being the Great Forest of Brecknock. The main purpose of enclosure in Wales is thought to have been the continuation of improvement of an essentially pastoral economy, in contrast to the enclosures in England which hastened the conversion, especially in the Midlands, from an arable to a mixed farming economy, with strong emphasis on the provision of livestock for the London market. Enclosure in Wales facilitated the use of marginal land at the edge of the upland moors, but also incorporated the reclamation of poorly-drained marshes and river valleys, together with coastal commons and wastes.

The situation in Scotland was different in respect of character and timing, with internal variations between the Highlands and the Lowlands, enclosure coming earlier in the latter. Small-scale enclosure of open fields in the Scottish lowlands, influenced it is thought as much by fashion for landscape design as for more utilitarian motives, had begun in the late seventeenth century, and continued more vigorously in the eighteenth century, possibly (though this is

debated) facilitated by a range of general enabling Enclosure Acts whose purpose included the afforestation of estates, the promotion of animal husbandry, and the removal of the open-field system variant known as run-rig. Parallel developments in the Highlands on the whole come later, with early examples of enclosure for the abolition of run-rig in the south-west Highlands in the late eighteenth century, with afforestation and the aesthetic improvement of landscape being a stronger factor in the later 'improvements' of the eastern and central Highlands. The experience of part of the Highlands was, it must additionally be remembered, conditioned by the context of attempted 'civilisation' of the Gaelic regions which had begun earlier in the eighteenth century and accelerated after 1745, through the means (though not entirely effective) of the 1746 Disarming Act and the 1752 Annexing Act.

80 Deserted crofts, with cultivation ridges, south-west of Balnacoil in Strath Brora, Sutherland. Symbolic of the several phases of depopulation of the Highlands of Scotland in the eighteenth and early nineteenth centuries, Strath Brora, was one of the foci of settlement which was profoundly affected by the major removal or clearance of tenants from the estates of the Marchioness of Sutherland in the first three decades of the nineteenth century, so that the cleared areas could be re-populated with sheep and deer.

The very different legal basis of land law in Scotland makes any attempt at statistical comparison with other parts of Britain almost impossible, but it seems that the general trend in the erosion of common land or commonties was one of high points of enclosure from 1750–80 and in the early nineteenth century.

The effects of enclosure on the landscape of different parts of Britain naturally varied with the nature of the land-use systems involved, the topography and terrain, and the means, motives and agents of enclosure. In the lowland areas, the major effect (in addition to the ubiquitous effect of radically changing ownership of and access to the enclosed land) was and is to be seen in the regular, generally square or rectangular-shaped fields. In the uplands the form of the enclosures was often linear, extending well up the hill slopes. The nature of the boundaries of the new fields varied, but hedges, stone walls, fences and ditches were the most common.

The social consequences of enclosure have been much debated, and views still vary, though it is recognised that some impoverishment was a consequence. In Scotland the social consequences of various types of enclosure had at times more obvious and dramatic consequences, especially as a result of the de-populating 'clearances' in the eighteenth and nineteenth centuries, many of the cleared lands being converted to extensive sheep farms, and the process reflected in the present landscape by the many abandoned settlements whose character-istics are easily seen from the air, as for example in the case of the deserted crofts west of Balnacoil in Strath Brora in Sutherland (photo 80). Strath Brora was affec-ted by the Sutherland clearances of 1819 and 1820 (part of a series of clearances which had begun in the eighteenth century), one purpose of which was to force crofters to migrate to settlements at the coast, such as Brora and Helmsdale, in order to turn the large estates into sheep-farms. In the 1820 clearances some of the Strath Brora tenants had moved to the coast, but many had gone to Caithness for agricultural holdings. The deserted crofts symbolise the new kind of agrarian capitalism, much influenced by the new ideas of the political economists of the late eighteenth century, and also the continuing hardships of those who sought a living in very marginal conditions, even of subsistence, which were frequently exacerbated by crop failure and famine, resulting in starvation and death for the unfortunate and emigration for others.

THE AGRICULTURAL REVOLUTION

The eighteenth and nineteenth centuries witnessed many more changes than those described above, and which, like enclosure, effected major transformations in landscape and in the social relations of production. These are generally charac-terised collectively as 'the agricultural revolution', but the chronology of agri-cultural change is complex and regionally varied, and the term is in some respects therefore unhelpful except as a general indicator of transition and change. The major innovations in agricultural practice are well known, and can only be briefly summarised here. They include the introduction of convertible husbandry, alter-nate husbandry, the incorporation of a range of new crops and grasses, the intro-duction of new types of implements and machinery, and the transformation of the use of labour. Convertible husbandry involved the alternation of grass and arable crops, and the efficiency of this practice, common in clay areas, scarp-and-vale regions and some of the lighter soil areas, was improved by the introduction of such grasses as trefoil, clover, sainfoin and lucerne. These increased the livestock capacity of land by improving the quality of pasture. Alternate hus-bandry involved the cultivation of fodder crops – roots, or in some cases sown grasses – in complex rotations also including cereals. The best known of such rotations was the Norfolk four-course, geared to the lighter soils of East Anglia, but variants evolved on the heavier clay soils of the west and north of England. The best known of the new crops was the turnip, incorporated into the Norfolk rotation early in the eighteenth century, but its use was not widespread until the end of the century, by which time it was in some areas being replaced by the swede.

The diffusion of agricultural innovations in Scotland followed a similar distance-related pattern to that experienced in England. An important centre for innovation was located in Berwick and East Lothian, where the new crops and rotations were to be found in the early eighteenth century, from whence they spread unevenly across the Lowlands and ultimately, by the end of the century to limited parts of the Highlands. In Wales the diffusion of innovations was largely a question of the lowlands, especially the Vale of Glamorgan and south Pembrokeshire (photo 81), having the earliest experiences of clover and other new crops and rotations.

While the major evidence of agricultural change in Georgian Britain is probably the significant increase in productivity, an important contributory factor was the increase in the amount of land for cultivation by means of various kinds of reclamation, including drainage of fens and marshes, and the 'reclamation' of areas of heath and moorland.

Significant attempts to drain the extensive areas of fen and marsh in Britain date back at least to the early middle ages, particularly under the influence of large monastic houses, but the technical means to effect drainage was limited, and was frequently offset by a combination of natural disasters such as sea and river flooding and a human reluctance to maintain drainage channels. During the course of the seventeenth century, however, a number of large-scale drainage schemes were undertaken, particularly for the Fens of Eastern England, by the Dutch engineer Vermuyden, whose basic techniques involved the straightening of slow-moving rivers and the raising of water from low-lying lands to the higher levels of the major rivers and drainage channels using windmills. By the beginning of the eighteenth century, however, areas such as the Fens had partly reverted to their wetland state, and the problem of drainage was not to be substantially solved until the advent of the steam-driven pump in the mid nineteenth century. The landscapes of these wetlands in the eighteenth and early nineteenth centuries, therefore, represent a fluctuating transition between late medieval and modern conditions of land management and agricultural production. On the uplands adjacent to the southern Fenlands, for example, there were still open arable fields in the early nineteenth century. In contrast, the black fens below the villages were the basis for a very different but complementary economy, involving the grazing of cattle, sheep, and horses, the cutting of turf and reeds for fuel and building materials, and fishing and wild-fowling. In the vicinity of Soham and Wicken (photo 82) in north-east Cambridgeshire, for example, there were in the eighteenth and early nineteenth centuries large areas of fen which provide examples of all these activities and of the hazards of living in such an adverse environment. The main means of drainage was the windmill, but there was frequent conflict of interest between those who wished to improve the efficiency of the drainage system and those who were primarily interested in waterways as means of transport. This is only part of a broader problem of administration. As Darby has put it, speaking of the Fenland in the eighteenth century, 'In the post-drainage Fenland, as in the pre-drainage Fenland, there was everywhere a chaos of authorities and an absence of authority. Nature, by many intersecting channels, had made all portions of the Level interdependent; and yet, when the eighteenth century began, a variety of separate interests was still very apparent'.[6] The reduction of scale of the areas for which the major drainage authorities were responsible had some temporary positive effect in the mid eighteenth century,

81 Panorama (of enclosed fields) near Fishguard, Pembrokeshire. The landscape of enclosure shown here is very different from the tidy landscapes of Parliamentary Enclosure. Farms are smaller than in the Englishry – the south of Pembrokeshire – and settlement is mainly in isolated farms or small hamlets. In the seventeenth, eighteenth and early nineteenth centuries, cattle were the mainstay of the farming economy, with barley and oats as the main crops. Enclosure of a spasmodic and irregular kind was underway in this period, and very little land was enclosed by act of parliament in the eighteenth or nineteenth centuries. The irregular size and shape of the enclosed fields thus testifies to a very different process of landscape evolution from that of lowland Wales and England.

with the creation, via acts of parliament, of new drainage districts and sets of commissioners, but in the case of the Fenlands it was not until the nineteenth century that major progress was made.

The nature of wetlands varied, however, both ecologically and geographically, and their history of reclamation also varied. Less continuous areas such as the Lancashire mosses were, for example, recovered on a more spasmodic and localised basis in the eighteenth century.

The reclamation of sandy heathland has on the whole a shorter and later history than that of fens and marshes. What had generally been waste areas occupied by rabbit warrens, for example the sands of north-west Norfolk, were transformed in the eighteenth century into model areas of new farming practice, of which the estate at Holkham is a very well known example. Another large area of sandy wasteland is the extensive area of heathland in Dorset, best known on account of the descriptions of the region in the novels of Thomas Hardy. Heathlands generally did not enjoy what now would be termed a good press, for their unkempt and unimproved appearance, together with their association with highwaymen and other less favourable members of society, including squatters, encouraged their transformation, often by means of parliamentary acts for enclosure of commons, to improved landscapes of trees, clover, and some arable farms. A more extensive erosion of such heaths has, however, been effected by the expansion of urban areas, such as Bournemouth, in the twentieth century, and by forestry plantation, though extensive areas still remain. From Wimborne Minster, on the River Stour, the view towards Bournemouth as seen on an air photograph shows the extent of Canford heath (photo 83).

82 Wicken and Soham, Cambridgeshire. This photograph shows part of the region of the southern Fenland known as the fen-edge; the point where the chalk and clay uplands meet the low-lying peat fens. The bottom half of the picture is largely fenland in the parish of Wicken (the village is at right centre). The extensive area of scrub-covered land in the lower centre is Wicken Sedge Fen, whose right-hand border is the old drainage and waterway channel, Wicken Lode. Wicken Fen is an area partly drained in the major Fenland drainage scheme in the late seventeenth century, but extensively used for the harvesting of sedge (*Cladium mariscus*) and, at its margins for the cutting of peat, through the eighteenth and nineteenth centuries. Wicken was enclosed in 1840. The adjacent area of Burwell was effectively drained in the eighteenth and nineteenth centuries. The oval area towards the top of the picture is Soham Mere, a former lake which was not drained until the late seventeenth century, and whose calcareous soils give it a distinct colour. At the top of the picture, to the left of the town of Soham, is a surviving open field – North Field – now farmed in severalty, but unfenced. Wicken Fen is now preserved as a nature reserve by the National Trust.

83 Heathland, near Wimborne Minster, Dorset. Canford Heath is one of the surviving portions of what was formerly a much larger area of heathland in South Central England, being very rapidly eroded by suburban growth in the twentieth century. Daniel Defoe, travelling from the town of Wimborne Minster to Poole in the 1720s described the area in between as 'a sandy, wild, and barren country'. This area, in contrast to the Norfolk and Suffolk light soil areas, underwent very little improvement in the eighteenth century.

Another major form of land reclamation was that of the ploughing up of marginal upland at times of increased demand for agricultural produce and of high prices. This was a characteristic of Scotland, Wales, and England in the late eighteenth and early nineteenth centuries, especially at the time of the Napoleonic wars. Cultivation margins had advanced and retreated in Britain over a much longer period of time. It has been suggested by Parry, for example, that in the English uplands there was uncoordinated advance to higher margins from 1550 to 1780, with more rapid extension of cultivation through parliamentary enclosure and the Napoleonic wars. Wales had a similar experience, and Scotland, having had a major early medieval advance and late medieval retreat, experienced another major advance of upland 'reclamation' in the eighteenth and nineteenth centuries, but much of it on land that had previously been cultivated and then abandoned.[7]

DESIGNED LANDSCAPES OF THE EIGHTEENTH AND EARLY NINETEENTH CENTURIES

While the landscapes resulting from enclosure symbolised a new relationship between people and land, their regular layout and pattern indicated more the land surveyor's art than specific landscape tastes. A very important and eminently observable feature of this period, however, was the change in landscape taste reflected in the design and layout of country houses and the parkland and estate land by which they were surrounded. The idea of landscape as a concept dated in Britain from the late sixteenth and early seventeenth centuries, and derived from the influences of the late Renaissance Italian architect Andrea Palladio as interpreted by the English architect Inigo Jones. The period from *c.*1710–1750 is in Britain the period of the Palladian movement, comprising a productive amalgam of landed capital and a particular kind of landscape taste and preference. The second generation of the Whig aristocracy, having rejected the architectural forms and emblems favoured by the Stuarts, embraced a nascent philosophy which, according to Summerson, 'was extremly propitious to a thesis which embraced, at one and the same time, a devotion to antiquity, a flexibility authorised jointly by Palladio and common sense, and a strong national loyalty in the figure of Inigo Jones'.[8]

The outcome was an intense submission to this new 'rule of taste', and the transformation of both rural and urban landscapes into forms and shapes that still dominate many parts of Britain to the present day. The carefully manicured rural landscapes involved an harmonious combination of the new Palladian architecture of the major country houses and the designed landscape gardens which surrounded them. The essence of these designs was a combination of the classical architecture of Greek and Roman antiquity through the perceptions of Vitruvius and the later interpretations of Palladio (the first English translation of whose *Four Books of Architecture* was published in 1715) and of the Scottish architect Colen Campbell, who published a volume of engravings (the first of three) of classical buildings in Britain, *Vitruvius Britannicus*, also in 1715. Campbell set a tone and style for the period with his designs for such houses as Wanstead House in Essex (1713–20), Houghton Hall in Norfolk (1721), built for Sir Robert

Walpole, and Stourhead in Wiltshire (1722), with bold classical porticos based on Campbell's interpretation of Palladian villas and a low, horizontal profile.

Another important figure at this time was Richard Boyle, Earl of Cork and Earl of Burlington, who had in 1719 solicited Campbell's help in the completion of the redesign, in a Palladian villa style, of his house, Burlington House, at Piccadilly in London. Burlington was a wealthy patron and architect who had studied Palladio's work at first hand in Vicenza, and who built a major Palladian villa for himself at Chiswick (1723–9). He had a close association with the painter William Kent, who initially assisted in the compilation and publication of collections of architectural drawings, but who also from the 1730s onwards began to design houses himself. One of Kent's most famous designs is that for Holkham Hall in North Norfolk (photo 84), conceived about 1725 and begun in 1734, for a patron, Thomas Coke (who later became the first Earl of Leicester), who had undertaken a Grand Tour in Europe between 1712 and 1718. The financing of the house itself was a problem, as Coke was in a difficult financial position after the bursting of the South Sea Company's heavy investment 'bubble', but a rise in the income from the Holkham estate and from some non-agricultural sources facilitated its initiation. Coke, on his Grand Tour, had first met William Kent in Rome in 1714, and after a long period of planning, the house and landscaped estate were built and created in the period from 1734 to 1765. The first Earl died in 1759. The second Earl of Leicester was the agricultural innovator known as 'Coke of Norfolk', who improved the estates and continued the building of the house. Holkham Hall itself shows strong influence of Burlington's preferred Palladian designs, including that of his Chiswick villa, and incorporates a central block with classical portico, with four wings or pavilions (kitchen, chapel, library, and guest wings), a palatial interior and a superb alabaster entrance hall, the Stone Hall. The house was built of light grey brick. The grounds and park were designed by Lancelot ('Capability') Brown in 1762. The grounds include a large lake to the west of the hall, an obelisk and temple.

The design of the landscape at Holkham indicates a change in landscape taste reflecting a change in ideology, from that in which houses and formal gardens symbolised the (mercantilist) state within an estate to one in which, as Cosgrove has put it 'The palladian country house and its enclosed parkland of sweeping lawns, artistically-grouped trees and serpentine lakes offers a synthesis of motifs owing their origins to a range of sources: late renaissance Italy, classical humanism, the literary pastoral and the seventeenth-century French painters in Rome... From a rather different perspective they represent the victory of a new concept of landownership, best identified by that favourite eighteenth-century word, *property*.'[9]

Landscape gardening is an interesting phenomenon of seventeenth-eighteenth- and nineteenth-century Britain. Formality of gardens and landscape design was characteristic of the seventeenth century, but changed in the eighteenth to a less formal concept associated with the notion of a series of picturesque perspectives and views. Thus the landscapes designed by William Kent bore close resemblance to those to be seen in the classical landscape paintings of the French painter Claude. Large acreages were planted with trees and adorned with temples, seats and urns, and large serpentine lakes and broad lawns were

84 (a) Holkham Hall, Norfolk. A well-known and splendid example of a Palladian house in a country estate, designed for Thomas Coke by William Kent, and begun in 1734. The hall is on the left of the group of buildings seen in the photograph, and comprises a central section with four wings attached. The central section includes the magnificent entrance hall, a state bedroom, a saloon, drawing room, gallery and two courts. The two wings to the rear are the Chapel Wing (nearest the lake) and the Library Wing, and those at the front the Kitchen Wing (nearest the lake) and the Guest Wing. The lake is part of the landscape gardening effected by Capability Brown in 1762.

(b) Holkham Park, Norfolk. The broader local context of the hall is seen in this view, including the north Norfolk coastline. This region of light soil was transformed by the new farming techniques and crops of the eighteenth century, popularised in this region by Thomas Coke. What had formerly been extensive areas of heath and warren became intensively cultivated agricultural land. The improvement of the eighteenth century was also registered in the landscape by the building of Palladian villas such as Holkham Hall and the landscaping of the estates of which they were the focus. The landscaping of the Holkham estate by Capability Brown is well registered in the photograph, including the long straight road to the hall from the south and the arrangement of the trees.

created. Capability Brown's designs were on a grander scale than those of Kent, and paid particular attention to contrasts of style and colour.

At Stourhead in Wiltshire there is a particularly fine example of a Palladian villa and a mid-eighteenth-century landscape garden. The estate was acquired in 1720 by Henry Hoare, who commissioned a design for a villa from Colen Campbell which was based on a Palladio-designed villa at Fanzolo in Italy. The villa was completed in 1722. Of equal importance, however, is the remarkable landscape garden, created at Stourhead by Hoare between 1741 and 1783. The central feature of the landscape is the serpentine lake surrounded by hills planted with beeches and conifers. The circumference of the lake contains a number of classical buildings and features, including a Temple of Flora, a Temple of the Sun, and a Pantheon, and the whole landscape is an example of Palladian rural gardening, reflecting both ancient classical and gothic styles.

Humphrey Repton, a landscape gardener of the later eighteenth and early nineteenth centuries, reflected a change in the understanding of the term 'picturesque', as exemplified in the writings of William Gilpin, and turned to a rougher and more rugged style of landscape. The combined effect of the work of such architects as Campbell, Burlington, Kent, and landscape gardeners such as Brown and Repton was an extensive and large-scale transformation of the face of many parts of rural Britain.

URBAN PLANNING

The Palladian influence extended also to the towns and cities of eighteenth-century Britain, and variations of the Classical mode of building design were extensively incorporated into many of the major planning schemes for new towns or for parts of existing towns and cities. The most famous work is that of the Wood brothers in Bath, Sir Robert Taylor and James Paine in London, of John Carr in York, and Craig, Adam, Reid, Sibbald and Graham in Edinburgh. Wood the Elder began work in Bath with the design of Queen Square in 1729, and the Circus in 1754, and Wood the Younger's impact is to be seen in the Royal Crescent,

built in the 1760s, and the New Assembly Rooms. In the second half of the eighteenth century, the major influences in classical style urban design and construction were James Stuart, Sir William Chambers, and Robert Adam. Their best-known works include Chambers' layout for Kew Gardens (1757–63) and Somerset House (1777–96) and Adam's Syon House (1762–9) and Kedleston Hall (1760s). Those who incorporated the Picturesque into their architecture included Sir John Soane, George Dance and John Nash, prime examples of whose work include Dance's Newgate Prison (1768–80). Soane's town house in Lincoln's Inn Fields (1792–1824) and Nash's Regent's Park (1811–13).

The two major types of urban development in the eighteenth century were the expansion and redevelopment of existing urban centres and – less frequently – the building of new towns. An interesting example of the combination, in a sense, of both types was the New Town of Edinburgh.

The new prosperity of the eighteenth century was not simply an English one. The New Town of Edinburgh, initiated by the arrangement of a competition in 1767 for its design by the Provost and motivated by a perceived need for them to emulate the developments in London, was sited to the north of the Old Town and laid out in a variant of a grid plan (photo 85). The site and the form, according to Reed, 'combine in an unambiguous and dramatic declaration of a new status for the Scottish capital and of new possibilities for a future based upon the prosperity of the bourgeoisie'.[10] The competition was won by James Craig, and his design for the new town involved the geometric layout of a series of squares and streets to the north of Castle Rock and its related glacial ridge, the pattern of the town being related to three east-west principal streets, Prince's Street, George Street and Queen Street. The main street was George Street, at each end of which there was to be a large square (St Andrew's in the east and St George's in the west). By 1790 Craig's plan was almost completed, with the exception of the large square at the western end of the New Town, the delay for the building of which was conditioned by difficulties presented by the neighbouring landowner. When this difficulty was resolved, the town council contracted Robert Adam to design the square, renamed Charlotte Square (1791), the building of which was not in fact finally completed until 1820, but which remains one of the finest and most elegant Georgian squares in Britain.

The main function of the New Town was residential, and part of the intention to offer a more spacious and gracious mode of living than that of the medieval Old Town. The scale of construction meant that much of the building was speculative, with investment recouped and profits made through sub-leasing or tenancy. The first two phases of development were largely completed by the end of the eighteenth century, and were followed by three further phases involving different styles. The third phase, which takes us to the end of the period covered by this essay, was influenced by the rapid growth of the city's population in the late eighteenth and early nineteenth centuries, and involved the work of Reid, Sibbald, and Graham, and the building of a second new town extending north beyond the first, together with Graham's plans for the property of the Earl of Moray, including Moray Place, similar to the design for the Crescent at Bath.

A very different development, and one which reflects a well-known phenomenon of social life in England in the eighteenth century – the spa town –

85 Edinburgh, Midlothian. The contrast between old Edinburgh and the New Town of the eighteenth and nineteenth century is very clear in this view. The New Town was developed on lands which first had to be drained – the former Nor' Loch, the draining beginning in 1759. The first major design for the New Town was that of James Craig in 1767, and his plan involved the geometric grid-plan layout, with three main streets as east-west axes. These streets, which run across the centre of the photograph (left-right) are Princes Street (nearest the castle), then George Street and Queen Street (in the linear belt of trees). Beyond Queen Street is the later section of the New Town, laid out in squares and circuses by Reid and others in the nineteenth century.

86 Buxton, Derbyshire. Buxton, with earlier but very modest traditions for the therapeutic properties of its waters, grew as a spa town in the eighteenth century, when the fifth Duke of Devonshire attempted to develop, using a site in the lower part of the town near the wells and springs, a midland equivalent of Bath. In 1778–80 the Crescent (lower left centre) was built by John Carr of York, opposite the site of St Ann's well. In 1785–90 a large stables area was built to the north (domed building), which became the Devonshire Hospital in the mid-nineteenth century. The dome dates from 1881–2.

is that of Buxton (photo 86), a small town in north-west Derbyshire in the valley of the river Wye, at an altitude of 300 m. Its thermal springs had been used for medicinal and therapeutic purposes in Roman times, with a revival of interest in the sixteenth century. The initiative for development in the late eighteenth century was that of the fifth Duke of Devonshire, who sought to provide more accommodation for those seeking cures, and to emulate developments at Bath. The architect employed by the duke was John Carr of York, a builder and later architect who worked very firmly in the classical Palladian tradition. In 1779–81 his major construction at Buxton was the Crescent, following the recently-established innovation of the crescent form as an element of urban design – Wood the Younger's Royal Crescent at Bath (1767–75). The Crescent was built in local stone and included three hotels, an assembly room and some shops. Stables and an exercise yard were built immediately to the north. Buxton's reputation was nowhere near as great as that of Bath, mainly on account of its relative inaccessibility until the coming of the railways in 1863, and the site of the new buildings was a depression, which gave them less visual prominence, but this development

174

does illustrate the way in which a particular style and fashion of building could be initiated in a remote place under the influence of an aristocratic patron.

The Georgian interest in urban planning is obviously reflected at a variety of scales and in a surprisingly widespread variety of locations. What might be deemed, from a metropolitan perspective, to be remote provincial places, were to a degree affected by the need of local landowners to express the fashions and tastes of the time, and also in some cases reflect strategies for control and development, in an almost colonial fashion, of areas which were thought to be potentially injurious to the peace of the nation. Some interesting examples are to be found in both Scotland and Wales. The town and fishing port of Ullapool (photo 87), on the east shore of Lough Broom in the north-west Highlands of Scotland, had been considered as a site for a possible fishing and manufacturing settlement in the early eighteenth century, but was in fact established in 1787 by the British Fisheries Society. Towns like Ullapool were established to stimulate the local economy, but also as a means of stabilising and civilising this remote region. As Withers has put it,

87 Ullapool, Ross and Cromarty. Founded in 1787 by the British Fisheries Society, which founded three planned fishing settlements in the late eighteenth century (the other two being Tobermory and Lochbay). There had been earlier ideas for a settlement at Ullapool to spread a range of employment, but the purpose of the 1787 settlement was to facilitate herring fishing, agriculture, and a range of artisan employment, including textiles. The grid-plan layout is characteristic of many other small Scottish coastal towns and villages of this period.

88 Fort George, Inverness, view eastwards. The fort is located at the end of Ardersier Point, which, with the opposite Chanonry Point, divides the inner Inverness Firth from the outer Moray Firth. The fort was one element in a general policy of garrisoning the Highlands from the late seventeenth century onwards, and was specifically built after 1745 (1745–63) to protect the entrance to the Great Glen at the Moray Firth. The engineer was Colonel William Skinner, and the design that of an irregular polygon with a curtain wall and six angle bastions.

The civil control sought for the Highlands through the harmony of economic social and political interests in these settlements was reflected in their ordered plan: the regular layout not only suited the aesthetic values of the time but represented in built form the rational and utilitarian philosophy of individual landowners and the social values of the improving class. Though clearly smaller scale than Edinburgh's New Town, the regular geometry of many planned villages symbolised the same control over space as Scotland's capital, and in the Highlands, stood in representation of the authority of capital and class over customary relations.[11]

The occupational basis was fishing (for herring), textiles, and farming. An SSPCK school and a school were built, and a doctor was provided. The strategic context of the construction of these planned villages and towns is well illustrated by the building of the garrison fort, Fort George in Inverness-shire (photo 88). The original Fort George, built by General Wade at Castle Hill in Inverness, having been destroyed in 1746, a new one was built in 1763 at Ardersier Point between 1748 and 1736, by Colonel William Skinner. The location on a promontory site and its design and fortifications leave a strong impression of its strategic purpose, namely the defence of the Great Glen routeway and of the entrance to the Moray Firth.

The town of Maryport in Cumberland (Cumbria) (photo 89) is a planned town of the eighteenth century which reflected the economic and town-planning energies of the Lowther family, who had developed the new town of Whitehaven, and Maryport was an imitation of this endeavour. Maryport was initiated in 1749 by the building of a coal dock by the estate-owner Humphrey Senhouse in the estuary of the River Ellen. A new town with the name of Maryport was built to the north of the river, with a grid-plan layout, and twenty years later its main economic activities centred around shipyards, an ironworks and an active coal trade.

Various manifestations of eighteenth- and early nineteenth-century planning energies, in relation to contemporary fashion and perception of economic development possibilities, were to be found also in Wales. An interesting example of local initiative leading to urban design is that of Aberaeron (photo 90), which is essentially an early nineteenth-century planned town. The initiative here came from the Rev. Alban Thomas Jones, who in 1805 inherited the estate at Aberaeron from Lewis Gwynne (with the condition that he took the surname Gwynne) and redeveloped the small harbour there in 1807. The small settlement had been in existence at the mouth of the River Aeron since late medieval times, but Gwynne saw the commercial possibilties for developing the harbour and town to serve west and mid Wales. The old harbour had been used by small ships in the

89 Maryport, Cumbria. Maryport had been the site of a Roman fort and settlement, south of the western end of Hadrian's Wall, and later of a small fishing settlement – Ellenfoot – but the planning of this Georgian new town at the mouth of the river Ellen began in 1749, with the initiation by Humphrey Senhouse of a coal dock to serve his estates in the area and of a new town, with grid-plan layout, on the north side of the estuary, named after his wife Mary. The design was similar to that of the nearby town of Whitehaven developed by the Lowther family in the late seventeenth century.

90 Aberaeron, Cardigan (Dyfed). A planned town in west Wales dating in its modern form from the early nineteenth century, the replanning of Aberaeron was initiated by the Rev. Alban Thomas Jones, who redeveloped the very small harbour (left centre) in 1807 to increase the town's commercial possibilities. The town's re-development began in 1811, and continued during the greater part of the nineteenth century, the initial model being, in theory, the Georgian planning at Bath and London. The older part of the town is that to the right of the harbour, on the seaward side of the main road.

eighteenth century for the export of herrings, grain and some lead ore, and imports included coal, slate, and limestone. The small ships also functioned as fishing boats. After the improvements to the quay and harbour, Gwynne began the development of the town from 1811 onwards, by developing a site with four houses and a courtyard, immediately to the north of the harbour. Subsequent buildings included Mynachy Row ('Bedlam Barracks') to house builders' labourers, and a school for poor children founded in 1818. The layout of the town, the style and colour of the buildings, were all prescribed by Gwynne, and the town when completed provided a good example of a Georgian and early Victorian planned town, including a large square. Two other early nineteenth-century planned towns in Wales which also were developed in a similar design tradition were Milford and Tremadoc.

Although urban and rural development in the eighteenth century is reflected in the varied styles of designed landscape which still, where preserved, attract much interested attention, it must not be forgotten that the period witnessed an increasing polarisation between rich and poor. The landscapes of poverty –

the urban hovels of the city centres and the basic cottages of the rural labourers – have largely disappeared on account of their flimsy and ephemeral nature, but they were a very significant feature of a capitalistic economy, the dark side of a landscape which is difficult to illuminate from survivals to the present day.

INDUSTRIAL LANDSCAPES

During the course of the eighteenth and nineteenth centuries the bases of non-agricultural production were gradually transformed by the discovery and application of new means of motive power, by greater concentration and specialisation, by the application of larger amounts of capital and the role of a new type of entrepreneur, and by major structural changes in the ways in which labour was employed – all this in the context of changing rates of population growth, leading to greater domestic demand for certain goods, together with a growing international demand. Such changes are symbolised in the new meaning attached to the word 'industry', which formerly had signified a commendable and energetic application to all kinds of work and tasks, but which increasingly took on the connotation of the processes, built environments and landscapes associated with manufacturing. This was, in effect, the period of the birth of modern industry.

The more dramatic industrial innovations of the later eighteenth century serve in some respects to conceal the fact that the balance of industrial activity in the first half of that century bore as much resemblance to the structure of the seventeenth century as to those of the 'Industrial Revolution'.

There were, however, major innovations that ultimately were to transform the nature of industrial economy and society, relating to the increase of new factors of production, including new fuels, new raw materials, new forms and sources of capital and new forms of organisation and management. Examples of major technological developments and inventions are Abraham Darby's smelting of iron with coke (1709), and innovations in the textile industry such as Kay's flying shuttle (1733), Hargreave's spinning jenny (1764), Arkwright's water-frame (1769), and Crompton's 'mule' (1779). The major concentrations of the growing industries of the eighteenth and early nineteenth centuries had a variety of locational factors, including water-power, the availability of coal near the surface, and existing traditions of production and labour forces.

Coalbrookdale (photo 91) was the site of a number of important technical and organisational experiments which were to have far-reaching effects. The originator of the early industrial complex at Coalbrookdale in Shropshire was Abraham Darby, born in 1678 of a Quaker family in Sedgley. He served an apprenticeship in Birmingham to a maker of malt mills and small machinery, and in 1699 set up his own company in Bristol for the manufacturing of malt mills. In 1708 he took over the lease of a blast-furnace at Coalbrookdale, and began smelting there in 1709. The reasons for this location are generally assumed to have been connected with the quality of the coke made from the local Clod coal, the transport facility provided by the River Severn, and the existing tradition of iron working in the area (since the early seventeenth century). Another important factor was the religious, social and business milieux provided by the Quaker connections in the region. The existing furnace at Coalbrookdale was repaired in 1708 and

91 Coalbrookdale, Shropshire. In the foreground, at the foot of the wooded slope, is the valley of the River Severn, into which (marked, centre and top of photograph, by its wooded slopes) runs Coalbrookdale, the location of the early iron-smelting industrial complex initiated by Abraham Darby in 1708. The earliest activities, and Darby's first house, were at the lower (Severn) end of Coalbrookdale, with warehouses and wharfage on the Severn, but as the iron-smelting and casting work expanded, the industrial complex spread further north up Coalbrookdale. On the right hand side of the picture is the western end of the town of Ironbridge.

began production of pig-iron in 1709, the iron being primarily used for casting cooking-pots and other small utensils. A second furnace was built in 1715, and the small industrial complex began to expand, with the production of a steam engine cylinder stimulating demand for this particular product from about 1732 onwards. Abraham Darby I died in 1717, and the management of the works was taken over by his son-in law Richard Ford, in partnership with Thomas Goldney. By 1736, Abraham II was in full partnership in the company, now called the Dale Company. Some guns were manufactured during the period of the Ford and Goldney management, but this ceased by the end of the eighteenth century, by which time the company was one of the biggest iron manufacturers in existence. Under the management of Abraham III, in the period from 1769 to 1789, developments included the rebuilding of the Old Furnace, the commencement of the building of Boulton and Watt steam engines, the construction of the Iron Bridge over the Severn, the construction of canals and inclined planes in the complex, and the construction of forty workmen's houses at Ketley. Later managers, up to 1850, included Richard Dearman, Edmund Darby, Barnard Dickinson, and Francis Darby. By the mid nineteenth century, the company had developed not only

a very wide range of industrial products, but had also established a reputation for the production of cast figures and sculptures. By this time the company employed about 4,000 workers, producing 2,000 tons of iron per week.

One of the spectacular innovations associated with Coalbrookdale was the erection of the world's first cast-iron bridge, across the Severn, begun in 1779, reflecting the unique capacity of the Coalbrookdale iron works to produce very large iron arches and spars.

Many of the early industrialists like the Darbys showed much concern for the well-being of their workers, related to religious, philanthropic and utopian views of society and human relationships. An interesting example of an industrial complex built to implement such principles is that of New Lanark, in Lanarkshire in Scotland (photo 92). This was a manufacturing village founded in 1783 by David Dale, an utopian philanthropist. He built a village to accommodate 1,000 people. The basis of this industrial and social experiment was cotton-spinning, undertaken by a closely-knit community, and by the end of the eighteenth century New Lanark's cotton mill was the largest in Scotland. The experiment was continued, for the first thirty years of the nineteenth century, in the role of

92 Cotton Mills, New Lanark, Lanarkshire, from south. New Lanark is located in Upper Clydesdale and the photograph shows the cotton mills (lower right) and workers' houses of this planned community. It was initiated by Richard Arkwright and David Dale, who founded the New Lanark Mills in 1783, and managed by Robert Owen, the philanthropist, between 1799 and 1827. The settlement included not only the mills and model housing (about 170 houses), but also schools, a church, and shops.

partner-manager, by the better-known Robert Owen, Dale's son-in-law. The population at the time of Owen's influence was over 2,000, living in model houses, working in 'ideal factory' surroundings, and experiencing a novel and advanced form of schooling. Owen claimed that he had established a community that was 'self-employing, self-supporting, and self-governing'. This was only one of a series of experiments by Owen and others in utopian social philanthropy.

These two instances of new types of industrial development are respectively, both typical and untypical of the new locations and characteristics of industry in Britain in the later eighteenth century. Coalbrookdale evidences a site of producation related to the newer factors of production: coal, iron ore, transport, and skilled capitalist entrepreneurship. New Lanark indicates the continuing importance of water-power, but also has a number of things in common with Coalbrookdale, including new machinery, and utopian principle. By the end of the century, however, the beginnings of the move of major, growing, heavier industries to the coalfields was clearly evident. Even so, small-scale rural or domestic industry continued to be an important feature of the industrial scene, especially in the textile industry, but was increasingly caught up in the newer capitalist relations of industrial production, including the vicissitudes of national and international market demand and price-changes.

TRANSPORT AND COMMUNICATIONS

Important elements of the changing landscapes of Britain in the eighteenth and early nineteenth centuries were the new and improved means of communication, conspicuously the turnpike roads and canals. According to Pawson,

> The major improvements in Britain's transport systems can be characterised as a series of innovation waves from the mid-seventeenth century onwards. As responses to the pressures of economic expansion, they proceeded hand-in-hand with it. The turnpike boom accompanied the upturn of the mid-century years, spilling into the first generation of canal construction, and then both slowed until the rapid take-off of the late 1780s, after which canal investment and port improvement rose to new heights. Yet the waves of river, road, and canal innovation all came to an abrupt halt with the emergence of the steam railway in the 1820s and 1830s.[12]

The turnpiking of roads began in the late seventeenth century in response to the need for a much better and more reliable system and surface for a growing rate of internal trade. Each trust, which was responsible for only relatively short sections of highway, was established by Act of Parliament, and though this process led to a complex multiplicity of enterprises, they did in practice form major linked networks in the most economically active regions of Britain, notably London and its environs, the West Midlands, and the North and north-western industrialising counties. The rate of growth of the turnpikes increased conspicuously in the period 1750–1840, there being some 22,000 miles of turnpike at the peak of development. Apart from the turnpikes, the only other conspicuous efforts at road development in the eighteenth and nineteenth century were the 'military' and Highland roads in Scotland.

The next major transport development was the canal, which offered a solution to the problem of transporting heavy goods such as coal. Although much coal was transported by sea, this was not a possible solution for all areas of coal-mining or of coal-consumption. The improvement of rivers by straightening and deepening was an old-established practice, but the cutting of artificial waterways essentially dates from the cutting of a canal alongside the Sankey Brook from St Helens to the Mersey in Lancashire, the canal being completed in 1757. This was followed by a more famous construction, the canal built for the Duke of Bridgewater to transport coal from Worsley to Manchester, the first part of the canal being opened in 1761, and linked in 1762, by a second canal, to the Mersey at Runcorn. In a short time the new Trent and Mersey canal provided a major link between the major river systems of the Trent, Mersey, and Severn. In spite of the episodic nature of canal construction in the eighteenth century, it has been estimated that by 1840 about 4,000 miles of canals and improved river navigations had been created in Britain. While the densest network of canals was in England, major developments also occurred in Wales and Scotland. In Wales the major canals were in the south, serving the coalfields and growing industrial regions, but outside the south the only other part of Wales well served was the north-east. In Scotland there were three major canals: the Forth and Clyde canal, begun in 1768 and finally completed to Dumbarton in 1790; the Crinan Canal, linking Glasgow with the Western Highlands by by-passing the Mull of Kintyre, which was completed in 1801; and the Caledonian Canal, constructed through the Great Glen and opened in 1822, but which was outdated (by steamships) almost as soon as it was opened.

The English network started with local canals and expanded to regional linkages between the Thames, Severn, Trent, Humber, and Mersey. The major canals included the Staffordshire and Worcestershire (1772), the Grand Trunk or Trent and Mersey (1777), the Thames and Severn (1793), the Kennet and Avon (1810), the Grand Junction (1815), and the Leeds and Liverpool (1815). This scale of construction was possible only by the introduction of large-scale and highly innovative techniques of civil engineering, including flights of locks, aqueducts, docks, and bridges. An interesting example of the scale of environmental conquest by means of the technical skills of civil engineers is the flight or staircase of 29 locks on the Kennet and Avon Canal at Devizes (photo 93) whose construction was started in 1794 and completed in 1810, the purpose of which was to lift the canal from the much lower-lying valley of the Bristol Avon to the higher Vale of Pewsey. The canal itself ran from Newbury to Bath, via Devizes, and was part of a network linking the Thames and Severn basin (and therefore London and Bristol) and was largely engineered by the Scots engineer John Rennie (1761–1821). The development of a dense canal system was therefore an important feature of eighteenth- and early nineteenth-century Britain, not only providing new and cheaper means of transport for the heavy goods of the industrial revolution and for agricultural produce, but also providing a testing-ground for new forms of financial investment and new types of expertise in engineering. This experience was continued with the later and newer form of transport, the railway.

In the sense of fixed wooden rails on which waggons could be pulled or propelled by animal or human power (generally known as tramways or waggonways),

93 Flight of 22 locks, Kennet and Avon Canal, west of Devizes, Wiltshire. A staircase of 29 locks on the Kennet and Avon Canal constructed between 1794 and 1810 by the Scots engineer John Rennie (1761–1821), to raise the level of the canal from the Bristol Avon to the Vale of Pewsey, and thus complete a link between London and Bristol. Rennie's canal work is noted for the high and imaginative quality of both engineering and architecture.

railways had existed since the seventeenth century. The advent of iron rails in the second half of the eighteenth century and the advent of the steam locomotive in the first few years of the nineteenth century introduced a new and revolutionary change in the history of transport and of landscape. Although pioneer experiments with steam locomotives had been conducted by Richard Trevithick at Coalbrookdale in 1802, the first major development was the use of such a locomotive in 1804 at the Penydarren Ironworks near Merthyr Tydfil. Here again the engineer was Richard Trevithick (1771–1833), a Cornishman by birth, who had initially worked on the application of steam engines for winding and pumping in mines. He built a railway locomotive for the owner of the ironworks (Samuel Homfray) which first ran on 13 February 1804. Further experiments were undertaken by a number of engineers, but the best-known developments are those of 1825, with the opening of the Stockton and Darlington Railway – in effect, an improved waggonway – for use by steam locomotives, the project engineered by George Stephenson. The first completely new railway, however, was that constructed by George and Robert Stephenson between 1826 and 1830, the Liverpool and Manchester Railway, which was opened on 15 September 1830. This marked the opening of a new era in transport, most of which falls outside the period studied in this chapter, but even by 1837 substantial progress had been made, involving approximately 300 miles of railway, much of it in south Lancashire and the North-East of England.

CONCLUSION

Georgian Britain and its survivals in present-day landscapes clearly symbolise an important and complex set of transitions and changes from late feudalism to early and maturing capitalism. The new social relations of production and power of that era are clearly marked in what are essentially privileged and minority landscapes, that is those artifacts of landscape, carefully designed and created in rural and urban environments, which reflect the changes in taste and in wealth of those with old money and the newer entrepreneurs, wealth used to acquire and extend the ownership of property. The wealth itself is also a symbol, of course, of changing modes of production and of increasingly larger scale commercial engagements, often at global level. Our contemporary aesthetic judgements of the Georgian Age tend, perhaps, to be excessively influenced by these generally admirable survivals of good taste, reflecting the tastes not only of the more influential inhabitants of Britain, but also their admiration of the work of architects and designers from elsewhere in Europe, notably Italy. There remains, however, the generally silent voice in the landscape of those by whose toil, and in many cases deprivation, the salient features of Georgian landscape were created. They cannot be seen from the air: they can only be imagined, read about, or viewed in some more sensitive paintings, but their existence, however short and painful, should not be forgotten.

FURTHER READING

M. Reed, *The Georgian Triumph: 1700–1830*, London, 1983.

R. S. Neale, *Bath: A Social History 1680–1850*, London, 1981.

A. J. Youngson, *The Making of Classical Edinburgh, 1750–1840*, Edinburgh, 1966.

I. Adams, *The Making of Urban Scotland*, London, 1978.

C. Chalkin, *The Provincial Towns of Georgian England: A Study of the Building Process 1740–1820*, London, 1984.

J. Summerson, *Georgian London*, London, 1962.

7 Victorian Britain: 1837 – *c*.1900

INTRODUCTION

Aerial photography is by no means the most extensive source of information on Victorian England but it is in many ways a rich one. Developed as a research tool by archaeologists anxious to learn more about prehistoric earthwork and crop and soil-mark sites, there is understandably relatively little aerial photography of the most conspicuous Victorian landscapes in the industrial north. Since the start of large-scale demolition of the fabric of Victorian England, industrial archaeologists are now more numerous, but while they have been thick on the ground they have only recently begun to create an aerial photographic record. So, as with most sources, the historical geographer must approach what aerial photographs there are of Victorian landscapes with a very different eye to that which took them. The great advantage of looking at Victorian landscapes from the air is precisely the greater sense of *landscape*, of a more comprehensive and systematic view, than is usually available from the ground. This is especially true for sites to which it is difficult to get access, such as quarries and docks (photo 94), but also for sites such as factory complexes and urban railway systems which are barely perceptible from the ground. What stand out on aerial photographs are examples of large-scale and spectacular Victorian planning – model factory villages, prisons, country houses, the large fields of late Parliamentary Enclosure – and I will discuss a number of photographs of sites such as these, not just because they make good pictures but because they disclose much about how Victorians, or at least those in power, saw themselves. I am aware that, in more senses than one, this represents a 'view from above' and privileges precisely the ideology of environmental coherence such Victorians valued, so I will also read these and other photographs in a way which questions such ways of seeing.[1]

How does a study focusing on aerial photographs of Victorian Britain relate to the historiography of the period, particularly to the approaches of historical geographers? Victorian studies took off in the 1960s, at a time when the physical evidence of Victorian Britain was being demolished and when its social as well as physical fabric was being discovered not to be as unremittingly brutal, ugly and monotonous as was conventionally thought. Asa Briggs' seminal *Victorian Cities* (1963) was intent to demolish the stereotypes and caricatures of such cities and recover them as places which were complex, highly particular and, above all, civilised.[2] However, Briggs' evocation of a sense of place in these cities was not expressed visually in maps, illustrations or photographs; indeed, there was more visual evidence, including aerial photographs, in an earlier book which reproduced precisely the negative stereotype of Victorian England which Briggs challenged – W. G. Hoskins' *The Making of the English Landscape* (1955).[3] If Hoskins' implied industrialisation destroyed any meaningful historical sense of

94 London Docks. The three docks of West India Dock (completed in 1880) occupy the centre of the picture and beyond on another bend on the river are the Surrey Docks (built in the 1870s). From the air, and before many were filled in, Dockland resembled a series of lakes and gave a good idea of what an achievement of engineering and hard labour (docks were dug out by pick and shovel by thousands of men) the creation of Dockland was. Housing was run up near the docks (much had already been demolished when the photograph was taken in 1972) although there was no assurance that the dockers who lived there would be employed every working day – that was one reason why housing had to be near possible employment. Note the absence of railway facilities, a peculiarity of the London docks compared with other large British ports. This is because much of the characteristically high value, low bulk cargo was destined for London or for premises such as bonded warehouses a short distance away. Water and horse drawn transport was adequate.

landscape, M. W. Beresford, a pioneer in using aerial photography, was no less attentive to the complex fabric of Victorian cities than to that of the deserted villages of medieval England.[4] When a self-conscious historical geography of Victorian towns and cities developed rapidly in the late 1960s and 1970s it did not do so in terms of the morphological tradition in the study of earlier and smaller settlements. It paid less attention to the visual evidence of the built environment, or indeed to what made one place characteristically different from another, than to sources such as the manuscript census, rate books and marriage records which lent themselves to statistical manipulation and to addressing general issues such as theories of modernisation or community formation. Moreover, the social space of such studies (representing indices of segregation, journeys to work, the patterns of marriage) was often only vaguely related to the physical environment (the configuration of streets, houses, relief and drainage) and often ignored it altogether. Also often missing was any sense of how Victorians themselves responded to their surroundings and to each other.[5]

Victorian historical geography is now less consciously 'urban'. The publication of major works on the Tithe Surveys has helped to redress the neglect of rural England.[6] Also, influenced by currents in social history, the historical geography of the period is now more consciously cultural – focusing on issues of social power and imagery and once more on the built environment in all its palpability and particularity. The discipline has again become archaeological in the sense not just of recovering the physical fabric of the past but of recovering modes of knowledge and power that may find expression in that fabric. Research is now less extensive than intensive; rather than taking representative samples of this or that data source to answer a positivistic hypothesis, historical geographers make so-called 'deep readings' and 'thick descriptions' of one or two sources. Aerial photographs, no less than public health reports or Victorian novels, all respond well to this approach.[7]

Historical geographers are now concerned as much with representation as reality. They are intent not only to reconstruct past landscapes or patterns of activity but also to reconstruct how people in the past perceived those landscapes or activities; moreover, some historical geographers have been unwilling to privilege their retrospective representations as more 'real' or 'objective' than contemporary ones. In its post-modern phase, historical geography is not so much an advance towards a more complete description or explanation of an independent entity like 'The Victorian City' than a negotiation between varying and conflicting representations. Moreover it does not necessarily seek to resolve this multiplicity by presenting one representation (say, a statistical one) as more 'real' than another (say, an artistic one). I should add that this post-modern historical geography is still more an article of faith than a practice. Even studies which recognise the constitutive power of representation do not entirely abandon empiricism.[8] And nor will this one.

A representation-conscious approach to the past has, not surprisingly, been concerned with periods that are representation-rich; and there is no richer period in this respect than the Victorian one. Not only are there abundant sources but the sensibility which informs those sources, especially official and sophisticated sources, is consciously observational – in pictures (paintings, photos, engravings), plans, maps and graphic descriptions (in novels, sermons, newspapers) but also statistical surveys conducted to project light (and sophisticated categories) upon areas like the living conditions of the urban poor which had become, and threatened to remain, shrouded in obscurity, not just because of any irregularity in the lives of the poor or instability of the built environment, but because of their representation in other, more impressionistic, sources.[9]

It is appropriate that aerial photographs be used as a source for the study of Victorian England because if Victorians did not invent the aerial view as a strategic source of knowledge, they developed it to a sophisticated degree. Vantage points were various, both imaginary ('bird's-eye') and real – balloons, towers, tall buildings, railway viaducts. New and higher vantage points gave surprising and, in many senses, rewarding views – for those intent on detailed surveillance and for those looking in a more relaxed and scenic way. Cities were the most frequent subject for aerial viewing. There was already a tradition of urban prospects but as Victorian cities expanded and were internally transformed

– often chaotically, it seemed to those on the ground – so the aerial view comprehended them in an orderly and optimistic way. A prospect of Manchester based on sketches from the top of the Exchange Station and issued by *The Graphic* in 1889 (see figure above) is one of many urban views emphasising, through lighting and perspective, buildings and streets which embodied civic pride and subduing those which did not. Less oblique views emphasised streets rather than architecture and helped make cities intelligible for mobile and investigative citizens. A popular view of London, as if from a balloon on Parliament Hill, and with street names on rooftops, was recommended by Henry Mayhew in his *Criminal Prisons of London* (1862) as 'more easily comprehensible to Strangers than the ordinary town plans of the London streets'.[10] As industrial enterprises spread horizontally so they commissioned prospects (often for engraving on company stationery) to enhance their expansion and their connections with traffic routes, especially railways.[11] Some city views also included 'less stately, more expressly utilitarian features' but all were broadly optimistic, informed by the ethos of 'improvement'. So when the paragon of late Victorian observation, Sherlock Holmes, passed Clapham Junction, he remarked to his unobservant companion:

> 'It's a very cheering thing to come into London by any of these lines which run high and allow you to look down upon the houses like this.'
> I thought he was joking, for the view was sordid enough, but he soon explained himself.
> 'Look at those big, isolated clumps of building rising up above the slates, like brick islands in a lead-coloured sea.'
> 'The Board Schools.'
> 'Lighthouses, my boy! Beacons of the future!...'[12]

Aerial photography has many of its roots in these conventions. The first air pilots and passengers in the 1920s and 1930s were as conscious as Victorians of the rewards of new vantage points. As a 1924 guide to air travel put it: 'Life expands in an aeroplane. The traveller is a mere slave in a train ... air travel

95 Halifax, West Yorkshire. The deeply incised valley of Ovenden Brook is filled with the spinning mills, dye works and weaving sheds of the two leading manufacturers in Victorian Halifax: Ackroyd (worsteds) and Crossley (carpets). Edward Ackroyd's villa and grounds are at the top left of the picture and to the right is the Gothic church (1856–59) which he commissioned Gilbert Scott to build to tower over his works and impress his workers. On the spur at the confluence of the two valleys is the public park he financed. The Crossley factory complex fills most of the valley. A painting of a view similar to this was commissioned by Crossleys in the late nineteenth century to emphasise the scale of their enterprise.

allows him to look around him freely and at never-ending variety. The earth speeds by him with nothing hidden and full of surprises, with its clear waters, its peaceful forests, its welcoming villages and fields.'[13] While amateur photographers went for such picturesque material, professionals concentrated on the utilitarian, including photographs of industrial and port complexes.[14] But while such photographs might reveal the logic of an industrial landscape as well as unsuspected beauties, in doing so they reproduced another of the conventions of Victorian aerial views, their purification of the environment, particularly their reduction or elimination of human presence. This needs to be borne in mind when using aerial photographs as a source for the Victorian period. Of course, at the time of taking such photographs most of the Victorians who lived and worked in such environments were long dead but precisely the point of much historical geography now is to recover the ways in which people, especially ordinary people, lived and thought, not just to recover the physical fabric of the environment. In contrast to the elevated sensibility of the aerial view, such studies seek more 'street credibility'. Such street-wise representations may be more populist than aerial views but are no more 'real'. Sophisticated Victorians, no less than late twentieth-century radical historians, were fascinated as much by the rough-and-tumble of life on the streets as by orderly prospects; arguably, these two views are two sides of the same inquisitive sensibility. So rather than emphasise one over the other I intend in this chapter to make each a foil for the other. If aerial photographs occlude the human element or the human scale they heighten awareness of contexts Victorians themselves were only dimly aware of and may disclose features that they consciously tried to hide.

CITIES

Cities set the tone of Victorian society in Britain. Indeed, to contemporaries the period was an 'Age of Great Cities'. In 1801 only London had a population over 100,000; by 1901, 32 other places did.[15] The cities which initially caught the imagination, both inspiring enthusiasm and provoking alarm, were the provincial industrial capitals, notably Manchester, Leeds, Birmingham and Bradford. These places did not mushroom overnight – the foundation for their take-off was laid in the eighteenth century – but their growth rates set them apart from provincial towns which did not industrialise so comprehensively. Leeds, already in 1775 a major town of 17,000 for the finishing and marketing of woollen cloth, was by 1831 a city of 123,000 in which all branches of woollen manufacture were conducted and where there was an increasing variety of other industries too. In contrast, Norwich, a city of 40,000 in 1786 but already experiencing a steep decline as a woollen textile centre, had by 1831 only modestly increased its population to 62,000. What mushrooming there was went on further down the urban hierarchy. Among the most precocious settlements was Middlesbrough. In 1801 it was a place of four houses, by 1841 a town of 5,000 people and by 1861 one of 19,500 as it developed an industrial base first in the export of coal and then in the production of iron.[16]

Contemporary observers emphasised the novelty of urban development and usually in terms which made the urban process seem barely coherent. Thus in

1840 William Cooke Taylor considered the new industrial towns of northern England to be based on 'a system of social life constructed on a wholly new principle yet vague and indefinite by developing itself by its own spontaneous force and daily producing effects which no human foresight had anticipated'.[17] In hindsight the process seems more orderly and the power of the past in directing patterns on the ground more apparent. The expansion of many large textile towns and cities in Lancashire and Yorkshire was essentially cellular; formerly isolated settlements built up around textile mills were eventually enfolded in a more continuous built-up area (photo 95). Such mill colonies often retained their insular identities in a cultural as well as an economic sense, their residents' pastimes remaining more rustic than civic. The urbanisation of culture could take longer than the urbanisation of bricks and mortar.[18] As tithe and enclosure maps often reveal, the pattern of streets and buildings was often moulded by an agrarian landholding system. Areas of early Victorian working class housing in West York-

96 Leeds, West Yorkshire. A fragmented pattern of later nineteenth-century working class housing characteristic of the East End of the city. The short disconnected streets and abrupt changes in alignment reflect the pattern of the small holdings which small speculative builders developed. The back-to-back house was prevalent throughout Leeds, even in more orderly developments on larger more compact holdings. Many of the back-to-backs of Leeds were demolished in the 1960s and at the bottom of this photograph of the time this is shown taking place.

shire textile towns (photo 96) often display a discordant pattern of unconnected roads, dead-ends and odd-shaped houses filling awkward corners which reflects the development of speculative housing on small holdings within a highly fragmented freehold pattern. Later developments tended to be more orderly as the supply of small holdings (which small builders preferred) became exhausted, as the larger holdings of leasehold estates came on to the market and as the construction and finance industries became sufficiently large to exploit them. Also prompting a more orderly pattern were the demands of minimum building standards for wider streets and by tram and bus companies for longer ones.[19]

By no means did all urban working people live in such legible landscapes. As housing reformers observed to their disgust, many were crowded into labyrinthine districts in, or adjacent to, the old centres of cities, in the cellars and attics of former middle-class dwellings or behind main streets in enclosed courts and yards that might only be reached by a tunnel entrance. In 1841 a quarter of Liverpool's population lived in courts and another 9 per cent in cellar dwellings.

Such people tended not to be factory workers but casual workers who needed to be close to employment opportunities at the centre of cities.[20] Many of the urban poor slept rough – on brickfields, under bridges – especially those who came to cities seasonally, in winter usually, after labouring for part of the year in the country.[21]

Not all industrial towns and cities were free to expand. Some Midland towns, notably Nottingham (photos 97, 98), were constricted by a girdle of commonable land. On the basis of the lace and hosiery industries the population of Nottingham expanded rapidly within its medieval confines causing gross overcrowding and some of the worst living conditions in the country. In 1832 4,283 people lived on just 9 acres of land, many in courts and alleys. There was nothing archaic or strictly agrarian about the refusal of Nottingham's commoners to cede their grazing rights. The largest and most powerful were urban rentiers with a stake in the slum conditions; they were reluctant to release a large amount of land on the market in the depressed conditions of the 1830s. In 1845 an Enclosure Act was passed and before the Award was made 20 years later 5,000 new houses had been built on the newly released land along with 200 factories and warehouses and shops. The Act stipulated minimum building standards – including a minimum of three bedrooms to new houses and no back-to-backs. These standards made houses too expensive for many working people but despite them 500 back-to-backs were built in the 1850s on former meadowland to the south of the city where many streets remained undrained and unpaved. The pattern of building on the enclosed areas was determined by the new allotments of the Enclosure Award but the pattern of streets followed the medieval footpaths and furlongs of the open fields.[22]

Freehold land tended to favour the development of poorer housing but it did not preclude the building of polite suburbs, especially in salubrious situations (photos 99, 100). For example, good-class housing continued to be developed on small freehold plots on the heights of London's Hampstead within reach of Hampstead Heath.[23] Nevertheless, Victorian suburbs tended to be built on larger estates whose landowners offered 99-year building leases hedged about with restrictive covenants. This pattern had been established as early as the seventeenth century on the Duke of Bedford's Bloomsbury Estate in London where it was perpetuated into the nineteenth century as squares of upper-middle-class terrace housing which stretched from St Giles to the new Euston Road. More private than their Georgian forebears the Victorian upper middle class preferred detached dwellings to terraces and by the mid nineteenth century every large town and city had its sanctum of middle-class villas. These areas were meticulously planned and managed. They included such amenities as a church, a park and a good school and excluded such developments as commerce, industry, pubs, poorer dwellings, public transport and through traffic. The restrictive covenants of the leases conditioned their exclusivity as did physical barriers such as walls and gates. Gasworks and slaughterhouses were invariably banished to lower class areas even if the residents in these areas might be too poor to make use of the gas or to purchase the meat.[24]

There was nothing new about the separation of the rich from the poor but contemporaries tended to regard this as a new development and to inflate its

97 The Meadows, Nottingham in 1926. As the name suggests a former area of pasture, one of the three great areas of common land surrounding Nottingham which were not enclosed until an Act of 1845. The main thoroughfare Arkwright Street stretching diagonally across the picture to Trent Bridge was built in 1848 but residential and industrial development did not spread extensively for at least another ten years when holdings were consolidated and reapportioned. At the centre of the photograph is St Saviour's Church (1863), opposite a factory listed on mid-nineteenth century maps as a cabinet works; at the bottom edge of the picture is a factory making hosiery machinery and interspersed elsewhere other engineering works, lace and hosiery factories. Apart from a square of almshouses bordering London Road on the left and a line of middle class houses facing the river, most of the houses are terraced working class dwellings but a close look will reveal some of the fine distinctions of size, style and position so important in calibrating residential status.

98 Nottingham in 1971. This high vertical view brings out the areas of spacious Victorian planning surrounding Nottingham, a city that until the mid-nineteenth century was hemmed in by unenclosed commonable land and which became severely overcrowded as a result. The crescent shaped development at the bottom left is The Park, an area of substantial villas developed for Nottingham's well-to-do. The site was the northern part of the Duke of Newcastle's deer park lying adjacent to his town mansion, The Castle. (The southern, more low lying part of the park, was sold for railway development and for an area of poor housing.) Planned around two circuses The Park was strictly residential but, as a close inspection of the photograph will reveal, development did not turn out to be as symmetrical as envisaged. To the north are examples of public planning, three areas of public recreation amounting to 130 acres allocated by Commissioners of the 1845 Enclosure: the largest an area of playing fields, to its south a smaller pleasure ground and arboretum connected to broad tree lined walks leading up to and down from a circus enclosing a new water works. The light area to the right of the circus shows the demolition of an area of working class housing developed in the wake of the Enclosure award. The subsequent redevelopment obliterated the former building pattern that was conditioned by the allotments of the award and the street pattern that followed the medieval footpaths and furlongs of the open fields.

99 East Heath, Hampstead, London. A classic site of conflicting pressures on land. The open area to the right of the ponds was a freehold part of the Maryon Wilson estate and since 1829 planned to be developed as an area of substantial middle class houses. However it was seen by local middle class residents as indistinguishable from Hampstead Heath to the east which had become defined by romantic tastes as a beauty spot and by local middle class residents as a public amenity. Up until the 1860s Maryon Wilson wanted to keep the Heath open, if only as a way to raise the value of the proposed residential area. In a remarkable trouncing of the rights of property – or rather the victory of one set of property owners over another – Maryon Wilson was prevented from acquiring leasing powers over his own freehold land. When after a protracted and unsuccessful legal battle Maryon Wilson threatened to enclose the Heath, milk his manorial rights by selling off sand and gravel and giving over land to laundry posts and then grant building leases short enough to turn it into a slum, the weight of Commons preservation sentiment was turned against him. The whole area was purchased by the Metropolitan Board of Works. There were insufficient funds to design and manage it as a municipal park so through judicious neglect and scatterings of gorse seed it was turned into the image of wild nature late Victorians so admired. While sophisticated nature lovers and literati trod its paths the area also became, after the arrival of the railway, more of a popular playground, 'Happy Hampstead', the crowds converging every Bank Holiday on the fair sited between the ponds and East Heath Road. As the photograph shows, the area did not remain fallow of houses. While Maryon Wilson was obstructed in his schemes Thomas Rhodes laid out South

scale or at least to regard it with newly anxious eyes.[25] Until late in the nineteenth century, cities were differentiated less by neighbourhood than by street and even within streets of the same type of housing there might be a range of occupational classes. A terrace of new two-bedroom dwellings might house a young clerk as the only breadwinner for a wife and baby and two doors along an older labourer with a working wife and children and perhaps also a lodger. The fine details of position and styling within any one street helped calibrate status but even so it is difficult to make simple connections between the physical and the social fabric of Victorian cities. Social patterns varied greatly between cities, according to their prevailing economic base, social structure, transportation system and not least to their topography. If in Manchester social and territorial divisions were most pronounced – or so seemed to be in view of the distance and often hostility between the big bourgeoisie who owned the great mills and warehouses and the extensive proletariat who worked in them – in Birmingham, a city of small work-shops with a reputation for social mobility and an atmosphere of class consensus, social geography seems to have been more integrated. Sheffield was also a city of small workshops but a more self-consciously working-class one than Birming-ham, not just because it lacked an integrating civic gospel but also, in contrast to Birmingham's relatively gentle terrain, its deeply incised valleys favoured the formation of more isolated working-class districts.[26]

If there was no overall plan to Victorian cities, there were from the mid ninteenth century an increasing number of schemes, both private and public, to reorganise their physical fabric and by extension their economic and social condition. These included new boulevards, housing estates and public parks.[27] These stood out in the landscape if only in contrast to the more *ad hoc* environ-ments which surrounded them and to which they were consciously opposed. Most of these schemes were informed by a belief that bad environments, ones that suffered a variety of conditions – dilapidation, poor drainage, overcrowding, multiple use, informal layout – were a prime cause of many ills, not just physical disease but improvidence, crime, laziness, irreligion, even political subversion. These characteristics made up the compound image of the 'slum'.[28] Wide streets were valued not only for ventilating slum districts they passed through (a strategy based on the theory that bad smells caused disease) but also for allowing the invigorating circulation of trade and for exposing such areas to the reproving presence of the higher classes and the police. What made a variety of schemes 'model' was not just the quality of their materials but their principles of social discipline[29] (photo 101).

Taking advantage of the provisions of the Cross Acts (1875) which allowed local authorities to purchase and demolish areas of unfit housing, private housing trusts built blocks of model dwellings for working people, most famously in London by the Peabody Trust set up in 1863. To compensate for their low economic return (5 per cent or less) relative to other investments, such schemes were designed to reap a high moral return in terms of the improved domestic habits and general demeanour of their tenants. They often ran to a strict regime, with long lists of dos and don'ts and close supervision. As much as the relatively high rents it seems it was the regime of such blocks and their barrack-like appear-ance (so reminiscent of a workhouse or prison) that made them unattractive to

Hill Park between 1870–71 on the lollipop shaped site of some 'escaped' copyholds and without suffering a squeak of protest. Furthermore this turned out to be a more taste-less scheme than the one Maryon Wilson envisaged, with tightly packed houses turning their backsides to public view.

100 Hove, East Sussex. Hove expanded rapidly from the 1870s as a consciously refined alternative to Brighton (made rougher by the railway), a 'Belgravia-sur-Mer' with broad avenues of substantial (if hardly elegant) terraces, which resisted incorporation by its larger and more vulgar neigh-bour. The centrepiece Brunswick Town does have a more Regency style and was begun much earlier in 1830 as an echo of Kemp Town devel-oped on the east side of Brighton but was not fully completed for another forty years. Beyond is the ground of Sussex County Cricket Club built in 1872, like county grounds in Edgbaston, Birm-ingham and West Bridgford, Nottingham a centrepiece of middle class surburban development.

101 Pentonville Prison, London. A monument to early Victorian social engineering, Pentonville was not only a model for other prisons but clarified principles informing other disciplinary institutions like workhouses, asylums, hospitals, factories and schools. Imprisonment at Pentonville was considered not just a penalty but a course of treatment. The building was designed as a machine for fabricating virtue from the raw material incarcerated there. All services and transactions were depersonalised, mechanised and centralised. At the pivot of the whole mechanism is a central hall from which every door of each of the 520 cells in the four radial wings could be seen. Each cell cost as much to build as a commodious new dwelling for an artisan and his entire family. Prisoners were kept in silence and profound isolation, most of the time in their cells but also in the two concentric exercise yards, walking around the paths in masks holding a knotted rope.

those displaced from the areas in which they were built. Their importance has been exaggerated by historians of housing. By 1914 in London there were less than 100,000 rooms in philanthropic dwellings of all kinds, not all of them inhabited.[30]

Many mill owners with factories in isolated locations built housing for their workers because no speculative builder would take the risk. Furthermore, to attract and secure a workforce this housing might be of better quality than usual. The relatively low return on house building might be more than made up for in other parts of the enterprise. A few well publicised and self-publicising factory owners, notably Titus Salt, attempted to do more than this and to provide a comprehensively planned community (photo 102, and see figure below), in the process allowing the residents less relaxation from the discipline of the workplace than they might enjoy in more down at heel and informal neighbourhoods. Some housing reformers saw home ownership as an instrument of moral reform. In the Pennine towns especially there was already a tradition of home ownership among better paid workers using building clubs, part of a tradition of self-respect. This tradition was reorganised by middle-class reformers, including industrialists such as the Crossleys of Halifax, who sponsored permanent building societies as vehicles for small investors as well as for those who wanted to own a home (photo 103, and see figure below).[31]

The State assumed relatively little responsibility for housing and what legislation there was tended to be permissive. There were great variations in the degree to which local authorities applied it. In the second half of the nineteenth century there were a series of housing reform acts – for example, to fix an owner's respon-

102 Saltaire, West Yorkshire. Built for Titus Salt by the River Aire three miles from Bradford, Saltaire is the largest and most famous model mill colony. Work began on building the factory in 1851 and when completed in 1876 Saltaire housed over 5000 people in over 800 dwellings and included a grandiose Congregational chapel (significantly opposite the mill gates), an adult education institute, schools, almshouses and public park. It thus provided all that a Victorian employer regarded as necessary for a useful life – work, health, education, moral instruction, space for respectable leisure and good houses – and excluded elements he would regard as inimical to it, including a pub, Irish people and any patch of ground where people might enjoy some impromptu fun. The social hierarchy of the mill was in theory replicated in the housing plan with separate rows of houses for overlookers (one with a look-out tower) and streets of successively smaller houses for lesser paid workers. But the census reveals that many streets were actually quite mixed and over time included residents who did not work for Salt. Many of Salt's workforce continued to live outside Saltaire perhaps because they were too independent, not just too poor. The 49 acres were purchased from a number of owners. The plan made little concession to the natural features of the site (apart from the river) or to previous geographical names and ownership patterns. With its grid iron street plan and functional zoning Saltaire was consciously opposed to the more informal patterns of local industrial villages and of central Bradford from where Salt had moved his enterprise.

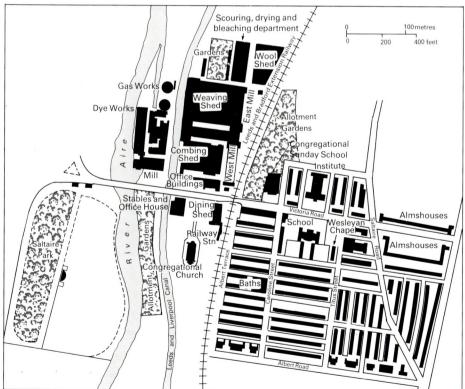

After Lockwood and Mawson's plan of Saltaire (1881).

103 Halifax, West Yorkshire. A suburban landscape largely financed by the Crossleys, the predominant employers in the town, and expressing their moral beliefs, Halifax was built up from a highly fragmented pattern of landholding. At the centre are the villa and grounds of Francis Crossley (built in the 1840s and remodelled in 1865–7), on its eastern side a row of gothic almshouses (1855), on its western side a Congregational chapel (1863). The owner of the land between villa and chapel refused to be bought out and so Crossley built the tower to hide it. To the south is the 12.5 acre People's Park (made up of closes from six different owners) donated by Crossley to the town in 1857 and which he enjoyed viewing from his villa as an arena of his benevolence. To the north, beyond the cemetery, is land (formerly a more loosely regulated park for political meetings and horse racing) purchased by Crossley in 1862 and sold to his brother to develop into a model residential estate funded by the Halifax Permanent Building Society of which the Crossleys were founding trustees.

sibility for maintenance (the Torrens Acts) and to select areas for clearance and reconstruction (the Cross Acts) – but it was not until an act of 1880 that local authorities were empowered to build houses. The first authority to do so under the Act was the London County Council with its Boundary Street scheme at Bethnal Green[32] (photo 104, and see figure on p. 202 which shows a slightly different angle).

As Victorian towns and cities expanded and infilled, so there was increasing concern about the disappearance of open space for recreation. There was pressure to open private gardens and parks to the public at least occasionally, to build new public parks and, later in the century, to preserve commons on the urban periphery. The public park movement was part of a wider campaign to remodel working-class leisure patterns, to promote what reformers called 'rational recreation'. Horse-racing, prize-fighting, pub-going were just some of the pursuits reformers wanted to wean the working class away from, either in favour of organised sports in playing fields or of more decorous promenading in family groups in pleasure gardens. With their battery of regulations and orderly (if informal looking) layout, such parks were in their way as disciplined an environment as a factory. The first public parks were financed by industrialists, like the 11-acre Derby Arboretum (1840) by Jedidiah Strutt and the 12-acre People's Park in Halifax by Francis Crossley. These parks were often located away from the areas in which most of the poor lived and indeed were used to stimulate suburban development for the better off. This helped to pay for the park and to promote social mixing on middle class terms, a central principle of social reform. These parks were eventually handed over to municipal corporations who later in the century were themselves active in creating parks, sometimes on a large scale.[33]

Public parks were one component in the effort of the leaders of towns and cities to improve their environment and their image, and to promote a sense of civic pride. This was expressed more monumentally in the centre of cities. On sites cleared of warrens of old buildings arose broad streets and squares lined with new town halls, museums, concert halls and banks designed in a variety of revivalist styles consciously echoing the atmosphere of rich, powerful and, above all, cultured cities in early modern Europe such as Venice or Bruges.[34]

The dominance of large industrial towns and cities in the Victorian imagination and on the ground can obscure the degree to which industrialisation still occurred in settings that seemed semi-rural. Recalling his upbringing in the mining country around Eastwood, Nottinghamshire in the late nineteenth century, D. H. Lawrence described the mines as 'an accident in the landscape' that was for him still resonant of 'the old England of the forest and agricultural past'. Life was 'a curious cross between industrialism and the old agricultural England of Shakespeare and Milton and Fielding and George Eliot' with a sense 'of intimate community' engendered by the butty system underground and a great love of nature among the colliers above, 'prowling for a rabbit, for nests, for mushrooms, anything'.[35] Arguably this is as much an urban as a rural sensibility, a reconstruction of the rural by those keenly aware of a growing disjunction between industry and the countryside. Those who worked in industry were no less aware of this than those who observed it. It is important to recall that, contrary to the pro-

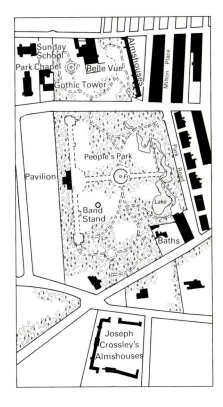

People's Park, Halifax. The upper section relates to photograph 103.

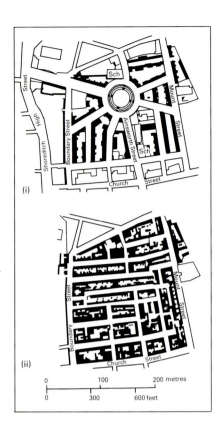

The Boundary Street scheme (i) after rebuilding, and (ii) before slum clearance. (After J. N. Tarn, *Five Per Cent Philanthropy*, Cambridge, 1973.)

104 Boundary Street Estate, Bethnal Green, London. Begun in 1893 on a site of 15 acres the Boundary Street Improvement Scheme was the first extensive local authority housing development and the first to exhibit comprehensive spatial control over the site as well as give the buildings some architectural taste. The scheme provided for clearing an area of narrow streets and courts known as the Jago, displacing a population of over 5,700. Separate workshops were included as well as provision shops and costermonger stores. The Jago had been an opaque area to the reforming imagination, a trap for all the noxious conditions that engendered a slum, but the Boundary Street scheme was a clear model of social and sanitary order.

nouncements for public parks, the inhabitants of even the largest industrial towns and cities were not permanently trapped within them. In West Yorkshire open moorland was often only a walk away from terraces of working class housing and while buses and trams extended the built-up area they also made more distant countryside accessible. Elizabeth Gaskell opens *Mary Barton*, her novel on industrial Manchester in the 1840s, with a historically accurate scene set in some fields outside the city, a place of popular resort for working people at holiday time. 'Here in their seasons may be seen the country business of haymaking, ploughing &c, which are such pleasant mysteries for townspeople to watch; and here the artisan deafened with the noise of tongues and engines, may come to listen awhile to the delicious sounds of rural life'.[36]

THE COUNTRY

Rural areas did not exercise such a strong hold upon the Victorian social imagination as did large towns and cities. This is in part a reflection of their relative and, in some places and periods, absolute social and economic decline. At the accession of Queen Victoria more than one in two of the population lived in rural areas, by her death in 1901 the figure was one in four; and this while the overall population quadrupled.[37] This is not to say that Victorian farming was inefficient – far from it in the 1860s and 1870s – or to say that Victorians did not care about the countryside; they did, often passionately. But unlike rural areas in the eighteenth century or urban areas in the nineteenth, the Victorian countryside was generally assumed to be empty of social or economic energies or tensions that it was imperative to resolve.[38] As rural areas became more dependent on the demands of towns for meat, milk and cheese – and as the agricultural landscape became more pastoral – so the countryside was also made over more in terms of urban or urban-funded ideals, for example in the preservation of wild areas, commonland and old cottages, the running up of picturesque villas and the building and remodelling of country houses in a variety of antique styles. The countryside became more rustic, less rural.[39] While this transformation did not begin in the Victorian period it did then become emphatic. Only in the later nineteenth century, in a period of agricultural depression, did metropolitan observers recognise that all was not sweetness and light in the countryside, in particular, that most rural labourers lived in conditions as bad as, if not worse than, those of urban labourers, that most cottages were insanitary hovels, not the rose-decked dwellings swarming with sun-bonnetted children so beloved of Victorian painters.[40]

While the rural population declined the social structure of landlords, tenant farmers and landless labourers remained more or less intact; indeed, landed estates accounted for almost 90 per cent of the agricultural land. Landlordly attitudes remained patrician, if now ostentatiously so. This self-consciousness (and the uncertainty that underlay it) is expressed in the size and style of Victorian country houses (photo 105). Landlords fashioned themselves as medieval barons, Renaissance princes, Tudor courtiers and Georgian squires. A thousand Victorian country houses survive, perhaps twice that many were built, and in view of the expense of building or radical remodelling (at least £30,000) it seems most of them

105 Penrhyn Castle, Gwynedd. A monumental 'Baronial' style house, a pastiche of military architecture of the fourteenth and fifteenth centuries, in which a genuinely medieval house is swallowed up. Designed in 1827 by Thomas Hopper for G. H. Dawkins Pennant and built when Pennant's slate quarries two miles away were at their most prosperous. The English hardwoods near the house are interspersed with large evergreens and exotics, including a Californian conifer planted by Queen Victoria in 1859. The garden is detached from the house and consists of a symmetrical Italianate terrace descending to a 'wild' garden originally stocked with plants from the furthest corners of the Empire.

must have been funded by revenue from urban rents or industrial enterprise. This revenue was enjoyed by many hereditary landowners but it seems that the entry of new men into landed society was accelerating. During the late Victorian depression there was a glut of country houses for sale. Many fell into ruin, others were detached from their estates for sale to professional men who wanted the convenience of a house in the country, not the burden of a country house, and only the most superficial trappings of country life.[41]

If country houses seemed feudal from the outside with their fanfares of turrets, underneath they were a precise and complex example of Victorian machinery. Aerial photographs can reveal some of the components which Victorians would rather not have had, in particular, the extent of the service block which, through the effects of screening, lowering, and laying out drives, was made barely apparent to members of the family and their guests (photo 106). The family block was serviced through a more secret landscape still, threaded between and below the main rooms and corridors, perhaps in places articulated by hydraulic lifts but relying for the most part on the labour of large retinues of servants. Country houses were designed to segregate different activities and to orchestrate them as quickly and efficiently as possible, whether in transporting a tureen of soup the length of two cricket pitches from kitchen to table or in making guests' luggage appear in their room before they did. The Victorian country house was a machine designed to produce both domestic comfort and propriety.[42]

The surroundings of country houses changed less radically. The area of park-land increased during the nineteenth century, with the creation of new parks (as the railway opened up new areas for country house building) and the incorporation of woodland in others. But the style of parkland was little altered from the century before. Most parks improved in the eighteenth century were left to mature with perhaps the addition of some evergreens and colourful exotics near the house. Entrances and drives might be moved to make houses more private. The most marked change was the creation of formal, finely detailed gardens near, and often adjacent, to the house. In the popular Italianate style, these gardens were made up of terraces laid out with elaborate parterres and filled with highly coloured bedding plants, each terrace usually bounded by stone balustrades and punctuated by urns and statuary. A little further away and more secluded in shrubbery might be rose gardens and specimen gardens to show off individual plants, a so-called 'gardenesque' style transplanted from suburban villas.[43] Indeed, overall there was a good deal of cross-fertilisation between the organisation and styling of polite suburbs and country houses, particularly in their combinations of private and public face. With their lodges, gates, drives and Gothic churches and their collection of villas with separate service quarters and perhaps a turret or two, new middle-class surburban developments presented a collective version of the country house landscape.

106 Thoresby House and Gardens, Nottinghamshire. Designed by Anthony Salvin, the house and gardens were built by 1871 for Lord Manvers, largely financed by profits from his collieries, and in a size and style reflecting the great houses built for Elizabethan courtiers. It re-placed a more modest Georgian house of red brick with a stone portico. Secluded to the north of the main block of the house, is the extensive area of domestic offices and court-yards supplying it. The tower over the main entrance gave an extensive view down the drive and allowed servants to be mobilized upon sighting a car-riage. The entrance courtyard is a little lower than the south terrace so that those in the gardens would be undisturbed by comings and goings.

Railways reorganised Victorian Britain, arguably transformed it. Their impact upon the landscape was often dramatic, their impact upon the Victorian imagination no less so. 'The iron rail proved a magician's road', declared Samuel Smiles, 'The locomotive gave a new celerity to time. It virtually reduced England to a sixth of its size. It brought the country nearer the town, and the town nearer the country. . . It energized punctuality, discipline and attention.'[44] While the building of the railway often seemed disruptive, not to say chaotic (especially to those with landed or rustic sensibilities), most observers recognised the emergence of a new order – in the standardisation of time throughout the country, in the extension of the hinterlands of industrial towns, in the monumental structure of railway building and in the new experience of railway travel.[45]

The first phase of railway development, the building of the main trunk routes from 1830 to the late 1840s, was the most dramatic and contentious. In retrospect, technical advances like the railway seem necessary breakthroughs but British industrialisation was proceeding satisfactorily within an infrastructure of waterways and roads. A major incentive was financial. There was in the 1830s and 1840s a glut of capital and the railway soaked it up like a sponge.[46] The railway certainly stimulated the economy, particularly the iron, coal and engineering industries, and did so more generally by dramatically lowering the costs of bulk transportation. Perhaps its most striking effect on consumption patterns was in transporting perishable foodstuffs. By the end of the century Londoners could buy fresh milk from the West Country and those with the money could enjoy broccoli from Cornwall, asparagus from the Vale of Evesham, strawberries from Hampshire and fresh cream from Devon.[47] While the railway did not play such a pioneering role in settlement formation as it did, for example, in North America, it did create towns like Crewe and Swindon, enlarged many others within commuting distance of major cities and reorganised residential patterns within large towns and cities. A striking measure of the railway's influence on urban development is the fate of those towns it passed by. Thus in 1841 Tewkesbury was a thriving town of 5,800 on the main highway from the north to the west of England but upon losing the Birmingham-to-Gloucester line to Cheltenham its growth was arrested and by 1901 its population had declined to 5,400.[48]

There were those who thought being bypassed by the railway was no bad thing, notably those with a stake in the old order. There was some well-publicised hostility to railway building by members of the landed gentry outraged at the prospect of the symbol of industrial progress crossing their land, or at least their parks. 'Physical objects and private rights were to be stamped under the wheels of the Fire King', complained a landed MP in the 1830s, 'the earth was to be tunnelled; parks, gardens and ornamental grounds were to be broken into'.[49] The very creation of those landscape parks perhaps less than a century earlier had often involved extensive excavation and a good deal of stamping on the rights of others but they were in the early railway age coming to a picturesque maturity which obscured the violence of their own making but heightened that of the railway. The Earl of Harborough successfully forced the line between Leicester and Peterborough to make a detour ('Harborough's curve') around Stapleford

Park and some other landed magnates forced the railway companies to further excavate their parks to hide the line.[50] The obstructive attitude of such landlords incurred the wrath of railway publicists who accused them of using sentiments about picturesque beauty as a ploy to raise the price of their land to the companies. 'Fancy prices for fancy prospects', complained John Francis in his 1851 *A History of the English Railway*; in contrast 'the imaginative vision of the [railway] shareholders beheld Titanic arches and vast tunnels; magnificent bridges and fine viaducts'.[51] Propagandists like Francis exaggerated the hostility of the landed interest, many of whom were railway shareholders and some of whom granted land free to railway companies. But objections on the grounds of landscape amenity continued to be made, most famously by Wordsworth. A railway shareholder himself Wordsworth had written in praise of railways and viaducts in general when they were still far from his beloved Lakes but in 1844 he complained bitterly about the projected Kendal and Windermere Railway, not so much for spoiling the view but for letting loose into the Lake District holiday crowds from the industrial towns of the north west.[52]

In the first phase of building trunk lines, companies paid great attention to the appearance of the railway both on the ground and in guidebooks. Viaducts were singled out for their magnificence (photo 107). Victorians preferred viewing them obliquely from ground level from where their power (and by extension

107 Ouse Viaduct, near Ardingly, West Sussex. The London to Brighton railway cut across the grain of the Weald; this viaduct over the valley of the Ouse, completed in 1841 stretches for 1,475 yards, and reaches a maximum height of 96 feet. It is part of a series of long tunnels, high embankments and deep cuttings on this stretch of the line; two miles to the north is the 1,141 yard Balcombe tunnel.

108 Charwelton, Northamptonshire. The ubiquity of embankments and cuttings tends to minimise the achievement of those who built the railway. Less formal traces of navvies' labours may emphasise it, notably where materials excavated from tunnels or cuttings were insufficient or superfluous for the building of embankments and where land on either side of the line was used to dig or dump it. This view of the abandoned railway line from Aylesbury to Rugby shows a spoil tip of material excavated from a tunnel north of Charwelton. The signs of slippage suggest it also functioned as a support for the steep embankment carrying the line.

that of the railway) was best appreciated. Railway travellers of course were scarcely aware of the viaducts they passed over and companies arranged for excursions to stop at major viaducts to allow passengers to disembark and scramble down to see them to advantage. The guide books that gave such views were more reticent about the laborious process of railway building, even when parts of the line they show are evidently unfinished; in fact, part of the point of this reticence was to assuage genteel fears of railway building stocked up by anti-railway propaganda featuring terrifying navvies and explosive locomotives.[53] And now it is more easy to forget the process as well as the scale of railway building (photo 108). The greatest earthworks since the Iron Age has been absorbed into the landscape and our liking for it, as has the labour that made them, each man shovelling up to 20 tonnes of material a day. Despite the protests of landowners and custodians of rural England the railway was readily accepted, even welcomed by most, including those who could not afford to use it, as a feature in the landscape. John Francis was making a political point when he reported that 'the clergy of Hampshire petitioned against the new power because the rustics kept away from church to see the train pass by';[54] but there is no doubt that the railway became a popular spectacle.

Both pro- and anti-railway propaganda emphasised the railway as a democratic symbol. For John Francis it was in every way a 'levelling' power; it 'gives the poor man the luxuries of the rich [and] placed the wealthy on a level with the poor'.[55] Arguably, the railway actually sharpened class differences – by segregating social ranks into different class carriages, by stimulating the growth of more exclusive suburbs (for artisans as well as for the ranks of the middle class) and by hemming in the districts of those who could not afford the fares. The impact of railway building upon cities was more striking than upon the countryside. It changed their physiography with bold strokes. 'The plans of British towns, no matter how diverse before 1830', observes J. R. Kellett, 'are uniformly superinscribed within a generation by the gigantic geometrical brush-strokes of the engineers' curving approach lines and cut-offs, and franked with the same bulky and intrusive termini, sidings and marshalling yards'.[56] The demand for space and the high cost of land at the centre of cities initially forced the planting of termini towards the periphery of cities but companies were anxious to move towards the centre despite the cost, if only for prestige, and many did so. The social cost of this is less calculable than the financial. Large areas of poor housing were demolished to make way for the railway, clearing the problem of slum housing in one place but probably aggravating it elsewhere.[57] Hemmed in by embankments, loomed over by viaducts, exposed to the smoke of locomotives and to the gaze of passengers, the poor Londoner's view of the railway was not so appealing as that enjoyed by the Hampshire rustic.

Station building decisively altered the geography of cities, changing the flow of traffic and population, attracting some forms of land use and repelling others (photo 109).[58] Over all this arose the most magnificent monuments of the railway age, the station buildings themselves. 'Railway termini and hotels are to the nineteenth century what monasteries and cathedrals were to the thirteenth century', declared the *Building News* in 1875, 'they are truly the only representative buildings we possess'.[59] Gateways to the Victorian city, railway stations mediated two worlds and were essentially two-faced: half-factory, half-palace. The sheds of steel and glass were daring examples of modernity pointed to open country and the regime of railway space; on the other hand the reception buildings of brick and stone evoked the past in a variety of revivalist styles and looked out to the older regime of horse-drawn and pedestrian traffic.[60]

If the railway made its distinctive mark on the landscape it also made its mark on travellers' perception of landscape. As the irregularities of terrain that were perceptible on old roads were replaced by the sharp linearity of the railway, so passengers experienced a loss of contact with the landscape, most acutely in tunnels and on high viaducts. Some found the shock of this dreadful, others found it exhilarating. The experience of looking at landscape from a speeding train was novel. Those who persisted in trying to hold the foreground in focus found it an unnerving, even nauseous, experience. Those who enjoyed the spectacle of moving panorama shows – a kind of proto-cinema – relished it.[61] The railway created new vistas on the landscape. As it reorganised Britain so it re-presented it.

FURTHER READING

S. Daniels and S. Seymour, 'Landscape design and the idea of improvement 1730–1914', in R. A. Dodgshon and R. A. Butlin (eds.), *An Historical Geography of England and Wales*, 2nd edn, London, 1990.

R. Dennis, *English Industrial Cities of the Nineteenth Century: A Social History*, Cambridge, 1984.

H. J. Dyos and M. Wolff (eds.), *The Victorian City: Images and Realities*, London, 1973.

G. E. Mingay (ed.), *The Victorian Countryside*, London, 1981.

M. Robbins, *The Railway Age*, Harmondsworth, 1965.

8 The twentieth century: *c.*1900–*c.*1960

INTRODUCTION

By and large, this book is concerned with the permanence of landscape, but this chapter is concerned with its impermanence. Most of the photographs used in earlier chapters were taken relatively recently and show features which survive from the often distant past. However, it would be difficult to claim that such photographs are a significant source for the historian of the present century; in particular, most of the man-made artifacts of this period are all too visible at ground level, and their arrangement well-recorded in maps and plans. By contrast, this chapter treats aerial photographs as historic artifacts in their own right, and as a record of landscapes no longer to be seen.

Whatever the concerns of historical geographers of earlier periods, it is hard to claim that the physical appearance of the landscape is a central theme in research on the twentieth century. Therefore, while this essay will touch on wider economic and social issues, the central narrative deals with the development of 'planning'. This introduction explores available photographic sources, and then suggests that the distinctive feature of the twentieth century is the extent to which new landscapes were the outcomes not of the hidden hand of 'economic progress' but rather of conscious, often aesthetically informed decisions – of design, public policy, or consumer choice. The emergence of two major forces are discussed at some length: the mass of the population as consumers, and the central state.

The use of contemporary aerial photographs as historical sources is an almost unexplored theme. The first aerial photographs were taken by Nadar (Gaspar-Félix Tournachon), who filed a patent on taking photographs from a balloon in 1853, and began experiments over Paris in 1858. The first attempts in Britain were made by James Glaisher of Greenwich Observatory in 1861 and 1862. However, these early attempts produced poor results due to the effects of the motion of the balloon on the long exposures required by early photographic techniques. Practical aerial photography began with the introduction of the gelatin dry plate in the 1870s, and the English inventor Walter Woodbury was the first to use these in a balloon, patenting a system for military reconnaissance in 1877.[1] Unfortunately, few aerial photographs of British locations survive from before 1900, and they only become abundant with the enormous development of technique and proliferation of equipment resulting from the First World War; in particular, abundant images of inter-war Britain can be found in the Aerofilms collection, while comprehensive vertical coverage was produced by the RAF just after the Second World War.

These photographs are arguably of interest to historians of all periods, and particularly to those interested in urban themes, as they pre-date the bombings of the Second World War and the still greater destruction of subsequent redevelopment. However, this chapter is principally concerned with creations of the period, and therefore with what has both come and gone during this century. As such, it is concerned with landscape not as something fixed, or a slow accretion, but rather with landscape as ephemera and, in some ways, as a matter of fashion. The technology which gave us the aerial photograph, something doubly impossible for most of the period covered by this book, also provided the capability, economic rather than strictly technological, to shape the landscape not merely as we needed – which the brawn of the Victorian navvy had already achieved – but as we wished.

Parks and landscape gardens, the designed landscapes of previous centuries, were a product and reflection of concentrated political and economic power, demonstrating the capacity of landowners to mould their domains as they wished, ignoring both pre-existing features and the wishes of other inhabitants; that they occupied a small fraction of the country and had little economic function was inherent in their role as environments for an elite. In the twentieth century, the attempt to design not just some but all environments has, conversely, been one of the most direct assaults on unbridled capitalist property relations. Further, attempts to impose aesthetic criteria on the entire landscape created inevitable conflicts with economic imperatives; the landscape became not merely a reflection of conflicts between different social classes and economic interests but one of the principal arenas of battle.

There is an obvious conflict between ravaging heavy industry or rampaging property developers, on the one hand, and those concerned for the glories of the countryside and the beautification of towns, on the other. A historical perspective also reveals both a growing distinction between giving the urban masses access to the countryside and an often elitist pressure for conservation *per se*, and very different aesthetics of how the landscape should be. Simplifying drastically, two main aesthetics can be identified: an urge for order, first classicist then modernist; and a quest for the picturesque, often tied to romantic notions of the rural past. The former provided much of the initial rationale for planning, and often presented itself in utilitarian terms, but one thesis of this chapter is that, as in so much of modernism, this utilitarian 'functionalism' proved disfunctional, and therefore a consequence of a sometimes confused aesthetic.

While the conflict between the ordered and the romantic is scarcely new, the scale of landscape change in the twentieth century has been wholly novel. If the principal motive force of the nineteenth century was the steam engine, seeking fuel to power itself, rails to run on, and very occasionally providing the muscle behind constructors' shovels and hammers, in the twentieth century the great power was the consumer, and the great invention 'leisure'. As electricity and the expansion of new consumer goods industries freed manufacturing from the coalfields, as the rise of the service sector made employment no longer synonymous with manufacturing, and as new transport systems permitted residence to be even further removed from employment, so the location of homes, of shops, and even of factories and whole towns, became increasingly a matter of whim.

In particular, while in the past the places of residence of most of the population were a direct function of their place of employment, and most waking hours were spent at work or doing basic daily chores, the home became increasingly the locus of consumption and leisure. For the growing middle class, the place of residence was selected for the leisure opportunities it offered, and the type of neighbours one would find; at the same time, levels of property ownership were rising and likely future values became a concern. In short, residential communities ceased to be simply adjuncts of centres of employment: their rise was promoted through advertising and their decline would come about through a loss of amenity, or a shift in what was desired. Nor were these trends restricted to the middle classes; some of the archetypal lost landscapes of the twentieth century were created by the rush of the better-off artisans and clerks to find a small piece of countryside for themselves.

While homes as centres of consumption, and as items of consumption in themselves, transformed the surroundings of towns and cities, 'leisure' more subtly changed the landscape as a whole. If place of residence was less closely tied to place of work, place of recreation was largely liberated from it, and self-evidently the holiday-maker and week-ender select locations in terms of image and aesthetics; the period also saw essentially the creation of 'retirement', as a time of leisure rather than mere decrepitude, and the retiree was increasingly footloose and sought-after, fuelling the rapid population growth of the south coast. The 'consumption' of places by those at leisure, whether temporarily or permanently, had a direct impact on the landscape through provision of transport, of accommodation, and of more specialised facilities. Further, in a country of predominantly urban employment the politicisation of the landscape and the emergence of environmental politics could never have happened whilst most of the population were preoccupied with work; while farming remained the predominant land-use, numbers directly employed in farming dwindled steadily and a growing fraction of the population felt some broader involvement in rural areas through their use of the countryside for leisure.

The rise of the consumer, and the conversion of places into consumer commodities, clearly shaped the twentieth-century landscape, but the other crucial new actor was the central state. The state has become so omnipresent it is hard to appreciate how little impact central government had on most localities before this century. While always reserving unto itself ultimate authority, its employees were few and its concerns mainly with military and trade matters; in local matters short of insurrection, it operated mainly through proxies: magistrates, turnpike trusts, Poor Law Guardians, and eventually town and county councils. In all of these what it provided was mainly a framework within which local interest groups vied for dominance, and commercial interests frequently had the final say.

The concerns of central government expanded rapidly from the 1880s onwards, as civil servants influenced by utilitarian ideals created the Local Government Board and the Boards of Education and Health, and moved the focus of the Board of Trade from international commerce to the labour market; note that these were all, in party political terms, peripheral ministries. However, the pervasive power of the central state, and in particular its role in shaping the landscape, is clearly a creation of the First World War. The conduct of war had always been part of the state's preserve but, since the defeat of Napoleon, wars had been limited affairs; colonial wars, in particular, were more a steady business for professionals than all-consuming conflagrations. The First World War placed quite new demands on an industrial society: as both sides in a relatively evenly-matched contest sought to mobilise more and more resources, the state became involved in more and more aspects of society.

In a war of attrition, the supply of munitions became crucial, and the state became a major industrial employer; vast new factories had to be thrown up, and new housing estates built to house the workers. These developments were on an unparalleled scale, and provided a model for later developments. Then overseas supply lines came under attack, and it was realised how dependent Britain had become on imported food and raw materials; self-sufficiency became a watchword, and planting wheat or growing pine trees were matters of state policy. Above all, total war meant total disruption of the peacetime economy, and the state found itself dragged into the direction of raw materials, of docks and railways, of industrial labour, of basic foodstuffs; ultimately, to the direction of almost all aspects of the economy, and while many politicians were aghast, a corporatist if not a Fabian ethos had already taken a firm hold at high levels of the Civil Service.[2]

While most of the wartime controls were rapidly dismantled after 1918, experience and much of the administrative machinery remained. Meanwhile, the 1911 National Insurance Act, and the extension of unemployment insurance to most of the industrial workforce in 1920, gave the state a continuing concern for the state of the economy. As the structural problems of the economy became more visible in the 1920s and 1930s, pressure grew for direct intervention. Despite Treasury resistance, the state became involved in schemes for industrial rejuvenation in depressed regions, and the wartime munitions plants became the model for new developments. Meanwhile, growing concern over the threat of new war led to the Barlow Commission of 1939–40, which sought to decant industry and population from 'congested' areas where they were likely to be vulnerable to bombing.[3]

The Second World War saw much more rapid moves towards total mobilisation; virginity had been lost. The needs of air power, of defence against a real threat of invasion, and the need to accommodate 3.5 million troops prior to D-Day meant that the direct impact of war on the British landscape was far greater; and this is not to even mention the effects of aerial bombardment. But the war also established the all-embracing responsibilities of the state: that if something was wrong, 'they' should do something about it. As a result, the vague notions of 'homes fit for heroes' of the First World War were replaced by detailed plans for 'reconstruction', in which national parks were as central as the repair of bombed cities. In particular, it was the war as much as the obvious excesses of inter-war sprawl which legitimised comprehensive physical planning. While the immediate post-war years were blighted by austerity, much of this 'Butskellite' consensus survived the more affluent 1950s. Obviously, a story which ends in 1960 scarcely brings us up to the present day, but that is a matter for the conclusion.

This chapter's central theme is the development of planning, and as a related volume is concerned with the changing environment,[4] an attempt has been made to avoid overlaps, particularly in photographic themes.

IMPROVING THE CITY

Britain in 1900 was an urban society, but one in which the city was more often seen as a threat to civilisation than as a monument to it. It is therefore unsurprising that the Edwardian years saw growing concern with urban form. While Victorian improvers had emphasised the physical elimination of the worst slums and the construction of individual civic buildings as foci for urban pride, the notion of the positive planning of whole towns began to gain strength. Two strands can be identified, an official school which sought to turn large towns into great cities and the Town and Country Planning movement which worked to replace cities by networks of country towns. Paradoxically, it was the latter who had greatest success, and certainly set the direction for state planning after 1945.

Perhaps because the empire itself was so splendid, Britain never really competed with Haussmann's Paris, Brandenburg Berlin, or even Mussolini's Rome in the construction of an imperial capital. While grandiose schemes abounded, many of these were picturesquely gothic rather than classical, and the actual impact on London very limited:[5] photo 110 of Trafalgar Square and surrounding

110 Trafalgar Square and Admiralty Arch, London. This photograph was taken from the balloon 'Corona' on 22 May 1909; as such, it is one of the earliest surviving aerial photographs of London. It also records some of the few completed attempts to give London the architecture to match its status as an imperial capital. The Admiralty Arch, completed in 1911, was designed by Sir Aston Webb as part of a national memorial to Queen Victoria which also involved the refacing of Buckingham Palace and the construction of the *rond-point* in front of it.

area shows one of the few completed examples. Most provincial cities did little beyond extending the Victorian town hall to accommodate a growing bureaucracy, or bracket it with civic offices. One clear exception is Cardiff, where Cathays Park was consciously developed as a capital complex for Wales, from the City Hall of 1904 to the Welsh Office of 1938. However, these developments generally exhibit an insipid architectural neo-classicism rather than any particular conception of urban design; for a more confident imperialism, we should perhaps look to Lutyens' work on New Delhi from 1912 onwards, which sought to assimilate Indian motifs into a European classical idiom to express our domination of the Orient.[6]

Given the status that the Town and Country Planning movement has since achieved, it is important to understand its original marginal position; consider John Buchan, barrister, MP, and eventually Governor General of Canada. In the first chapter of *Mr Standfast*, one of Buchan's sequels to *The Thirty-Nine Steps* set during the First World War, his hero Richard Hannay is ordered home from the front and instructed to

> sink down deep into the life of the half-baked, the people whom this war hasn't touched or has touched in the wrong way, the people who split hairs all day and are engrossed in what you and I would call selfish little fads. . . You won't live in an old manor like this but in gimcrack little 'arty' houses. You will hear everything you regard as sacred laughed at and condemned, and every kind of nauseous folly acclaimed, and you must hold your tongue and pretend to agree.

This purgatory proves to be the 'Garden City of Biggleswick', very obviously Letchworth Garden City, and Buchan provides a short sketch of the town.

> The house – or 'home' as they preferred to name it at Biggleswick – was one of some two hundred others which ringed a pleasant Midland common. It was badly built and oddly furnished; the bed was too short, the windows did not fit, the doors did not stay shut. The inn at Biggleswick was a reformed place which sold nothing but washy cider. . . About half [the inhabitants of Biggleswick] were respectable citizens who came there for the country air and low rates, but even these had a touch of queerness and had picked up the jargon of the place. There seemed to be an abundance of young men, mostly rather weedy-looking but with one or two well-grown ones who should have been fighting. The young men were mostly Government clerks or writers or artists. There were quantities of young women too, most of them rather badly dressed and inclining to untidy hair.[7]

Hannay was sent to Biggleswick because it was a centre of opposition to the war, and this was true of Letchworth; Frederic Osborn (1885–1978) could easily be one of Buchan's characters. A member of the Independent Labour Party and the Fabians, he was appointed Secretary Manager of the Howard Cottage Society at Letchworth in 1912, but went into hiding in 1916 to avoid conscription and published various new town polemics under pseudonyms. He was company secretary for Welwyn Garden City Ltd between 1919 and 1936, and lived in Welwyn for over fifty years. Osborn was never a 'planner', more a constant lobbyist for

Ebenezer Howard's original vision, serving on the 1945 Reith Committee on new towns and keeping alive the Town and Country Planning Association.[8]

Raymond Unwin (1863–1940) became a more establishment figure, but began as an active member of William Morris's Socialist League; his father was a friend of the Oxford reformer, T. H. Green. Trained as an engineer rather than an architect, his essential ideas were embodied in *The Art of Building a Home* (1901): either urban quadrangles of cooperative housing, modelled on Oxford colleges, or village greens; these units were seen as expressions of communal living. Following the 1901 Garden City Association conference, attended by George Bernard Shaw and Seebohm Rowntree, he became involved in designing several schemes, including New Earswick, established by Joseph Rowntree from 1902 on the outskirts of York, and Letchworth, from 1903. The ideologies underlying such communities are visible in the planned facilities of New Earswick: a Library and Institute, an Art School, a Church and Chapel, and shops and a Temperance Inn.[9]

In 1912 Unwin published *Nothing Gained by Overcrowding*, but perhaps his greatest impact came through the World War. The Ministry of Munitions had to house enormous new workforces employed at its plants; for example, Well Hall Estate in south-east London, containing 1,200 homes for workers from Woolwich Arsenal, was built in $10\frac{1}{2}$ months in 1915.[10] The Director General of the Ministry of Munitions was Hubert Llewellyn Smith, a former resident of Toynbee Hall and assistant of Charles Booth, as well as a pioneer of state involvement in the labour market, which perhaps explains the ministry's pioneering role in adopting new principles of urban design.[11] Unwin was in charge of the planning of munitions settlements and worked on a number of major schemes, most notably at Gretna, and this led to plans for post-war reconstruction. He served on the 1917 Tudor Waters Committee, which concluded that 300,000 houses should be built within twelve months of the end of the war. The standards laid down by Tudor Waters, replacing narrow-frontage terraces by wide frontage cottages, generous gardens, and curving tree-lined roads, had a wide impact on the inter-war period but were increasingly debased by speculative builders or cash-limited councils into the archetypal semi-detached.[12]

In examining the work of the early town planning movement, there is a danger that we over-emphasise the new towns, Letchworth and Welwyn. By 1914, there were over fifty housing schemes on Garden City lines,[13] but most were suburbs rather than the free-standing towns advocated by Ebenezer Howard.[14] In this sense, Hampstead Garden Suburb (photo 111) is a better archetype, founded in 1906 and now containing over 5,000 houses. Unwin was the overall planner but Edwin Lutyens designed the central features on rather different principles. The Garden Suburb was an explicit experiment aimed at improving the lives of the poor, and altering the relations between social classes, but in retrospect it appears somewhat naive. Its founder, Dame Henrietta Barnett, stated her ambition thus:

> If we could buy a large estate and build so that all classes could live in neighbourliness together, the friendships would come about quite naturally and the artificial bridges need not be made.[15]

However, given that the Suburb contains sections of houses designed for specific groups such as artisans, this vision was more corporatist than socialist.

BRITAIN AND THE BEAST

These early developments in planning were the work of a small group of enthusiasts, and matter mainly because of their later consequences; their impact on the landscape of inter-war Britain was very constricted. Much the most striking change was the explosion in the size of towns, and in this planning played little role. Population growth, smaller households, and the expansion of the south's population relative to the north all had some part, but the crucial factor was a wish to live at lower densities, so that between 1914 and 1939 London's population grew from 6.5 million to 8.5 million, but the urban area trebled.[16] Over 4 million new houses were built in the inter-war period, comprising over a third of the total housing stock. The prime agent of this new urban sprawl was not the private car; as the table below suggests, relatively few households possessed a car in 1930, and the suburban commuter travelled by electric train or tube in London, or by bus elsewhere. In particular, surface extensions of the London Underground into west and north London, and the electrification of the Southern Railway, led suburbs such as Hendon and Wembley to double or even treble in population during the 1920s.[17]

MOTOR VEHICLE OWNERSHIP IN BRITAIN 1903–88

DATE	MOTOR VEHICLES CURRENTLY LICENSED IN GREAT BRITAIN (000s)	VEHICLES PER THOUSAND POPULATION
1903	18	0.5
1909	144	3.6
1920	650	15.4
1930	2272	50.9
1940	2325	49.5
1950	4409	89.6
1960	9439	185.3
1970	14950	276.3
1980	19210	350.8
1988	23302	420.0

Source: Department of Transport, *Transport Statistics Great Britain* (various dates).

The shift of population to the south was encouraged by the growth of new consumer-oriented manufacturing industry, but it is perhaps more correct to see the latter as an effect: the greatest expansion in employment, particularly in London, was in the service sector, and the new jobs clerical or managerial. These new consumers, with both the money to buy new products and the larger homes to keep them in, created new markets for consumer durables, and so we see new mass production industries, often dominated by particular firms: bicycles (Raleigh), sewing machines (Singer), vacuum cleaners (Hoover) and so on. By establishing brands and securing dominant market shares, these firms achieved the volumes where the economies of scale inherent in assembly line production were attainable.

There was often a substantial delay between the creation of an industry and this mass production stage; for example, 59 motor manufacturers had been established by 1900, but most catered quite literally to the carriage trade. Ford began to assemble cars in 1911 in Manchester (photo 112), from imported components, and rapidly dominated the market through its massive advantage in engine power for the price.[18] The combination of firms which dominated their markets and assembly line methods led to the appearance of very large and extensive industrial sites; the later Ford plant at Dagenham, with an integrated steel plant and employing 25,000 workers, is one of the best known. Smaller firms, freed by the bus from a need to be near their workers' homes, gathered together on industrial estates to share amenities; for example, Slough trading estate grew to employ 30,000 on 600 acres. However, it is important to note that the first of these giant sites, although based on mass production, scarcely catered to consumers: Woolwich Arsenal, at its peak nearly three times the size of Dagenham, is illustrated (photo 113). Similarly, Slough began as an army transport repair depot.[19]

The growth of the London suburbs was a planned process, if only due to the managed development of the Underground and railway systems; in addition, much development was on a large scale and actively marketed, placing some premium on the overall aesthetics of a development.[20] The greatest criticism at the time concerned not the destruction of the countryside by the sprawl of Metroland but more specific eyesores, many of which have since been banished: road-

111 Hampstead Garden Suburb, London. The Garden Suburb was established in 1906 by Dame Henrietta Barnett, wife of Canon Barnett the founder of Toynbee Hall. Its location on the then edge of London, adjacent to Golders Green, was a matter of controversy within the town planning movement which generally favoured the promotion of free-standing towns. Its growth embodied a striking contradiction, well illustrated in this 1935 photograph. Overall planning was the responsibility of Raymond Unwin, who favoured winding lanes and vernacular 'cottages', but the consulting architect Edwin Lutyens was responsible for the central square and public buildings at Temple Fortune. The contrast between Unwin's rural romanticism and Lutyens' classical formalism is a visual reflection of the divide between Unwin's romantic socialism and the more authoritarian vision of the Barnetts, in which the central school and church, on the highest point of the site, were instruments of social control.

112 The Ford Motor factory at Trafford Park, Manchester, photographed in 1926. The Ford Motor works has some claim to be the birthplace of mass-market motoring in Britain. While in the inter-war period the motor industry became highly concentrated in the West Midlands and South-East, in the Edwardian period it was more scattered and most producers were very small scale, catering quite literally to the carriage trade. This factory assembled 6,139 Model T's in 1913 and captured a large share of the market. Note that although modern in the use of single-storey buildings, the buildings are huddled together on a cramped site close to workers' housing: production was 'Fordist', but the workforce was pre-Fordist and certainly were not expected to arrive in their own Model T's.

113 Woolwich Royal Arsenal and Plumstead, London. One of the most remarkable, if least known industrial sites in Britain, the Arsenal dated from the seventeenth century and by the 1900s employed 16,000 workers; in 1907, the Thames-side site was three miles long and a mile wide. However, most of the buildings shown here date from the extra-ordinary expansion during the First World War, when employment on this one site reached 74,467; all the industrial buildings in this 1961 photograph as far as Plumstead High Street were part of the Arsenal, and it does not show the older part of the site, to the right, or the extension over the Plumstead marshes to the left where dangerous processes were carried out in isolated buildings; this area has now been re-developed as part of Thamesmead new town.

side advertising in rural areas, which now so strikes the British visitor to America, was banned by the Advertisement Regulation Act of 1900; similarly, ribbon development (photo 114) was controlled by the Restriction of Ribbon Development Act passed in 1935. Perhaps the greatest outrages, however, were the attempts by the working class and lower middle class to make their own escape from the city.

Given cheap land, cheap public transport, and no planning controls, higher wages meant that many urban workers could afford to buy a small plot and visit at weekends. For example, at Peacehaven on the Sussex coast (photo 115), plots measuring 25 by 100 feet sold for between £25 and £75, and in the 'plotlands' of south Essex, where competition between railway companies meant particularly low fares, prices were even lower. Building was also economical: one solution was old railway carriages, some of which are still to be seen at Dungeness, or tramcars.[21] To right-thinking people, and most historians of planning, these were nothing but rural slums, but there is a clear class dimension: the impulses behind Pinner and Laindon Hills were similar, and what distinguished them was the means of the inhabitants.

The bulk of the south Essex plotlands were removed as part of the construction of Basildon new town, deliberately sited there with this aim and replacing inde-

114 Ribbon development on the western edge of Hereford. While many of the threats to the British countryside campaigned against in the inter-war period persist, some have been eliminated by planning controls. One was road-side advertising in rural areas, which now so startles the British visitor to the United States; another was ribbon development, unplanned constructions of houses directly fronting onto main inter-urban roads. The example shown, photographed in 1961, has now essentially vanished, as new housing estates on either side of the main road have eliminated the ribbon form.

pendent plot owners by council house tenants (photo 116). In the debate on the new town, the local MP gave a different perspective:

> These freeholders . . . are, almost without exception people of slender means and owning comparatively small plots of land. In many cases their homes are the result of the labour from their own hands. These people came from the East End of London . . . in the 1920s, and they built their own homes during the week-ends. In all cases their property represents a lifetime of abstinence and thrift . . . Whatever their means, these people possess something of infinite value to themselves. They possess their homes, their freeholds and their pride and self-reliance.[22]

At the time, these developments were severely criticised. One of the most passionate critics was the Welsh architect, Clough Williams-Ellis, author of *England and the Octopus* (1928) and editor of *Britain and the Beast* (1937); the latter includes contributions by Keynes and E. M. Foster, while the former contains a 'Devil's Dictionary': Advertisements, Borough Engineers, Bungalows,

115 Peacehaven, East Sussex. The archetypal uncontrolled inter-war development, on the cliffs east of Brighton and here photographed in 1933. As Pevsner put it: 'What is one to say? Peacehaven has been called a rash on the countryside. It is that, and there is no worse in England. Peacehaven derives its name from the end of the First World War. Whose haven was it? Whose haven is it?... Small plots, yet nothing semi-detached, let alone in terraces. Every man his own house, even if only a few feet from the neighbours.' Perhaps two comments can be added: firstly, a sequence of photographs would show that even this monstrosity has mellowed, with infilling and the growth of trees; secondly, the ideological commitment to the detached house, however small, has returned to be a hallmark of private estates in the 1980s and 1990s.

116 Plotlands at Basildon, Essex. If Peacehaven was built for the new retired population, the 'plotlands' of south Essex, perhaps the only true shanty towns of Britain, were built for themselves by East Enders seeking to escape London: individuals bought a small plot and then constructed a shack for themselves. Their flimsiness made them truly ephemeral landscape features; in par-ticular, Basildon new town, about twenty-five miles east of central London, was created to replace the plotlands of Laindon and Pitsea. This 1965 photograph shows an area of plotlands being progressively built over by the new town, its new roads imposing a different geometry; Pitsea railway station and junc-tion are visible at the bottom.

Electric Power Distribution, and so on.[23] Williams Ellis' deliberate counterpoint to all this 'urban beastliness' was Portmeirion (photo 117), the 'village' he created on the north Wales coast. However, it seems arguable that the impulse behind its location, on a prominent coastal site, was very similar to that behind Peacehaven, and what distinguished it from the latter or from Laindon Hills was the resources, and ultimately the class background, of its builders.[24] There are two great ironies: firstly, it seems doubtful whether Portmeirion, as a 'new village', would be any more likely than the plotlands to receive planning permission today; secondly, Portmeirion is now essentially a tourist attraction and contains little reference to its founder, while Basildon has a plotlands museum, including a restored bungalow.[25] Ultimately, all is heritage.

WAR AND RECONSTRUCTION

The direct impact of the Second World War on the landscape of Britain was very substantial. In particular, Britain as a whole became a potential, and in the Battle of Britain actual, theatre of war for the first time since the Jacobite rebellion. The coastal defences, already strong, were greatly strengthened and supplemented by lines of defences stretching across the Weald between London and

117 Portmeirion, developed on the north Wales coast near Portmadoc by Clough Williams-Ellis from 1926 on was a deliberate counter-blast to exurban dystopias such as Peacehaven. In its whimsicality it is also an explicit rejection of the formalism, whether classical or modernist, of British planning: the vernacular employed is Italian rather than Unwin's old English cottages. It was also implicitly elitist: for years its actual function was as an exclusive hotel, the casual visitor deterred by a prohibitive entrance charge; perhaps ironically, it has now become a mass tourist attraction more concerned with the 1960s 'Prisoner' television series than with Williams-Ellis' ideas. This photograph was taken in 1950.

118 Manston Airfield, Kent, in 1942. Given the difficulty of obtaining photographs of wartime sites, the best example of a Battle of Britain airfield was photographed by the Luftwaffe, on 13 July 1942. This is taken from a set of German 'target folders' captured after the war and now held by the Imperial War Museum. The folders contain photographs, maps and other information. For obvious reasons, the photograph is from a high altitude, and only limited details of the airfield can be seen. In particular, note that the runways are of grass, but the peripheral buildings, ammunition dumps and so on are extensive; Manston, just west of Ramsgate, was one of the airfields closest to France, and therefore crucial to the interception of German attacks on London.

the sea. Observation posts and radar towers occupied hilltops across the country; 'old airfields' now litter the countryside, their triangular runways visible on maps and old hutments to be seen on the ground. Less visibly, much of central government went underground, in new tunnels under Whitehall.[26] Later, when the threat of attack had dwindled, Britain became an enormous military encampment, as both British and American forces prepared to invade Europe; all across southern England military hutments were erected at high speed, and were later pressed into other uses, from government offices to chicken farms.

To the student of ephemeral landscapes, military facilities, with their geometric patterns and quite different locational rationale, are of central interest, but sources are regrettably scarce. To a quite extraordinary extent, aerial photographs of any type of military installation remain classified; one explanation was that it requires a colonel or equivalent to declassify photographs, and it is precisely because old photographs of wartime RAF stations are so unimportant that time cannot be found to release them.[27] It is perhaps unsurprising that the RAF collection admits to no verticals showing the Hawthorne complex in Wiltshire, apparently still a main centre for command and control during nuclear war,[28] but similarly almost all oblique photographs of Woolwich town centre were taken looking away from the arsenal. Fortunately, one group of flyers was relatively undeterred by British government restrictions, and therefore photo 118 makes use of a Luftwaffe photograph of one of the main Battle of Britain fighter bases.

119 The City of London before the blitz. This 1939 photograph shows the traditional City, with a largely medieval street plan, where Wren's churches, and above all St Paul's, dominated the various temples of mammon; the closest competitors were organs of the state, the Central Criminal Court at the Old Bailey in the bottom left hand corner, and the Bank of England in the middle distance beyond St Paul's.

If air photographs of wartime construction are hard to trace, the evidence for destruction is more obvious. Until now, the street plans of British cities had evolved through a process of slow accretion, the old burgage plots easily discernible from the air in cities such as Southampton. Area bombing caused enormous destruction, as shown in the sequence of photographs of the City of London (photos 119, 120, 121) but what is perhaps more important is that, whereas Wren's plans for rebuilding London after the Great Fire were completely frustrated by existing property owners eager to rebuild, 'reconstruction' came to mean not so much re-creation of what had been there before, as replacement not only of the rubble but of the pre-existing pattern by something more rational: Donald Gibson, architect of the new Coventry, commented after the 1940 bombing that 'many citizens had despaired of the possibility of having a dignified and fitting city centre . . . Now, in a night, all this was changed . . . like a forest fire the present evil might bring forth riches and beauty.'[29]

In 1940 and 1941, the 'enlightened establishment' in Britain was seized with the notion of a 'New Jerusalem', a vision of a 'sun-lit garden city'.[30] The underlying impulse was as much Christian as Socialist, with Archbishop William Temple

227

120 The blitzed City. By 1944, the destruction seems almost total, with the miraculous exception of St Paul's; it is important to remember that this area suffered exceptionally, and in most bombed towns the majority of buildings survived and the subsequent total clearance which occurred in many city centres was far more a matter of policy rather than necessity. However, what was not necessary even in the City was the complete change in scale of the replacement buildings.

a central figure. One product was the Beveridge Report; another strand concerned physical reconstruction of cities. For example, Ralph Tubbs' *Living in Cities*, published in 1942 by a pillar of the modernist architectural establishment, discusses 'how others have dealt with destruction', complaining that Ypres had been rebuilt after almost total destruction in 1914–18 as 'an imitation of the old. Narrow streets, dark rooms, and traffic congestion have been re-created'. He then makes an impassioned plea:

LARGE SCALE ORGANISATION

If the cities of the future are to be places of beauty where everyone can live happily . . . it will require organisation and planning on a very large scale, combined with enthusiasm and determination. In war, the nation unites in a common effort, everyone plays his part to hasten victory. In peace we must work together on the same scale for our common good. It must not be every man for himself but every man working to further civilisation. To succeed, we must have the necessary organisation.

WE MUST PLAN NOW[31]

121 The City reborn. This 1967 photograph pre-dates the more spectacular outrages, such as the Stock Exchange and NatWest towers and, according to taste, the high-tech Lloyd's building of the 1980s; most of the Barbican is out of view, although the slab blocks of London Wall are just visible on the left hand side. What stands out is the replacement of the small scale pre-war city by numerous eight to ten storey blocks utterly lacking in distinction. It is indicative of how far taste has swung in recent years that Pevsner, writing about the Paternoster Square development in 1973, speaks of 'Lord Holford's outstandingly well conceived precinct', seen here immediately to the left of the cathedral; today, the same buildings stand condemned by Prince Charles, and are scheduled for replacement: another ephemeral landscape.

What is remarkable is not the plea for a better world, but the emphasis on large scale planning (and wider streets!) to achieve it; to ensure we do not miss the point, the above declaration is accompanied by photographs of tanks, planes, and guns being mass-produced. The *Daily Mirror* made the same point:

> Housing will have to be tackled like a problem of war. We can make . . . tanks, aircraft, battleships, pipelines, harbours! Are we, then, incapable of building houses? No. But to get those precious products of peace we must show the same energy, the same brain power, the same spirit by means of which we made the fearful engines of war.[32]

One result was the comprehensive redevelopment of bombed city centres; note that while reconstruction often facilitated later pedestrianisation by providing rear service roads, this was not part of the original plan even in Coventry, and the new wide high streets were designed for the car. Tubbs urged that 'the motorist must be planned for, not regarded as a criminal', and noted, apparently slightly regretfully, that 'it appears unlikely that planes will be able to land inside the town for some time to come'.[33] Just as the Barlow Report had attacked 'con-

gested areas' on a regional scale, so creating greater space within cities was an aim of reconstruction. In the 1940s and 1950s, this could only be achieved in areas such as the East End of London by reducing total population. Accommodation of the displaced households led to an official new town programme on vastly expanded lines, involving fourteen towns, eight around London; by 1971, new towns housed nearly a million people.[34]

To emphasise rebuilt town centres and new towns misrepresents the post-war planning system. The most important components were controls on developers rather than state initiatives, and their effect on the visible landscape was therefore more indirect. The cornerstone was the 1947 Town and Country Planning Act, which required that new developments have 'planning permission', to be granted by local government committees; many other aspects of the post-war planning system, such as Green Belts and National Parks, operated in large part through this system of development control. The Act provided that the developer should pay a 'development charge' in return for permission, equal to the increase in site value through development, but the charge was abolished in 1953. Thereafter, the system did not so much socialise the development process as politicise it. Major developments came about through complex bargaining between developers, who needed permission, and councils who could only achieve planning goals through developers, and in this process street widening was far easier to specify as a goal than aesthetic improvement.

It is easy to criticise the post-war planning system for failing in its aims, but we must also recognise how much aesthetics have changed. Compare Tubbs' vision, and criticisms of Ypres, with Prince Charles' comments on the reconstruction of one of the most heavily blitzed areas of London:

> Just look at Paternoster Square! Did modern planners and architects in London ever use their eyes? Those planners swept away the lanes and alleys, hidden-away squares and courtyards which in most other European countries would have been lovingly rebuilt after the war . . . In devastated Warsaw, they used the paintings of . . . Bellotto as blueprints so that they could create the intimacy of the lost city. Lost, but found again; they brought it back from the dead. *We* buried the dead deeper.[35]

It was precisely this intimacy, associated with congestion and squalor, that the dreamers of the new Jerusalem rejected.

THE AFFLUENT SOCIETY

The immediate post-war period was a time when planners might dream, but the reality of Britain's situation was extreme economic weakness, reflected in 'austerity', and a continuation of wartime rationing; the war created new technologies, but they had little impact on ordinary lives. Two events perhaps most clearly mark the end of this period: the coronation of Queen Elizabeth II in 1953, notable among other things for the first surge of television ownership, and the Festival of Britain (photo 122) two years earlier. The latter is remarkable in that the state actively sought to promote a particular visual style, a notion of modernity – Ralph Tubbs designed the centrepiece Dome of Discovery – but also for its frivolity.

122 The Festival of Britain, London, 1951. A definitively transient yet influential landscape. The Festival celebrated the International Exhibition of 1851, but it also marked the end of post-war austerity, and provided a model for much of the architecture of the 1950s and 1960s. This photograph shows the Festival in full swing in May 1951: Waterloo Bridge is in the top right corner, and the Charing Cross railway bridge runs diagonally across the site. The Royal Festival Hall, just beyond the railway, is the one permanent building; also prominent is the Dome of Discovery, designed by Ralph Tubbs, and behind it the Skylon, by Powell and Moya who later designed the Barbican. The Festival was a celebration of modernism, both in the design of the individual buildings and the informal layout of the entire site: neither neo-Georgian details nor axial symmetry.

123 Heathrow Airport, London. This picture, taken in July 1954 and looking towards central London, captures the airport in a transitional phase: the control tower, Terminal 2 and the Queen's Building are visible (centre), and the tunnel linking the central area to the Bath Road at the left of the picture was complete, but the outline of the Second World War airfield is still clearly visible. The standard airfields of the later part of the war had three runways, arranged in a triangle to ensure one would always lie close to the prevailing wind, but Heathrow was always intended to be converted to a civilian airport and had six runways in two triangles, linked to form a Star of David. However, as the airport developed, the two east–west runways, seen here stretching away from the camera, were extended to over two miles in total length while the lateral runways were partly built over by extensions to the terminals.

Battersea Pleasure Gardens, with Emmett's Far Twittering and Oyster Creek Railway, marked an obvious break with austerity: 'state-organised fun'.[36]

The post-war Labour government fell as the Festival closed, reflecting just such a popular rejection of austerity. The Tory-governed 1950s now tend to be labelled as the 'never had it so good' era, but much was aspiration rather than achievement. As the table on p. 219 shows, car ownership doubled during the 1950s but even in 1960 it was less than half that of today; the first section of motorway only opened in 1958. The car-born invasion of the countryside had therefore barely started, and similarly the transformation of the countryside through a succession of systems of subsidy was just beginning; most of Britain's hedges remained in 1960. Similarly, only 43 per cent of all dwellings in 1961 were owner-occupied (compared to 65 per cent in 1988), 84 per cent of households lacked telephones in 1960 (compared to 16 per cent in 1987), and 32 per cent lacked televisions in 1961 (compared to 1 per cent in 1987). Further, while the 1950s gave greater emphasis to individual consumption and the autonomy of private industry, most of the state machinery constructed during the Second World War remained; the new towns programme really only got under way under the Tories, and the basic utility industries remained nationalised.

By comparison with what had gone before, therefore, the 1950s and the subsequent two decades were a period when Britain was transformed through planning. However, planning can be viewed as either passive development control or active anticipation of future needs. The final theme to be explored here is the ultimate failure of most planning of the period when viewed as anticipation, and the class bias present in development control. Three examples will be considered:

Firstly, Heathrow Airport (photo 123) was first built in 1943 as a heavy military transport field, using the site of an earlier private aerodrome. It was always planned for conversion to peacetime use, and the site was very flat and had, for the time, excellent road links to central London. However, because of prevailing winds and the location of surrounding developments, the main approaches lay directly over west London. Planning here failed totally to anticipate the growth of aircraft, and of the noise they created; air travel was seen as a matter of convenience for an elite rather than a mass activity. Policy for London's airports has remained confused, and at the time of the Roskill Commission of 1968–70 it was suggested, in jest, that their cost-benefit criteria, emphasising travel costs rather than amenity, should lead to an optimal location on Hyde Park and St James's Park; we should perhaps be grateful to the occupiers of the large house at the head of the Mall for blocking an otherwise ideal runway site, and so preventing the realisation of Tubbs' desire to see aircraft landing within cities.[37]

The second example concerns some of the largest items of government expenditure, and has led to a spectacular impact on the landscape. Until 1947, electricity generation was mainly market-based, with relatively small power stations within or on the edge of towns. This was economically rational since technical progress gave each generator a relatively short life meeting the constant base load demand, older stations being used only at times of peak demand. However, in 1947 it was decided that substantial improvements in energy efficiency were at an end, and that new stations would contribute to base load for their entire life. This

meant that it would be cheaper to move energy as electricity on a super grid than as coal by rail, and new stations were located along the Trent valley, adjacent to the most efficient mines and with a ready supply of cooling water.[38]

However, thermal efficiency in fact continued to improve; after all, it was only about 30 per cent in 1950. The consequences of this incorrect decision are perhaps as follows. Firstly, Britain became festooned by power lines, while the railways lost freight traffic. Secondly, the Trent valley became dominated by giant cooling towers, despite which the river was warmed to the point where further stations became impractical. Thirdly, the rural locations of the stations meant that waste heat could not be used to heat surrounding housing, so achieving far greater thermal efficiency; the earlier Battersea power station needed no cooling towers because hot water was pumped under the river to the Churchill Gardens

124 The Green Belt at Stanmore, London (formerly Middlesex). This is one of the classic examples of where the growth of London was stopped dead by the Green Belt, created by the Town and Country Planning Act of 1947. The railway station is the northern terminus of what is now the Jubilee line, just west of the Edgware Road. The striking effect of the legislation is clear in a sequence of photographs taken betwen 1946 and 1955: in 1946, the railway station is still relatively isolated, with considerable vacant land to the south; in 1947, as shown here, building is going on adjacent to the station; by 1955, development of the area south of the station is almost complete; but throughout there is no development north of the railway. While the costs and benefits of the Green Belt are a matter of debate, this detailed history shows how effective the policy was in bringing the outward physical expansion of London to a halt.

housing estate. The one obvious gain of this policy was that the giant stations were imposed on a part of the country far from the anonymous civil servants who conceived this 'plan'.[39]

The third example is much the largest: the core project of the post-war planning system, the 'containment of urban England', the mastery of Clough Williams-Ellis' 'octopus' of sprawl. This was the goal of the new towns programme, the Green Belt, and so on, and can be looked at on two levels. There can be no doubt that in terms of development control the Green Belt has worked, although the area has not been actively enhanced for recreational use; photo 124 shows Stanmore, Middlesex, one of the points on the edge of London where housing construction was halted in the 1940s, and the line has broadly been held. However, in wider social terms the verdict must be more mixed. The system led to a greater division of homes and workplaces, and so to a rise in commuting: those who might otherwise have travelled to London from Greater Elstree must now come in from Luton. By constraining the cities, it encouraged the inflation of land prices, and consequently of housing costs, while by diverting industrial development it may have retarded economic growth. Above all, the gains and losses varied greatly between social classes; Hall and his collaborators commented:

> the new suburban communities of owner-occupied homes in the small towns and villages cater for a narrow spectrum of social classes. Coupled with the concentration of municipal housing in the cities, the result is the development of a new form of publicly-sanctioned, publicly-subsidised *apartheid*.

Among the rural population, the poor and those who might have sold land for development lost, while affluent ex-urbanites for whom the country was a way of life rather than a place of work perhaps gained more than any other group. The inhabitants of the new suburbs gained through a higher specification of homes, and through the subsidy of mortgages, but lost through the squeezing together of houses and cramped gardens, and through long journeys to work. Council house occupants benefited again through raised standards, but urban containment led increasingly to unpopular high-density developments within towns; those moved to new towns, however, may have benefited substantially. Those who came off worst were those living in older properties in the urban cores, often privately rented: unable to escape to 'slums of hope' in the admittedly unattractive shape of the plotlands, the system largely passed them by.[41]

Finally, it is impossible to criticise *the* plan for the countryside, as there were so many: the Ministry of Agriculture sought to maximise food output, to stave off the U-Boat menace; the Forestry Commission worked to cover the uplands with conifers, growing pit-props to combat the Kaiser. More formally within the planning system, the National Parks and Access to the Countryside Act of 1949 was a minimalist response to popular pressure: the National Parks it created were designated areas with, in principle, stricter planning controls, rather than publicly-owned areas as in America, and despite its name the Act created no new public rights of access. The pressure for such rights began with the Kinder mass trespasses of the 1930s, and the foundation of the Ramblers Association in 1935; the same battle is still being fought through Forbidden Britain Days.

The duties placed upon National Parks Authorities embodied a further contradiction: they were enjoined both to conserve the countryside and promote access. In the immediate post-war period, this posed no great problem, as rural areas contained few facilities for trippers in charabancs. However, the rise in car ownership placed steadily growing pressure on National Parks and the like. Photo 125, taken in 1972, shows the effects on one such site, Stonehenge.[42] Whereas in the inter-war period, the fear was that the urban octopus would consume the countryside by turning it into town, by the 1960s town dwellers were beginning to consume the countryside as country: metaphorically to satisfy a demand for the space denied them in their contained cities, in practice through the impact of their feet and tyres, and the new roads they demanded. Discussion of this new 'problem' was once again permeated with the language of class, the new ex-urban villagers seeking to repel this new threat: as with Peacehaven and Portmeirion, enjoying the countryside was acceptable if in good taste.[43]

CONCLUSION

The twentieth century has seen greater changes to the British landscape than any previous century, but we take most of these changes for granted; hillforts excite our curiosity, but power stations are just there, even if the history behind their location is at least as notable. This essay has sought to bring out the role of conscious decision making, identifying elements of an intellectual history of landscape change. In particular, the state and 'planning', even more than the market, were the crucial agents of change, but they reflected the class society from which they emerged. Planning clearly has helped preserve the visual amenity of much of rural England, but the better-off have been the main beneficiaries. This is beginning to be recognised now as NIMBY-ism – 'not in my back yard' – but the solution is unclear.

Given that so much of the development of planning was the work of Labour governments and of individual 'socialists', this account draws attention to a basic shortcoming of British socialism: the objective was to establish proper relationships between classes, not eliminate class divisions. From the social engineering of Hampstead Garden Suburb to the much larger experiment of the London Green Belt, putting people in their place often promoted segregation in the name of tidiness. Further, planning frequently worked to transfer real income from the poor to the rich, just as 'progressive' taxation subsidised the opera-goer at the expense of the beer-drinking smoker.

It would be naive to expect state controls of land use to eliminate the conflict between different groups and needs; unsurprisingly, competing demands mediated through the market became political struggle. However, it is alarming how little real democracy was introduced in the process. The progressive elite who gave Britain its planning system knew what was good for the country, and that ambition was at least as much an aesthetically-defined vision of modernism as a concept of social justice. Modernism wore only a fig-leaf of functionalism: rationales could always be invented for tower blocks or, as we have seen, for giant power stations, but their real attraction was simply size, and an appearance of organisation. Much was done in the name of the working class, but somehow they were never asked what they wanted. Thatcherism, if it meant anything, was a rejection of the Butskellite consensus of the post-war elite, and it is perhaps significant that the greatest swings to the Tories in 1979 came from the London new towns such as Basildon. On the night of the 1992 General Election, the first indication of the failure of Labour's challenge was the result for Basildon. Should we see the rise of 'Essex Man', and the Conservative hegemony of the 1980s and 1990s, as the plotlanders' final revenge?

125 The impact of tourists at Stonehenge, Wiltshire. Taken in 1972, this is a good final photograph for this book: much of the grandeur of Stonehenge comes from its isolation on an otherwise empty plain, but the arrival of car-born mass tourism has transformed this. This photograph shows the arterial road, the car park, and the broad path created by visitors; aerial photographs are particularly revealing both of archaeological remains below the ground and the impact of millions of feet upon it. Since this photograph was taken, a new car park and visitor centre have been built some distance away and visitors can no longer wander among the stones: where once they could be isolated *with* the remains of the distant past, they are now isolated *from* them.

Notes

Introduction

1 For a full discussion of cropmarks and of the techniques of photographing and interpreting them, see D. R. Wilson, *Air Photo Interpretation for Archaeologists*, London, 1982.

2 O. G. S. Crawford, 'The Stonehenge avenue', *Antiquaries Journal*, 4 (1924), pp. 58–9.

3 D. Riley, 'Great monuments – wide landscapes', *Current Archaeology*, 74 (Nov. 1980), cover photograph and p. 71.

4 D. Knowles and J. K. S. St Joseph, *Monastic Sites from the Air*, Cambridge, 1952, pp. 270–1, and J. K. S. St Joseph (ed.), *The Uses of Air Photography*, 1st edn, London, 1966, p. 127 and Plate 61.

5 B. Hope-Taylor, *Yeavering: An Anglo-British Centre of Early Northumbria*, London, 1977.

6 J. N. Hampton, 'Some aspects of interpretation and mapping of archaeological evidence from aerial photography', in G. S. Maxwell (ed.), *The Impact of Aerial Reconnaissance on Archaeology*, C.B.A. Research Report No. 49, 1983, fig. 88.

7 J. K. S. St Joseph, 'Air reconnaissance: recent results', *Antiquity*, 49 (1975), pp. 293–5 and 50 (1976), p.57.

8 S. S. Frere and J. K. S. St Joseph, *Roman Britain from the Air*, Cambridge, 1983, pp. 193–5.

9 Frere and St Joseph, *Roman Britain*, pp. 126–7, and St Joseph, *Uses of Air Photography*, plates 54 and 55.

10 Aerial photographs nos. 40 and 41 in Peter Wade-Martins (ed.), *Norfolk from the Air*, Norwich, 1987.

11 Maurice Beresford and John Hurst, *Wharram Percy: Deserted Medieval Village*, London, 1990.

12 P. Everson, 'Aerial photography and fieldwork in north Lincolnshire' in G. S. Maxwell (ed.), *Impact of Aerial Reconnaissance*, p. 20 and fig. 13.

13 D. Knowles and J. K. S. St Joseph, *Monastic Sites*, and R. Allen Brown, *Castles from the Air*, Cambridge, 1989.

14 T. Bayliss-Smith and S. Owens (eds.), *Britain's Changing Environment from the Air*, Cambridge, 1990.

Chapter 1

1 Radiocarbon dating methods are widely employed in studies of the prehistoric period. However, since considerable problems exist in the calibration of radiocarbon dates with calendar years, the chronological framework used here is based on uncalibrated radiocarbon dates, conventionally expressed as *bc*. Actual calendar dates BC or AD have been used only for the later prehistoric period, that is from 800 BC onwards. For a discussion of radiocarbon timescale calibration, see G. W. Pearson, 'How to cope with calibration', *Antiquity*, 61 (1987), pp. 98–103.

2 O. G. S. Crawford, 'Celtic fields on the Long Mynd', *Antiquity*, 28 (1954), pp. 168–70.

3 C. A. Sinker, J. R. Packham, I. C. Trueman, P. H. Oswald, F. H. Perring and W. V. Prestwood, *Ecological Flora of the Shropshire Region*, Shrewsbury, 1985, pp. 164–5.

4 G. Lambrick (ed.), *Archaeology and Nature Conservation*, Oxford, 1985; P. L. Owens, 'Leisure and the countryside', in T. Bayliss-Smith and S. Owens (eds.), *Britain's Changing Environment from the Air*, Cambridge, 1990, pp. 100–32.

5 D. R. Wilson, *Air Photo Interpretation for Archaeologists*, London, 1982.

6 G. W. G. Allen, 'Discovery from the air', *Aerial Archaeology*, 10 (1984), pp. 1–97.

7 R. Whimster, 'Aerial reconnaissance from Cambridge: a retrospective view 1945–80', in G. S. Maxwell (ed.), *The Impact of Aerial Reconnaissance on Archaeology*, London, 1983, pp. 92–105.

8 D. N. Riley, 'The frequency of occurrence of crop marks in relation to soils', in Maxwell (ed.), *Impact of Aerial Reconnaissance*, pp. 59–73; R. Palmer, 'Aerial archaeology and Sampling', in J. F. Cherry, C. Gamble and S. Shennan (eds.), *Sampling in Contemporary British Archaeology*, Oxford, 1978, pp. 129–48.

9 F. Pryor, *Excavations at Fengate, Peterborough, England: The Fourth Report*, Northampton and Toronto, 1984.

10 B. and J. Coles, *Sweet Track to Glastonbury: The Somerset Levels in Prehistory*, London, 1986.

11 The Somerset Levels Visitor Centre at The Willows Garden Centre, Westhay 3 kms west of Glastonbury provides a display of recent archaeological research. A reconstructed section of the Abbots Way trackway can also be visited nearby.

12 H. C. Bowen and P. J. Fowler (eds.), *Early Land Allotment*, Oxford, 1978.

13 P. J. Fowler, *The Farming of Prehistoric Britain*, Cambridge, 1983.

14 A. Fleming, 'Coaxial field systems: some questions of time and space', *Antiquity*, 61 (1987), pp. 188–202.

15 P. J. Fowler, 'Secretarys' Report to the Commissioners', *Annual Review: Royal Commission on Historical Monuments of England 1984–85*, London, 1985, pp. 2–11.

16 A. Fleming, 'The prehistoric landscape of Dartmoor, part 2: north and east Dartmoor', *Proceedings of the Prehistoric Society*, 49 (1983), pp. 195–241.

17 A. Fleming, 'The prehistoric landscape of Dartmoor: wider implications', *Landscape History*, 6 (1984), pp. 5–19; A. Fleming, *The Dartmoor Reaves: Investigating Prehistoric Land Divisions*, London, 1988.

18 O. Rackham, *The History of the Countryside*, London, 1986.

19 P. J. Drury and W. Rodwell, 'Settlement in the later Iron Age and Roman periods', in D. G. Buckley (ed.), *Archaeology in Essex to AD 1500*, London, 1980; T. Williamson, 'Early co-axial field systems on the East Anglian boulder clays', *Proceedings of the Prehistoric Society*, 53 (1987), pp. 419–31.

20 H. C. Bowen, '"Celtic" fields and "ranch" boundaries in Wessex', in S. Limbrey and J. G. Evans (eds.), *The Effect of Man on the Landscape: The Lowland Zone*, London, 1975, pp. 115–23.

21 D. N. Riley, *Early Landscapes from the Air: Studies of Crop Marks in South Yorkshire and North Nottinghamshire*, Sheffield, 1980.

22 D. A. Spratt, 'Prehistoric boundaries on the North Yorkshire Moors', in Graeme Barker (ed.), *Prehistoric Communities in Northern England*, Sheffield, 1981, pp. 87–103; D. A. Spratt, *Linear Earthworks of the Tabular Hills, North-east Yorkshire*, Sheffield, 1989.

23 D. A. Spratt (ed.), *Prehistoric and Roman Archaeology of North-East Yorkshire*, Oxford, 1982.

24 M. Robinson, 'Landscape and environment of central southern Britain', in B. Cunliffe and D. Miles (eds.), *Aspects of the Iron Age in Central Southern Britain*, Oxford, 1984, pp. 1–11; P. V. Waton, 'Man's impact on the chalklands: some new pollen evidence', in M. Bell and S. Limbrey (eds.), *Archaeological Aspects of Woodland Ecology*, Oxford, 1982, pp. 75–91.

25 M. Bell, 'Valley sediments as evidence of prehistoric land-use on the South Downs', *Proceedings of the Prehistoric Society*, 49 (1983), pp. 119–50.

26 For comparative purposes, see R. Palmer, '*Danebury, An Iron Age Hillfort in Hampshire: An Aerial Photographic Interpretation of its Environs*, London, 1984.

27 P. J. Reynolds, *Iron Age Farm: The Butser Experiment*, London 1979; P. J. Reynolds, *Iron Age Agriculture Reviewed*, London, 1985. The farm operates as an open air working museum, presenting the results of the project to visitors.

28 R. Bradley, *The Social Foundations of Prehistoric Britain: Themes & Variations in the Archaeology of Power*, London, 1984.

29 R. W. Chapman, I. Kinnes and K. Randsborg (eds.), *The Archaeology of Death*, Cambridge, 1981.

30 A. Henshall, 'The chambered cairns', in C. Renfrew (ed.), *The Prehistory of Orkney 4000 BC–1000 AD*, Edinburgh, 1985, pp. 83–117.

31 D. V. Clarke, T. G. Cowie and A. Foxon, *Symbols of Power at the Time of Stonehenge*, Edinburgh, 1985.

32 B. Cunliffe, 'Iron Age Wessex: continuity and change', in Cunliffe and Miles (eds.), *Aspects of the Iron Age*, pp. 12–45.

33 B. Cunliffe, *Danebury: An Iron Age Hillfort in Hampshire, The Excavations of 1969–78*, vols. 1 and 2, London, 1984.

34 B. Cunliffe, 'Man and landscape in Britain 6000 BC–AD 400', in S. R. J. Woodell (ed.), *The English Landscape*, Oxford, 1985. Contains model of land-use within an Iron Age chalk landscape.

35 B. Cunliffe, 'Relations between Britain and Gaul in the first century BC and the early first century AD', in S. Macready and F. H. Thompson (eds.), *Cross Channel Trade between Gaul and Britain in the Pre-Roman Iron Age*, London, 1984.

36 P. Turnbull, 'Stanwick in the northern Iron Age', *Durham Archaeological Journal*, 1 (1984), pp. 41–9. P. Turnbull and L. Fitts, 'The politics of Brigantia', in J. Price and P. R. Wilson (eds.), *Recent Research in Roman Yorkshire*, Oxford, 1988, pp. 377–87. An excavated portion of the ramparts has been reconstructed and is open to the public.

37 S. S. Frere and J. K. S. St Joseph, *Roman Britain From the Air*, Cambridge, 1983.

38 J. Wacher, *The Towns of Roman Britain*, London, 1979, pp. 375–89.

39 J. Percival, *The Roman Villa: An Historical Introduction*, London, 1976; Malcolm Todd (ed.), *Studies in the Romano-British Villa*, Leicester, 1978.

40 D. R. Wilson, 'Romano-British villas from the air', *Britannia*, 5 (1974), pp. 251–61.

41 C. O'Brien, 'Iron Age and Romano-British settlement in the Trent Basin', in B. Burnham and H. B. Johnson (eds.), *Invasion and Response: The Case of Roman Britain*, Oxford, 1979, pp. 299–313.

42 P. Clay, 'A survey of two crop mark sites in Lockington-Hemington parish, Leicestershire', *Transactions of the Leicestershire Archaeological Society*, 59 (1984–1985), pp. 17–26.

43 C. W. Phillips (ed.), *The Fenland in Roman Times*, London, 1970.

44 R. Prescott, *Hampshire's Countryside Heritage 6: Chalk Grassland*, Winchester, 1983.

45 Burghclere Beacon SSSI originally notified by the Nature Conservancy in 1954. Renotified and reduced in area in 1984 under section 28 of the Wildlife and Countryside Act, 1981. Ladle Hill and Burghclere Old Limeworks SSSIs similarly notified in 1978 and renotified in 1984. SSSI boundaries in the figure on p. 40 are reproduced with the permission of the NCC South Region.

46 T. Darvill, *Ancient Monuments in the Countryside: An Archaeological Management Review*, 1987; M. Hughes and L. Rowley (eds.), *The Management and Preservation of Field Monuments*, Oxford, 1986.

47 The Historic Buildings and Monuments Commission for England (HBMC)/English Heritage, established under the National Heritage Act of 1983, advises the Secretary of State for the Environment on the scheduling of monuments and the designation of Areas of Archaeological Importance. Scheduled areas in the figure on p. 40 are reproduced with permission of HBMC.

48 S. Piggott, 'Ladle Hill – an unfinished hillfort', *Antiquity*, 5 (1931), pp. 474–85.

49 T. Darvill, *The Archaeology of the Uplands*, London, 1986.

50 J. Coles, *The Archaeology of Wetlands*, Edinburgh, 1984.

51 D. Hall, C. Evans, I. Hodder and F. Pryor, 'The fenlands of East Anglia, England: survey and excavation', in J. M. Coles and A. J. Lawson (eds.), *European Wetlands in Prehistory*, Oxford, 1987, pp. 169–201; F. Pryor, *Flag Fen, Prehistoric Fenland Centre*, London, 1991. The exhibition centre at Flag Fen provides tours of the excavations of the Bronze Age lake village and a reconstruction of the Bronze Age landscape.

52 See special review section, 'Survey, environment and excavation in the English Fenland', *Antiquity*, 62 (1988), pp. 306–80. Detailed reports of The Fenland Project including The Lower Welland Valley, The Peterborough–March area, and Marshland and the Nar Valley are published in *East Anglian Archaeology*, volumes 27 (1985), 35 (1987) and 45 (1988) respectively.

53 Archaeological Areas were designated in York, Chester, Hereford, Exeter and Canterbury in 1984. B. Jones, *Past Imperfect: The Story of Rescue Archaeology*, London, 1984, reviews destructive forces within town and country and the measures adopted to safeguard the archaeological record.

Chapter 2

1 B. Cunliffe, 'Settlement and population in the British Iron Age: some facts, figures and fantasies', in B. Cunliffe and T. Rowley (eds.), *Lowland Iron Age Communities in Europe*, Oxford, 1978, pp. 3–24; C. J. Arnold, *An Archaeology of the Early Anglo-Saxon Kingdoms*, London, 1988.

2 H. C. Darby, 'The Anglo-Scandinavian foundations', in H. C. Darby (ed.), *A New Historical Geography of England Before 1600*, Cambridge, 1976, pp. 1–38.

3 M. Gelling, *Place-names in the Landscape*, London, 1984;
M. Gelling, *Signposts to the Past*, London, 1978; G. J. Copley,
Archaeology and Place-names in the Fifth and Sixth Centuries,
Oxford, 1986.

4 D. Hooke, *Anglo-Saxon Landscapes of the West Midlands: the
Charter Evidence*, Oxford, 1981; D. Hooke, 'Regional
variation in southern and central England in the Anglo-
Saxon period and its relationship to land units and
settlement' in D. Hooke (ed.), *Anglo-Saxon Settlements*,
Oxford, 1988, pp. 123–51; and D. Hooke, *Worcestershire
Anglo-Saxon Charter Bounds*, Woodbridge, 1990.

5 H. C. Darby, *Domesday England*, Cambridge, 1977.

6 D. R. Wilson, *Air Photo Interpretation for Archaeologists*,
London, 1982; see also D. Riley, *Air Photography and
Archaeology*, London, 1987.

7 Darby, 'The Anglo-Scandinavian foundations'.

8 G. R. J. Jones, 'Multiple estates and early settlement', in
P. H. Sawyer (ed.), *Medieval Settlement*, London, 1976,
pp. 15–40; G. R. J. Jones, 'Multiple estates perceived',
Journal of Historical Geography, 11 (1985), pp. 352–63;
Hooke, 'Regional variation'.

9 R. A. Hall, 'The topography of Anglo-Scandinavian York',
in R. A. Hall (ed.), *Viking Age York and the North*, London,
1978, p. 32.

10 T. Tatton-Brown, 'The topography of Anglo-Saxon London',
Antiquity, 60 (1986), p. 22.

11 G. C. Boon, *Silchester: the Roman Town of Calleva*, 2nd edn,
Newton Abbot, 1974; see also further aerial photographs
and commentary in S. S. Frere and J. K. S. St Joseph, *Roman
Britain from the Air*, Cambridge, 1983, pp. 151–5.

12 M. Alexander, *The Earliest English Poems*, Harmondsworth,
1977, p. 28.

13 G. R. J. Jones, 'Multiple estates and early settlement'; G. R.
J. Jones, 'Multiple estates perceived'; D. Bonney, 'Early
boundaries and estates in southern England', in P. H.
Sawyer (ed.), *Medieval Settlement*, London, 1976, pp. 72–82;
Hooke, 'Regional variation'.

14 P. J. Fowler, 'Farming in the Anglo-Saxon landscape: an
archaeologist's view', *Anglo-Saxon England*, 9 (1981),
pp. 263–80.

15 D. N. Riley, *Early Landscapes from the Air: Studies of Crop
Marks in South Yorkshire and North Nottinghamshire*,
Sheffield, 1980.

16 T. Unwin, 'Townships and early fields in north
Nottinghamshire', *Journal of Historical Geography*, 9 (1983),
pp. 341–6.

17 T. Williamson, 'Parish boundaries and early fields:
continuity and discontinuity', *Journal of Historical
Geography*, 12 (1986), p. 241; see also T. Williamson,
'Settlement chronology and regional landscapes: the
evidence from the claylands of East Anglia and Essex', in D.
Hooke (ed.), *Anglo-Saxon Settlements*, Oxford, 1988,
pp. 153–55.

18 Bede, *A History of the English Church and People*,
Harmondsworth, 1968, p. 58; see also S. Bassett (ed.), *The
Origins of Anglo-Saxon Kingdoms*, Leicester, 1989.

19 A. Fox and C. Fox, 'Wansdyke reconsidered', *Archaeological
Journal*, 115 (1960), pp. 1–48.

20 J. N. L. Myres, 'Wansdyke and the origins of Wessex', in
H. Trevor-Roper (ed.), *Essays in British History Presented to
Sir Frank Feiling*, London, 1964, pp. 1–27.

21 P. Wormald, 'Offa's Dyke', in J. Campbell (ed.), *The Anglo-
Saxons*, Oxford, 1982, pp. 120–1; D. Hill, 'Offa's and Wat's

Dykes: some aspects of recent work 1972–1976',
*Transactions of the Lancashire and Cheshire Antiquarian
Society*, 79 (1977), pp. 21–33.

22 M. U. Jones and W. T. Jones, 'The crop-mark sites at
Mucking, Essex, England', in R. Bruce-Mitford (ed.), *Recent
Archaeological Excavations in Europe*, London, 1975, p. 134;
see also M. U. Jones, 'Saxon Mucking – a post excavation
note', *Anglo-Saxon Studies in Archaeology and History*, 1
(1979), pp. 21–38.

23 M. U. Jones, 'Early Saxon settlement finds', *Medieval
Archaeology*, 27 (1983), pp. 141–3.

24 P. V. Addyman and D. Leigh, 'The Anglo-Saxon village at
Chalton, Hampshire: second interim report', *Medieval
Archaeology*, 17 (1973), pp. 1–25; P. V. Addyman, D. Leigh
and M. J. Hughes, 'Anglo-Saxon houses at Chalton,
Hampshire', *Medieval Archaeology*, 16 (1972), pp. 13–31.

25 B. Cunliffe, 'Saxon and medieval settlement-pattern in the
region of Chalton, Hampshire', *Medieval Archaeology*, 16
(1972), pp. 1–12. See also Arnold, *An Archaeology of the
Early Anglo-Saxon Kingdoms*; and T. Unwin, 'Towards a
model of Anglo-Scandinavian rural settlement in England',
in D. Hooke (ed.), *Anglo-Saxon Settlements*, Oxford, 1988,
pp. 75–98.

26 A. Meaney, *A Gazetteer of early Anglo-Saxon Burial Sites*,
London, 1964.

27 J. K. S. St Joseph, 'Sprouston, Roxburghshire: an Anglo-
Saxon settlement discovered by air', *Anglo-Saxon England*,
10 (1982), pp. 191–9.

28 R. Bruce-Mitford, *The Sutton Hoo Ship Burial: a Handbook*,
London, 1979. Sutton Hoo is currently under re-excavation
in a programme directed by Professor Martin Carver.

29 J. H. Williams, M. Shaw and V. Denham, *Middle Saxon
Palaces at Northampton*, Northampton, 1985; P. Rahtz, *The
Saxon and Medieval Palace at Cheddar: Excavations 1960–62*,
Oxford, 1979.

30 B. Hope-Taylor, *Yeavering, an Anglo-British Centre of Early
Northumbria*, London, 1977.

31 J. Campbell, 'The first Christian kings', in J. Campbell (ed.),
The Anglo-Saxons, Oxford, 1982, p. 58.

32 G. R. J. Jones, 'Multiple estates perceived', p. 354.

33 Tatton-Brown, 'The topography of Anglo-Saxon London'
p. 24.

34 P. Holdsworth, 'Saxon Southampton', in J. Haslam (ed.),
Anglo-Saxon Towns in Southern England, Chichester, 1984,
p. 335.

35 P. Holdsworth, 'Saxon Southampton; a new review',
Medieval Archaeology, 29 (1976), pp. 26–61; see also
J. Bourdillon, 'Countryside and town: the animal resources
of Saxon Southampton', in D. Hooke (ed.), *Anglo-Saxon
Settlements*, Oxford, 1988, pp. 176–95.

36 J. Haslam, 'Introduction', in Haslam (ed.), *Anglo-Saxon
Towns*, Chichester, 1984, p. xiv; see also D. Hill, 'Towns as
structures and functioning communities through time: the
development of central places from 600 to 1066', in D. Hooke
(ed.), *Anglo-Saxon Settlements*, Oxford, 1988, pp. 197–212.

37 G. Astill, 'The towns of Berkshire', in Haslam (ed.), *Anglo-
Saxon Towns*, Chichester, 1984, p. 65.

38 H. R. Loyn, *The Governance of Anglo-Saxon England 500–
1087*, London, 1984, p. 71.

39 L. Alcock, '*By South Cadbury is that Camelot...*': The
Excavation of Cadbury Castle 1966–1970*, London, 1972.

40 M. Biddle and D. Hill, 'Late Saxon planned towns',
Antiquaries Journal, 51 (1971), pp. 70–85; see also M. Atkin,

'The Anglo-Saxon urban landscape in East Anglia', *Landscape History*, 7 (1985), pp. 27–40.

41 J. Haslam, 'The towns of Wiltshire', in Haslam (ed.), *Anglo-Saxon Towns*, Chichester, 1984, p. 113.

42 Gelling, *Place-names in the Landscape*, London, 1984.

43 C. D. Morris, 'Viking Orkney: a survey', in C. Renfrew (ed.), *The Prehistory of Orkney*, Edinburgh, 1985, pp. 210–42.

44 Morris, 'Viking Orkney'.

45 Bede, *A History of the English Church and People*, pp. 128–9.

46 R. Hall, *The Viking Dig*, London, 1984, p. 49; see also R. Hall, 'The making of Domesday York', in D. Hooke (ed.), *Anglo-Saxon Settlements*, Oxford, 1988, pp. 233–47.

47 A. MacGregor, 'Industry and commerce in Anglo-Scandinavian York', in R. Hall (ed.), *Viking Age York*, pp. 37–57.

48 D. Whitelock, D. C. Douglas and S. I. Tucker (eds.), *The Anglo-Saxon Chronicle*, London, 1961, p. 46.

49 D. Hall, 'The late Saxon countryside: villages and their fields', in D. Hooke (ed.), *Anglo-Saxon Settlements*, Oxford, 1988, pp. 99–122.

Chapter 3

1 M. M. Postan, *Essays on Medieval Agriculture and General Problems of the Medieval Economy*, Cambridge, 1973.

2 E. Miller, 'The English economy in the thirteenth century: implications of recent research', *Past and Present*, 28 (1964), p. 39.

3 J. C. Holt, '1086', in J. C. Holt (ed.), *Domesday Studies*, Woodbridge, 1987, p. 56.

4 H. C. Darby, *The Domesday Geography of Eastern England*, Cambridge, 1952, p. 1.

5 H. C. Darby, *Domesday England*, Cambridge, 1977, pp. 87–94.

6 The subject of an earlier volume in the Cambridge Air Survey series, *Medieval England: An Aerial Survey*, Cambridge, 1958 (2nd edn, 1979), edited by M. W. Beresford and J. K. S. St Joseph.

7 B. M. S. Campbell, 'Agricultural progress in medieval England: some evidence from eastern Norfolk', *Economic History Review*, 2nd series, 36 (1983), pp. 26–46.

8 H. S. A. Fox, 'The alleged transformation from two-field to three-field systems in medieval England', *Economic History Review*, 2nd series, 39 (1986), pp. 526–48.

9 A. R. H. Baker and R. A. Butlin (eds.), *Studies of Field Systems in the British Isles*, Cambridge, 1973.

10 See also R. Butlin in this volume, chapter 6 below.

11 S. R. Eyre, 'The curving plough strip and its historical implications', *Agricultural History Review*, 3 (1955), pp. 80–94.

12 D. H. Hall, 'Modern surveys in medieval field systems', *Bedfordshire Archaeological Journal*, 7 (1972), pp. 53–66, and his discussion of the archaeological evidence in T. Rowley (ed.), *The Origins of Open-Field Agriculture*, London, 1981, pp. 22–38.

13 O. Rackham, *Ancient Woodland: Its History, Vegetation and Uses in England*, London, 1980, pp. 177–80 and fig. 12.2.

14 O. Rackham, *The History of the Countryside*, London, 1986, p. 131 and fig. 6.5.

15 Darby, *Domesday England*, pp. 171–207, especially figs. 61, 62, 63. Maps of the returns of woodland for the English counties are included in the five regional volumes of Darby's series on the Domesday geography of England.

16 O. Rackham, *The History of the Countryside*, pp. 122–6, and

L. Cantor (ed.), *The English Medieval Landscape*, London, 1982, pp. 56–85.

17 C. C. Taylor, *The Cambridgeshire Landscape*, London, 1973, pp. 56–8.

18 For a recent survey of the work on this site, see M. Beresford and J. Hurst, *Wharram Percy: Deserted Medieval Village*, London, 1990.

19 H. Thorpe, 'The green villages of County Durham', *Transactions of the Institute of British Geographers*, 15 (1949), pp. 155–80.

20 L. Dudley Stamp, 'The common lands and village greens of England and Wales', *Geographical Journal*, 130 (1964), pp. 457–69.

21 Beresford and St Joseph (eds.), *Medieval England*, 1958, pp. 103–6.

22 M. Aston (ed.), *Aspects of the Medieval Landscape of Somerset*, Bridgwater, 1988, p. 76.

23 P. Warner, *Greens, Commons and Clayland Colonization: The Origins and Development of Green-side Settlement in East Suffolk*, Leicester, 1987.

24 R. Allen Brown, *Castles from the Air*, Cambridge, 1989.

25 B. Hope-Taylor, 'The excavation of a motte at Abinger, Surrey', *Archaeological Journal*, 107 (1950), pp. 15–43.

26 E. S. Armitage, *The Early Norman Castles of the British Isles*, London, 1912.

27 R. E. Glasscock, 'Mottes in Ireland', *Chateau-Gaillard*, 7 (1975), pp. 95–110.

28 For comprehensive lists, see D. Knowles and R. N. Hadcock *Medieval Religious Houses: England and Wales*, London, 1953, and D. E. Easson, *Medieval Religious Houses: Scotland*, London, 1957. Aerial photographs of over 100 religious houses were published in the first of the Cambridge Air Survey series, D. Knowles and J. K. S. St Joseph, *Monastic Sites from the Air*, Cambridge, 1952.

29 Beresford and St Joseph (eds.), *Medieval England*, 1979, part III.

30 Beresford and St Joseph (eds.), *Medieval England*, 1979, pp. 215–17.

31 M. Lynch *et al.*, *The Scottish Medieval Town*, Edinburgh, 1988; I. Soulsby, *The Towns of Medieval Wales*, Chichester, 1983.

Chapter 4

1 F. M. Page, *The Estates of Crowland Abbey*, Cambridge, 1934, p. 121.

2 J. Z. Titow, *English Rural Society*, London, 1969, p. 70.

3 Titow, *English Rural Society*, p. 71.

4 Z. Razi, *Life, Marriage and Death in a Medieval Parish*, Cambridge, 1980, p. 103.

5 C. Dyer, *Lords and Peasants in a Changing Society*, Cambridge, 1980, pp. 237–8.

6 *Victoria County History, Staffs*, VI, pp. 37–8.

7 J. Hatcher, *Plague, Population and the English Economy 1348–1530*, London, 1977, p. 25.

8 A. R. Bridbury, 'The Black Death', *Economic History Review*, 2nd series, 26 (1973), p. 584.

9 H. C. Darby (ed.), *An Historical Geography of England before AD 1800*, Cambridge, 1936, p. 232.

10 P. J. P. Goldberg, 'Urban identity and the poll taxes of 1377, 1379, and 1381; *Economic History Review*, 2nd series, 43 (1990), pp. 194–216.

11 J. C. Russell, *British Medieval Population*, Albuquerque, 1948, p. 146.

12 Hatcher, *Plague, Population and the English Economy 1348–1530*, p.14.

13 J. Cornwall, 'English population in the early sixteenth century', *Economic History Review*, 2nd series, 23 (1970), pp. 32–44.

14 B. M. S. Campbell, 'The population of early Tudor England: a re-evaluation of the 1522 Muster Returns and the 1524 and 1525 Lay Subsidies', *Journal of Historical Geography* 7 (1981), pp. 145–54.

15 M. W. Beresford. 'The poll tax and census of sheep, 1549', *Agricultural History Review*, 1 (1953), pp. 9–15; 2 (1954), pp. 15–29.

16 M. W. Beresford and J. K. S. St Joseph, *Medieval England: An Aerial Survey*, 2nd edn, Cambridge, 1979, p. 123 and fig. 46.

17 M. Reed, *The Buckinghamshire Landscape*, London, 1979, p. 155.

18 H. Thorpe, 'The lord and the landscape', *Transactions of the Birmingham Archaeological Society*, 80 (1965), p. 51.

19 W. G. Hoskins, 'The deserted villages of Leicestershire', *Transactions of the Leicestershire Archaeological Society*, 22 (1946), pp. 241–64 (revised in *Essays in Leicestershire History*, 1950). M. W. Beresford, 'The deserted villages of Warwickshire', *Transactions of the Birmingham and Midland Archaeological Society*, 66 (1945–6) (published 1950), pp. 49–106.

20 C. Dyer, *Lords and Peasants*, pp. 244–63.

21 M. W. Beresford, *The Lost Villages of England*, London, 1954.

22 A distribution map produced by the Deserted Medieval Village Research Group has been reproduced in several publications. See, for example, fig. 18, p. 74 in T. Rowley, *The High Middle Ages, 1200–1550*, London, 1986.

23 M. Batey, 'Nuneham Courtenay: an Oxfordshire 18th-century deserted village', *Oxoniensia*, 33 (1968), pp. 108–24.

24 J. Thirsk (ed.), *The Agrarian History of England and Wales, IV: 1500–1640*, Cambridge, 1967, ch. I, esp. pp. 46–9, 54, 67–9, and 'Industries in the countryside', in F. J. Fisher (ed.), *Essays in the Economic and Social History of Tudor and Stuart England in Honour of R. H. Tawney*, Cambridge, 1961, pp. 70–88.

25 See also different photographs of this site in Beresford and St Joseph, *Medieval England*, and K. Hudson, *Industrial History from the Air*, Cambridge, 1984, p. 24.

26 M. W. Beresford, *New Towns of the Middle Ages*, London, 1967, pp. 457–9.

27 For a detailed account of this borough, see Beresford and St Joseph, *Medieval England*, 1979, pp. 242–5.

28 See maps for Norfolk by D. Dymond in *The Norfolk Landscape*, London, 1985, fig. 14, and for Suffolk by N. Scarfe in D. Dymond and E. Martin (eds.), *An Historical Atlas of Suffolk*, London, 1988, p. 61.

29 A. R. Bridbury, *Economic Growth*, London, 1962, p. 79 and appendices II and III.

30 N. Scarfe, *The Suffolk Landscape*, London, 1972, p. 190.

31 C. Phythian-Adams, *Desolation of a City*, Cambridge, 1979, p. 281.

32 J. W. F. Hill, *Medieval Lincoln*, Cambridge, 1948, pp. 242, 286.

Chapter 5

1 K. Wrightson, *English Society 1580–1680*, London, 1982; J. Sharpe, *Early Modern England: A Social History 1550–1760*, London, 1987.

2 W. G. Hoskins, *The Age of Plunder: The England of Henry VIII 1500–1547*, London, 1976, p. 1.

3 See the debate between D. Gregory and J. Langton on 'The production of regions in England's industrial revolution', in *Journal of Historical Geography*, 14 (1988), pp. 50–8 and pp. 170–6.

4 For example, C. Clay, *Economic Expansion and Social Change: England 1500–1700*, 2 vols., Cambridge, 1984.

5 E. A. Wrigley, 'Urban growth and agricultural change: England and the continent in the early modern period', *Journal of Interdisciplinary History*, 15 (1985), pp. 683–728, reprinted in Wrigley, *People, Cities and Wealth: The Transformation of Traditional Society*, Oxford, 1987, pp. 157–93.

6 For example, M. Dunford and D. Perrons, *The Arena of Capital*, London, 1983.

7 J. Youings, *Sixteenth-Century England*, London, 1984, pp. 154–77.

8 J. Leland, *Itinerary*, quoted by D. Knowles, *Bare Ruined Choirs: The Dissolution of the English Monasteries*, Cambridge, 1974, p. 270.

9 D. H. Williams, *White Monks in Gwent and the Border*, Pontypool 1976, pp. 94–146.

10 L. Stone, 'The fruits of office: the case of Robert Cecil, first Earl of Salisbury, 1596–1612', in F. J. Fisher (ed.), *Essays in the Economic and Social History of Tudor and Stuart England in Honour of R. H. Tawney*, Cambridge, 1961, pp. 89–116.

11 J. Summerson, 'The building of Theobalds, 1564–1585', *Archaeologia*, 97 (1959), pp. 107–26.

12 J. Gerarde, *The Herball, or General Description of Plants*, London, 1597.

13 M. Overton, 'Agricultural revolution? Development of the agrarian economy in early-modern England', in A. R. H. Baker and D. J. Gregory (eds.), *Explorations in Historical Geography*, Cambridge, 1984, pp. 118–39; J. Yelling, 'Agriculture 1500–1730', in R. A. Dodgshon and R. A. Butlin (eds.), *Historical Geography of England and Wales*, 2nd edn, London, 1990.

14 H. C. Darby, *The Changing Fenland*, Cambridge, 1983.

15 J. Thirsk, *England's Agricultural Regions and Agrarian History, 1500–1750*, London, 1987, pp. 54–5.

16 J. Bettey, 'The development of water-meadows in Dorset during the seventeenth century', *Agricultural History Review*, 25 (1977); G. G. S. Bowie, 'Water-meadows in Wessex – a re-evaluation for the period 1640–1850', *Agricultural History Review*, 35 (1987), pp. 151–8.

17 J. Wordie, 'The South', in J. Thirsk (ed.), *The Agrarian History of England and Wales, Volume 5, 1640–1750, part 1, Regional Farming Systems*, Cambridge, 1984.

18 W. G. Hoskins, 'The rebuilding of rural England, 1570–1640', in *Provincial England*, London, 1965, pp. 130–48.

19 R. Machin, 'The great rebuilding: a reassessment', *Past and Present*, 77 (1977), pp. 33–56.

20 For an introduction to vernacular materials and styles, see R. W. Brunskill, *Illustrated Handbook of Vernacular Architecture*, London, 1978.

21 J. Goodman and K. Honeyman provide a European overview in *Gainful Pursuits: The Making of Industrial Europe 1600–1914*, London, 1988.

22 Wrigley, 'Urban growth'.

23 J. Ellis, 'The decline and fall of the Tyneside salt industry, 1660–1790: a re-examination', *Economic History Review*, 2nd series 33 (1980), pp. 45–58.

24 M. Flinn, *History of the British Coal Industry 1700–1830*, Oxford, 1981; P. Cromar, 'The coal industry on Tyneside, 1715–1750', *Northern History*, 14 (1978), pp. 193–207.

25 J. Hatcher and F. Barker, *A History of British Pewter*, London, 1974.

26 P. Glennie, 'Industry and Towns 1500–1730', in R. A. Dodgshon and R. A. Butlin (eds.), *An Historical Geography of England and Wales*, 2nd edn, London, 1990, pp. 199–222; L. Clarkson, *Protoindustrialisation*, London, 1986.

27 J. Thirsk, 'Industries in the Countryside', in F. J. Fisher (ed.), *Essays in the Economic and Social History of Tudor and Stuart England in Honour of R. H. Tawney*, Cambridge, 1961, pp. 70–88.

28 J. Smith, *A List of Men and Armour for Gloucestershire in 1608*, reprinted London, 1980.

29 D. J. Gregory, *Regional Transformation and Industrial Revolution: A Geography of the Yorkshire Woollen Industry*, London, 1982, ch. 2.

30 M. Rowlands, *Masters and Men: The West Midlands Metalware Trades Before the Industrial Revolution*, Manchester, 1975.

31 D. Hey, *The Rural Metalworkers of the Sheffield Region*, Leicester, 1972; and 'The origins and early growth of the Hallamshire cutlery and allied trades', in J. Chartres and D. Hey (eds.), *English Rural Society 1500–1700: Essays in Honour of Joan Thirsk*, Cambridge, 1990, pp. 343–67.

32 J. Chartres (ed.), *Agricultural Markets and Trade, 1500–1750*, Cambridge, 1989.

33 N. Goose, 'In search of the urban variable: towns and the English economy 1500–1650', *Economic History Review*, 2nd series, 39 (1986), pp. 165–85.

34 A. Beier and R. Finlay (eds.), *The Making of the Metropolis: London 1500–1700*, London, 1986.

35 Wrigley, 'Urban growth'.

36 *An Essay . . . Concerning the Growth of the City of London with the Measures, Periods, Causes and Consequences thereof*, London, 1698, reprinted in 'Sir William Petty on the causes and consequences of urban growth', *Population and Development Review*, 10 (1984), pp. 127–33.

37 P. Borsay, *The English Urban Renaissance: Culture and Society in the Provincial Town 1660–1770*, Oxford, 1989.

38 P. Borsay, 'Culture, status and the English urban landscape', *History*, 67 (1982), pp. 1–12.

39 P. Corfield, 'The role of small towns in eighteenth-century England', *British Journal for Eighteenth Century Studies*, 11 (1988).

40 M. Spufford, *Contrasting Communities: English Villagers in the Sixteenth and Seventeenth Centuries*, Cambridge, 1974.

41 V. H. T. Skipp, *Crisis and Development: An Ecological Case-Study of the Forest of Arden*, Cambridge, 1978.

42 C. Husbands, 'Standards of living in north Warwickshire in the seventeenth century', *Warwickshire History*, 4 (1980), pp. 203–15.

43 R. Dodgshon, *Land and Society in Early Scotland*, Oxford, 1981.

Chapter 6

1 G. L'E. Turner, 'The physical sciences', in L. S. Sutherland and L. G. Mitchell (eds.), *The History of the University of Oxford*, vol 5, Oxford, 1986, pp. 674–5.

2 R. Lawton, 'Population and society 1730–1900', in R. A. Dodgshon and R. A. Butlin (eds.), *An Historical Geography of England and Wales*, 2nd edn, London, 1990, pp. 292–8.

3 J. Barrell, *The Idea of Landscape and the Sense of Place*, Cambridge, 1972.

4 M. Turner, *English Parliamentary Enclosure*, Folkestone, 1980.

5 Turner, *English Parliamentary Enclosure*, pp. 26–7.

6 H. C. Darby, *The Changing Fenland*, Cambridge, 1983, p. 118.

7 M. L. Parry, 'Changes in the extent of improved farmland', in M. L. Parry and T. R. Slater (eds.), *The Making of the Scottish Countryside*, London, 1980, pp. 179–80.

8 John Summerson, *Architecture in Britain 1530–1830*, 6th rev. edn, Harmondsworth, 1977, p. 318.

9 D. Cosgrove, *Social Formation and Symbolic Landscape*, Beckenham, 1984, p. 199.

10 P. Reed, 'Form and context: a study of Georgian Edinburgh', in T. Markus (ed.), *Order, Society and Space*, Edinburgh, 1987, p. 118.

11 C. W. J. Withers, *Gaelic Scotland*, London, 1988, p. 95

12 E. Pawson, *The Early Industrial Revolution*, London, 1978, p. 152.

Chapter 7

1 S. Daniels and S. Seymour, 'Landscape design and the idea of improvement 1730–1914', in R. A. Dodgshon and R. A. Butlin (eds.), *An Historical Geography of England and Wales*, 2nd edn, London, 1990.

2 A. Briggs, *Victorian Cities*, London, 1963.

3 W. G. Hoskins, *The Making of the English Landscape*, London, 1955.

4 M. W. Beresford, *Time and Place*, Leeds, 1961; 'Prosperity street and others: an essay in visible urban history', in M. W. Beresford and G. R. J. Jones (eds.), *Leeds and its Region*, Leeds, 1967; M. W. Beresford, *The Lost Villages of England*, London, 1954.

5 R. Dennis, *English Industrial Cities of the Nineteenth Century: A Social Geography*, Cambridge, 1984, refers to much of this literature and offers a chapter (pp. 48–109) on contemporary perceptions of Victorian cities.

6 R. J. P. Kain and H. C. Prince, *The Tithe Surveys of England and Wales*, Cambridge, 1985.

7 Daniels and Seymour, 'Landscape design'; A. R. H. Baker and D. Gregory (eds.), *Explorations in Historical Geography*, Cambridge, 1984; D. Cosgrove, *Social Formation and Symbolic Landscape*, London, 1984.

8 D. Cosgrove and S. Daniels (eds.), *The Iconography of Landscape: Essays in the Representation, Design and Use of Past Environments*, Cambridge, 1988.

9 H. J. Dyos and M. Wolff (eds.), *The Victorian City: Images and Realities*, London, 1973.

10 R. Hyde, *Gilded Scenes and Shining Prospects: Panoramic Views of British Towns 1575–1900*, New Haven, 1985.

11 A. Föhl, 'Factories from the air: birds eye views on company stationery', *Daidalos*, 11 (1984), pp. 89–97.

12 Quoted in Y. F. Tuan, 'The landscapes of Sherlock Holmes', *Journal of Geography* (1985), pp. 56–60.

13 Quoted in K. Hudson, *Industrial History from the Air*, Cambridge, 1984.

14 'The flying photographers', *The Photographic Journal*, June 1974, pp. 288–93.

15 R. Lawton, 'Population and society 1730–1914', in Dodgshon and Butlin, *Historical Geography of England and Wales*, pp. 285–321.

16 Briggs, *Victorian Cities*, pp. 11–58, 134–83, 214–76.

17 W. C. Taylor, *Notes on a Tour of the Manufacturing Districts of Lancashire*, London, 1848, p. 16.

18 P. Joyce, *Work, Society and Politics: The Culture of the Factory in later Victorian England*, Brighton, 1980.

19 D. Ward, 'The pre-urban cadastre and the urban pattern of Leeds', *Annals, Association of American Geographers*, 52 (1962), pp. 50–66; D. Ward, 'A comparative historical geography of streetcar suburbs in Boston, Massachusetts and Leeds, England 1850–1929', *Annals, Association of American Geographers*, 54 (1964), pp. 477–89.

20 Dennis, *English Industrial Cities*, p. 237.

21 R. Samuel, 'Comers and goers', in Dyos and Wolff (eds.), *The Victorian City*, pp. 123–60.

22 Hoskins, *The Making of the English Landscape*, pp. 282–5.

23 F. M. L. Thompson, 'Hampstead 1830–1914', in M. A. Simpson and T. H. Lloyd (eds.), *Middle Class Housing in Britain*, Newton Abbot, 1977, pp. 86–113.

24 Simpson and Lloyd, *Middle Class Housing*, passim.

25 Dennis, *English Industrial Cities*, pp. 48–109.

26 Dennis, *English Industrial Cities*; Briggs, *Victorian Cities*, pp. 88–138, 184–240.

27 W. L. Creese, *The Search for Environment*, New Haven, 1966.

28 D. Ward, 'The Victorian slum: an enduring myth?', *Annals, Association of American Geographers*, 66 (1976), pp. 323–36.

29 Daniels and Seymour, 'Landscape design', pp. 510–13.

30 J. N. Tarn, *Five Per Cent Philanthropy: An Account of Housing in Urban Areas between 1840 and 1914*, Cambridge, 1973; Dennis, *English Industrial Cities*, pp. 142–3.

31 Daniels and Seymour, 'Landscape design', pp. 511–16; Dennis, *English Industrial Cities*, pp. 176–83.

32 E. Gauldie, *Cruel Habitations: A History of Working Class Housing 1780–1914*, London, 1974, pp. 239–310.

33 Daniels and Seymour, 'Landscape design', pp. 513–16.

34 Briggs, *Victorian Cities*, pp. 139–83.

35 D. H. Lawrence, 'Nottinghamshire and the mining country' (1930), in *Selected Essays*, Harmondsworth, 1950, pp. 114–122 (117).

36 E. Gaskell, *Mary Barton* (1848), Harmondsworth, 1970, p. 39.

37 G. E. Mingay, 'Introduction: rural England in the industrial age', in G. E. Mingay (ed.), *The Victorian Countryside*, 1981, pp. 3–4.

38 J. Barrell, *The Dark Side of the Landscape: The Rural Poor in English Painting 1730–1840*, Cambridge, 1980, pp. 32–3.

39 H. Prince, 'Victorian rural landscapes; in Mingay (ed.), *The Victorian Countryside*, pp. 17–29.

40 E. Gauldie, 'Country Homes', in Mingay (ed.), *The Victorian Countryside*, pp. 530–41.

41 D. C. Moore, 'The gentry', in Mingay (ed.), *The Victorian Countryside*; J. Franklin, 'The Victorian Country House', in Mingay (ed.), *The Victorian Countryside*, pp. 399–413.

42 M. Girouard, *Life in the English Country House*, New Haven and London, 1978, pp. 300–18.

43 Franklin, 'The Victorian Country House'; Prince, 'Victorian Rural Landscapes'. p. 27.

44 Quoted in F. Klingender, *Art and the Industrial Revolution*, London, 1972, p. 122.

45 W. Schivelbusch, *The Railway Journey: Trains and Travel in the 19th Century*, Oxford, 1986.

46 E. J. Hobsbawm, *Industry and Empire*, London, 1968, pp. 88–92.

47 J. B. Harley, 'England circa 1850', in H. C. Darby (ed.), *A New Historical Geography of England after 1600*, Cambridge, 1976, pp. 227–94 (271–6).

48 J. Simmons, 'The power of the railway', in Dyos and Wolff (eds.), *The Victorian City*, pp. 227–310 (292–3).

49 Quoted in S. Daniels, 'Images of the railway in nineteenth century painting and prints', in Castle Museum Nottingham, *Trainspotting: Images of the Railway in Art*, Nottingham, 1985, pp. 5–19.

50 M. Robbins, *The Railway Age*, Harmondsworth, 1965, p. 58; T. Warner, 'Early landscape preservation in the Dukeries: the 5th Duke of Portland and the coming of the railways', *East Midland Geographer*, 12, 1 (1989), pp. 34–43.

51 J. Francis, *A History of the English Railway*, 2 vols., London, 1851, vol. 1, p. 245.

52 W. Wordsworth, *Guide to the Lakes* (1835 edn), Oxford, 1970, pp. 146–66.

53 Daniels, 'Images of the railway'.

54 Francis, *A History of the English Railway*, vol. 1, p. 292.

55 Francis, *A History of the English Railway*, vol. 2, p. 245.

56 J. R. Kellett, *The Impact of the Railway upon Victorian cities*, London, 1969, p. 294.

57 Kellett, *Impact of the Railway*, pp. 287–382.

58 Simmons, 'The power of the railway', pp. 277–310 (281–2, 301–2).

59 Quoted in Daniels, 'Images of the railway', p. 17.

60 M. Girouard, 'All that money could buy', in A. Clifton Taylor *et al.*, *Spirit of the Age*, London, 1975, pp. 151–88 (183–7).

61 Schivelbusch, *The Railway Journey*, pp. 18–26.

Chapter 8

1 R. M. Doty, 'Balloonists', in R. Martin (ed.), *The View from Above: 125 Years of Aerial Photography*, London, 1983.

2 R. Dangerfield, *The Strange Death of Liberal England*, London, 1935.

3 Royal Commission on the Distribution of the Industrial Population (P.P. 1939–40, IV).

4 T. Bayliss-Smith and S. Owens (eds.), *Britain's Changing Environment from the Air*, Cambridge, 1990.

5 For a spectacular assortment, see F. Barker and R. Hyde, *London as It Might Have Been*, London, 1982.

6 T. R. Metcalf, *An Imperial Vision: Indian Architecture and Britain's Raj*, London, 1989, esp. ch. 7.

7 J. Buchan, *Mr Standfast*, London, 1918.

8 M. Hebbert, 'Frederic Osborn', in G. E. Cherry (ed.), *Pioneers in British Planning*, London, 1981.

9 M. G. Day, 'The contribution of Sir Raymond Unwin (1863–1940) and R. Barry Parker (1867–1947) to the development of site planning theory and practice c.1890–1918', in A. Sutcliffe (ed.), *British Town Planning: The Formative Years*, Leicester, 1981; M. Miller, 'Raymond Unwin', in Cherry (ed.), *Pioneers in British Planning*.

10 B. Cherry and N. Pevsner, *The Buildings of England: London 2: South*, Harmondsworth, 1983.

11 R. Davidson, 'Sir Hubert Llewellyn Smith and Labour Policy 1886–1916', unpubl. PhD Dissertation, Cambridge University, 1971.

12 Day, 'Raymond Unwin'.

13 G. Darnley, *Villages of Vision*, London, 1975.

14 For some lesser known northern examples, including Oldham Garden Suburb, see S. M. Gaskell, 'The suburb salubrious: town planning in practice', and M. Harrison, 'Housing and town planning in Manchester before 1914', both in Sutcliffe (ed.), *British Town Planning*.

15 Quoted in Darnley, *Villages*.

16 P. Hall, *Urban and Regional Planning*, Harmondsworth, 1975.

17 P. Oliver, I. Davis, and I. Bentley, *Dunroamin: The Suburban*

Semi and its Enemies, London, 1981; P. Hall, *London 2001*, London, 1989.

18 S. B. Saul, 'The motor industry in Britain to 1914', *Business History*, (1962), pp. 22–44.

19 E. Jones, *Industrial Architecture in Britain 1750–1939*, London, 1985.

20 Oliver *et al.*, *Dunroamin*.

21 D. Hardy and C. Ward, *Arcadia for All: The Legacy of a Makeshift Landscape*, London, 1984.

22 Bernard Braine, MP, speaking in Parliament in 1950; quoted by Hardy and Ward, *Arcadia for All*.

23 C. Williams-Ellis, *England and the Octopus*, London, 1928.

24 P. Gruffudd, 'Taming the Octopus: Portmeirion and the inter-war landscape ideal', *Loughborough Occasional Papers*, no. 12, 1987.

25 Hardy and Ward, *Arcadia for All*.

26 D. Campbell, *War Plan UK*, London, 1982.

27 Imperial War Museum, photographic section, personal communication.

28 Campbell, *War Plan UK*.

29 *Coventry Standard*, 7 December 1940.

30 C. Barnett, *The Audit of War*, London, 1986.

31 R. Tubbs, *Living in Cities*, Harmondsworth, 1942.

32 *Daily Mirror*, 14 June 1945 (quoted in Barnett, *Audit of War*).

33 Tubbs, *Living in Cities*.

34 P. Hall, *Urban and Regional Planning*, Harmondsworth, 1975.

35 Speech by HRH the Prince of Wales, at The Mansion House, 1 December 1987.

36 M. Banham and B. Hillier (eds.), *A Tonic to The Nation: The Festival of Britain 1951*, London, 1976, esp. A. Forty, 'Festival Politics'.

37 P. Hall, *Great Planning Disasters*, London, 1980.

38 For a contemporary aerial photograph of the Trent Power Stations, see Bayliss-Smith and Owens (eds.), *Britain's Changing Environment from the Air*.

39 G. Manners, *The Geography of Energy*, London, 1964.

40 R. Munton, *London's Green Belt: Containment in Practice*, London, 1983.

41 P. Hall *et al.*, *The Containment of Urban England*, London, 1973. See esp. vol. 2, ch. 12.

42 See also Bayliss-Smith and Owens (eds.), *Britain's Changing Environment from the Air*, p. 110–11.

43 J. A. Patmore, *Land and Leisure in England and Wales*, Newton Abbot, 1970.

Photographs

The photographs in this volume are drawn from the Cambridge University Collection of Air Photographs, except where noted differently below. Photographs from the Collection are in the copyright of the University of Cambridge, with the exception of those noted as 'Crown ©' which are reproduced by permission of the Controller of Her Majesty's Stationery Office.

A   Roman town, Caistor St Edmunds, Norfolk CRG 13 June 1989

B   Roman villa, Chignall St James, Essex BZ 49 July 1976

C   Garden earthworks, Harrington, Northamptonshire SB 56 March 1956 Crown ©

D   Longton, Staffordshire ABA 24 June 1960 Crown ©

1   Plowden, the Long Mynd, Shropshire AMR 50 December 1965

2   Berghill, Whittington, Shropshire CJX 9 July 1979

3   Fengate, Peterborough, Cambridgeshire RC8–BO 244 June 1976

4   The Polden Hills, Somerset MI 3 July 1953 Crown ©

5   Yar Tor Down and Holne Moor, near Dartmeet, Dartmoor, Devon RC8–HL 80 April 1985

6   The Scamridge Dykes, Yorkshire AUH 51 May 1968

7   Beacon Hill and Ladle Hill, Hampshire RC8–DH 106 and 108 October 1979

8   The Butser Ancient Farm Project, Bascomb Copse, Chalton, Hampshire Photo courtesy G. F. Barrett

9   Maes Howe, Mainland, The Orkney Islands GR 43 July 1951 Crown ©

10   The Milfield Basin, Northumberland BKC 39 July 1972

11   Dyke system at Stanwick, North Yorkshire BEV 57 February 1971

12   Dere Street, near Ancrum, Borders Region MT 86 July 1953 Crown ©

13   Roman Fort at Llanio, Ceredigion District, Dyfed KI7–AI 175 July 1975

14   Caerwent, Gwent CQH 11 July 1984

15   Iron Age settlement and Roman villa, Lockington, Leicestershire BYL 46 June 1976

16   Silchester, Hampshire KI7–U 193 June 1970

17   Harworth, Nottinghamshire CJO 43 July 1979

18   Tan Hill, All Cannings, Wiltshire BOV 32 October 1973

19   Llanfair, Waterdine, Shropshire VE 6 June 1957 Crown ©

20   Mucking, Essex ADF 42 June 1961

21   Drayton, Berkshire BTT 60 July 1975

22   Chalton, Hampshire RC8–AD 157 September 1972

23   Sprouston, Roxburghshire BEE 42 August 1970

24   Sutton Hoo, Suffolk BPK 29 February 1974

25   Yeavering, Northumberland DN 54 July 1949 Crown ©

26   Old Windsor, Berkshire VO 91 July 1957

27   South Cadbury, Somerset FC 46 July 1950 Crown ©

28   Malmesbury, Wiltshire PM 87 April 1955 Crown ©

29   Brough of Birsay, Orkney AMD 26 August 1965

30   York, Yorkshire RC8–AI 30 April 1973

31   Hound Tor, Devon BFF 50 May 1971

32   Lowesby, Leicestershire CFG 67 February 1978

33   Chalk downs, near Mere, Wiltshire AY 31 July 1948

34   Elsworth, Cambridgeshire RC8–HV 193 July 1985

35   Braunston, Northamptonshire AGV 21 April 1963

36   Eltisley, Cambridgeshire ADO 50 July 1961

37   Castle Hill, Hallaton, Leicestershire AKO 81 March 1965

38   Orford, Suffolk HC 54 August 1951

39   Caerlaverock, Dumfriesshire AGO 39 July 1962

40   Beaumaris Castle, Anglesey BO 62 July 1948

41   Whissendine, Rutland (now Leicestershire) CFF 57 February 1978

42   Cistercian house, Waverley, Surrey CX 30 June 1949 Crown ©

43   Upper Teifi valley, near Aberystwyth AUC 9 April 1968

44   Sweetheart, Dumfriesshire DU 24 July 1949 Crown ©

45   Battle, Sussex MA 61 July 1953 Crown ©

46   Salisbury, Wiltshire NP 3 April 1954 Crown ©

47   Crail, Fife CEC 97 August 1977

48   Pembroke Castle, Pembrokeshire BX 51 July 1948

49   Hillesden, Buckinghamshire AGV 50 April 1963

50   Hamilton, Leicestershire CFG 63 February 1978

51   Gainsthorpe, Lincolnshire CFM 54 February 1978

52   Knapwell, Cambridgeshire AEF 90 May 1962

53   Kersey, Suffolk HC 31 August 1957

54   Furnace Pond, Lower Beeding, West Sussex WT 20 June 1958 Crown ©

55   Barnack, Northamptonshire AAP 71 April 1960

56   Bentley Grange, Emley, North Yorkshire GV 35 July 1951 Crown ©

57   Queenborough, Isle of Sheppey, Kent BIW 43 June 1972

58   Newtown, Isle of Wight KW7–N 233 September 1968

59   Totnes, Devon FL 44 August 1950 Crown ©

60   Compton Wynyates, Warwickshire EY 67 June 1960 Crown ©

61   Titchfield Abbey, Hampshire AUM 21 June 1968

62   Tintern Abbey, Gwent CHR 72 September 1978

63   Hatfield House, Hertfordshire ON 58 July 1954 Crown ©

64   Bedford Level, Norfolk CFW 74 May 1978

65   Britford, near Salisbury, Wiltshire NM 56 April 1954 Crown ©

66   Stanton, Gloucestershire AIO 26 April 1964

67   Chapelfell, near Forest, County Durham BEW 3 February 1971

68   St Hilary, Cornwall AOP 92 June 1966

69   'Golden Valley', Minchinhampton, Gloucestershire AN 42 June 1948

70   Ddyle, north of Abbeycwmhir, Powys AUB 54 April 1968

71   Berwick-upon-Tweed, Northumberland CHS 97 September 1978

72   Stamford, Lincolnshire BK 52 July 1948

73   Orwell, Cambridgeshire BKY 22 October 1972

74   Willingham, Cambridgeshire ALE 99 June 1965

75   District of Knowle, Warwickshire FS 1 June 1951 Crown ©

76 District of Nuneaton, Warwickshire PI 34 March 1955 Crown ©
77 Port Ellen, Isle of Islay BOX 92 October 1973
78 South Field, Laxton, Nottinghamshire DW 50 July 1949 Crown ©
79 Padbury, Buckinghamshire AGV 57 April 1963 Crown ©
80 Near Balnacoil, Strath Brora, Sutherland AZL 39 July 1969
81 Fishguard, Pembrokeshire CHU 52 September 1978
82 Wicken and Soham, Cambridgeshire BSL 48 May 1975 Crown ©
83 Heathland near Wimborne Minster, Dorset CM 51 June 1989 Crown ©
84 (a) Holkham Hall, Norfolk FQ 30 June 1951 Crown ©
   (b) Holkham Park, Norfolk FQ 78 June 1951 Crown ©
85 Edinburgh, Midlothian AWB 70 July 1968
86 Buxton, Derbyshire OS 92 July 1954 Crown ©
87 Ullapool, Ross and Cromarty AGJ 74 July 1962 Crown ©
88 Fort George, Inverness AAH 18 July 1959
89 Maryport, Cumbria BRI 54 August 1974
90 Aberaeron, Cardigan (Dyfed) CDP 73 July 1977
91 Coalbrookdale, Shropshire YP 42 June 1959
92 Cotton mills, New Lanark, Lanarkshire BKE 64A July 1972
93 Kennet and Avon Canal, west of Devizes, Wiltshire CQZ 89 1986
94 London Docks BIJ 76 May 1972
95 Halifax, West Yorkshire Aerofilms Ltd August 1974
96 Leeds, West Yorkshire Aerofilms Ltd April 1952
97 The Meadows, Nottingham Aerofilms Ltd April 1926
98 Nottingham RC8-Z 155 July 1971
99 East Heath, Hampstead, London Aerofilms Ltd April 1981
100 Hove, Sussex Aerofilms Ltd May 1952
101 Pentonville Prison, London Aerofilms Ltd November 1965
102 Saltaire, West Yorkshire CRA 58 December 1986
103 Halifax, West Yorkshire Aerofilms Ltd September 1968
104 Boundary Street Estate, Bethnal Green, London Aerofilms Ltd July 1964
105 Penrhyn Castle, Gwynedd ML 32 July 1953
106 Thoresby House, Nottinghamshire DW 031 July 1949
107 Ouse viaduct, near Ardingly, Sussex Aerofilms Ltd April 1949
108 Charwelton, Northamptonshire BSD 57 March 1975
109 St Pancras Station, London Aerofilms Ltd June 1947
110 Trafalgar Square and Admiralty Arch, London The Royal Aeronautical Society May 1909
111 Hampstead Garden Suburb, London Aerofilms Ltd June 1935
112 The Ford Motor factory, Trafford Park, Manchester Aerofilms Ltd July 1926
113 Woolwich Royal Arsenal and Plumstead, London Aerofilms Ltd June 1961
114 Ribbon development on the western edge of Hereford June 1961 Crown ©
115 Peacehaven, Sussex Aerofilms Ltd May 1933
116 Plotlands at Basildon, Essex RAF Collection/photo: Royal Commission on Historical Monuments of England September 1965
117 Portmeirion, Gwynedd Aerofilms Ltd June 1950
118 Manston Airfield, Kent Trustees of Imperial War Museum, London July 1942
119 The City of London before the blitz Aerofilms Ltd June 1939
120 The blitzed City August 1944 Photo: RAF Collection Crown ©
121 The City reborn Aerofilms Ltd April 1967
122 The Festival of Britain, London Aerofilms Ltd May 1951
123 Heathrow Airport, London Aerofilms Ltd July 1954
124 The Green Belt at Stanmore, London June 1947 Crown ©
125 Stonehenge, Wiltshire BHU 84 April 1972

The Cambridge University Collection of Air Photographs currently holds about 400,000 photographs taken by members of the University's staff since 1945. Most are of the British Isles, including the Irish Republic, but there is also more limited coverage of Denmark, the Netherlands and northern France. The Collection is housed in the Mond Building, Free School Lane, Cambridge, CB2 3RF (Tel: 0223-334578) and may be visited by members of the public. Opening hours: 9.00–1.00, 2.00–5.00 (4.00 on Fridays); closed on Saturdays and Sundays. Copies of photographs in the Collection are available to order.

Notes on Contributors

Gillian Barrett, a Senior Lecturer in Geography at Wolverhampton Polytechnic, graduated from University College, Swansea. She completed her PhD in geography and landscape archaeology at Queen's University, Belfast. Her major research interest is the development of interdisciplinary approaches in the interpretation and analysis of aerial photography for archaeological and historical purposes. She is actively engaged in archaeological air survey and photography in England and Ireland.

Robin Butlin is Professor of Geography at Loughborough University. He was an undergraduate and postgraduate student at Liverpool University. He lectured in Geography at the University College of North Staffordshire (Keele), University College Dublin, and Queen Mary College, London, where he became Reader in Historical Geography. He has been visiting professor at the University of Nebraska, and Visiting Professorial Fellow at Wolfson College, Cambridge. His research interests include: the historical geography of rural England *c*.1600–1900; the historical geography of the Fenland of north-east Cambridgeshire, and the history of historical geography. He is author of *The Transformation of Rural England*, co-editor of *Studies of Field Systems in the British Isles, Change in the Countryside*, and *An Historical Geography of England and Wales*.

Stephen Daniels is Senior Lecturer in Geography at the University of Nottingham. He graduated from the University of St Andrews, obtained a Masters degree from the University of Wisconsin and his doctorate from the University of London. He has published a number of articles and exhibition catalogue essays on English and American landscape representation and design, is co-editor (with Denis Cosgrove) of *The Iconography of Landscape* (1988) and author of *Fields of Vision: Landscape Imagery and National Identity in England and the United States* (1992). He is presently directing research projects on 'The Making of Constable Country' and 'Picturesque Landscaping and Estate Management'.

Robin Glasscock is a Lecturer in Geography at the University of Cambridge and a Fellow of St John's College. He graduated from University College London and subsequently completed a PhD: his thesis concerning taxation and wealth in early fourteenth-century England led to his edition of *The Lay Subsidy of 1334* published by the British Academy in 1975. From 1960 to 1975 he was on the staff of the Geography Department at The Queen's University of Belfast from where he published papers on medieval Ireland and co-edited *Belfast: the origin and growth of an industrial city* (1967) and *Irish Geographical Studies* (1970). Since moving to Cambridge his research has again been on aspects of the settlement and economy of medieval England. He is co-editor of *Villages, Fields and Frontiers* (1988).

Paul Glennie is a Lecturer in Geography at the University of Bristol, having previously been Research Fellow at Jesus College, Cambridge. He has published one book and several papers on medieval and early modern agriculture, industry and social change. He is currently working on books on the emergence of modern consumption (with Nigel Thrift), and on early modern English artisan households.

Humphrey Southall is a Lecturer in Geography at Queen Mary and Westfield College, University of London. He was an undergraduate and postgraduate student at St Catharine's College, Cambridge; his doctoral thesis concerned the geography of pre-1914 unemployment and the origins of the depressed regions of Britain. He has published a series of papers on the economic geography of pre-1914 Britain, on the development of trade union organisation, and on artisan mobility in mid-nineteenth century Britain; he is co-author (with Noel Whiteside) of a forthcoming study of the history of unemployment insurance, and the role of organised labour in the development of the Welfare State.

Tim Unwin is a Senior Lecturer in Geography at Royal Holloway and Bedford New College, University of London. Having graduated from the University of Cambridge he completed his PhD at Durham on medieval settlement and society in Nottinghamshire. Since then he has continued to work on Anglo-Scandinavian society in Britain, but has also undertaken research on agrarian change in the Middle East and Mediterranean Europe. He is the author of *Wine and the Vine: An Historical Geography of Viticulture and the Wine Trade*, and is currently working on an examination of the relevance of critical theory to geographical action.

Index

Photographs are indicated by page numbers in italics